CHANGING THE CHANNEL

Dear Wendy!
Here's to your
continued success
& happiness!.
Cheers,
Murugathu

CHANGING THE CHANNEL

12 Easy Ways to Make Millions for Your Business

MICHAEL MASTERSON
MARYELLEN TRIBBY

WILEY

John Wiley & Sons, Inc.

Published by John Wiley & Sons, Inc., Hoboken, New Jersey.
Published simultaneously in Canada.

For general information on our other products and services or for technical support, please contact our Customer Care Department within the United States at (800) 762-2974, outside the United States at (317) 572-3993 or fax (317) 572-4002.

Wiley also publishes its books in a variety of electronic formats. Some content that appears in print may not be available in electronic books. For more information about Wiley products, visit our web site at www.wiley.com.

Library of Congress Cataloging-in-Publication Data:

Masterson, Michel.
   Changing the channel: 12 easy ways to make millions for your business / Michael Masterson, Mary Ellen Tribby.
      p.   cm.
   Includes bibliographical references and index.
   ISBN 978-0-470-37502-0 (cloth)
   1. Marketing–Management.   2. Marketing channels.
I. Tribby, Mary Ellen.   II. Title.
   HF5415.13.M3657 2009
   658.8–dc22   2008032171

Printed in the United States of America.

10 9 8 7 6 5 4 3 2 1

To all my partners, protégés, and mentors who have made my career possible. And to my family and friends, who have made my career worth having.

—Michael Masterson

To my wonderful husband Patrick, whose everlasting love and commitment allows me to continually learn, teach, and enjoy life; and to our three miracles: Mikaela, Connor, and Delanie, who make every day a spectacular day.

—MaryEllen Tribby

CONTENTS

FOREWORD

In the "good old days," a lot of lip service was given to the idea that you could make more money in business by being a "multi-channel merchant"—meaning that you sold your product through multiple channels of distribution and promotion instead of only one.

It sounded good in theory. But at that time, in practice, the options for multi-channel marketers were severely limited because there were so few channels. A multi-channel marketer was typically a catalog marketer who also opened a small retail store near his headquarters. Or maybe a restaurant or retail bakery that did a small business selling gourmet food by mail.

But the Internet changed all this. It has created a plethora of new channels for distribution, promotion, and commerce. The challenge today is not whether to be a multi-channel marketer. It's knowing *which* channels to select and how to use them to multiply your sales and profits.

In this regard, there are no better teachers of how to use multi-channel marketing to maximize profits than Michael Masterson and MaryEllen Tribby. They have built, individually and as a team, a number of healthy multi-channel businesses with annual revenues of $10 million to $100 million or more. In their newsletters, articles, reports, books, and conferences, they've taught thousands of entrepreneurs, both aspiring and experienced, to do the same. In *Changing the Channel*, the authors offer a unique combination of real-world experience, proven results, and teaching ability unduplicated in any other multi-channel marketing book or course.

Both Michael and MaryEllen originally made names for themselves in old-school direct-response marketing, particularly in direct mail, a field in which they are both famous. Both are masters of the hard-sell and have created mailers generating untold millions of dollars in direct orders—one of the most difficult feats in marketing. (If you can write sales letters that make a lot of money in the mail, most other marketing is a breeze by comparison.)

When the Internet came along, Michael and MaryEllen immediately saw the potential, especially in the Internet's ability to quickly and repeatedly reach thousands or millions of prospects at minimal cost. Both were early pioneers in making the transition from offline to online direct marketing. And their innovative approach to online marketing, detailed in Chapter 3, helped double or triple their revenues, while dramatically reducing marketing costs.

Unlike many old-school direct marketers, Michael Masterson and MaryEllen Tribby eagerly embraced the new forms of marketing that have emerged in the past half decade or so. But also unlike so many new media evangelists, who serve as cheerleaders for new technology simply because it *is* new, Michael and MaryEllen put all of the new media they used to the ultimate direct-response test: Does spending a dollar on these new marketing channels generate two dollars or more in sales?

Therefore, in this book, you'll find a lot of advice on both old and new media. In Chapter 4, the authors cover today's favorite flavor of the month: social media. In Chapter 12, they explore the now exploding world of joint venturing. And in Chapter 13, they tackle another favorite of the new media evangelists, event marketing.

But Masterson and Tribby discuss all these multiple channels with two important differences from the way you might see these topics treated in other articles and books. First, everything Masterson and Tribby write about is based on extensively tested and measured results. They spend literally millions of dollars each year testing copy and marketing methods for their various companies. Therefore, they remove subjective judgment from the discussion of which tools are best. Their recommendations and strategies are based strictly on the ROMD (return on marketing dollars) that each channel generates, not on whether they think it's a neat idea or a cool technology.

Second, Michael and MaryEllen are media agnostics. Because they are successful business owners, managers, and entrepreneurs—and not consultants with a vested interest in promoting and selling their expertise in a specific channel (e.g., blogging, podcasts)—*Changing the Channel* gives you a high degree of objectivity and honesty rarely seen today in books, blogs, and columns written by consulting specialists with an ax to grind and a service or speech to sell.

Michael Masterson and MaryEllen Tribby have no interest in convincing you that e-mail marketing is better than MySpace, or vice versa, because they are not trying to sell you either one. Their sole objective is to help you use multiple marketing channels in your business to turn one dollar into two dollars, as fast as you can, and often as you can.

You have heard the old expression, "Those who can, do; those who can't, teach." Much of the rah-rah marketing advice I read today, especially concerning new media and other emerging marketing channels, is written by people who teach and "talk the talk," but who do not "walk the walk." They may advise clients to invest in their ideas and beliefs about marketing, but that investment is made with the client's money, not their money. These advisers get paid whether their multi-channel marketing experiments work or not.

Michael Masterson and MaryEllen Tribby are the real deal. They test and refine their ideas in actual marketing campaigns, using their own money to fund the experiments. They understand how important it is for your marketing to make money for you, and how painful it is for your marketing to fail to produce sales. Therefore, this dynamic duo of multi-channel marketing won't always tell you to use what's trendiest, coolest, or hippest. But, they will always share with you those multi-channel marketing methods that work best, generating the maximum results with the least risk. That's what I want. And I assume it's what you want, too. And in this book, that's exactly what you get. So if you want your multi-channel marketing to make you more money (regardless of whether it gets you on the cover of *Fast Company* magazine or wins you a creative award from your local ad club), you've come to the right place. Here's to happy—and profitable—reading!

—Bob Bly

ACKNOWLEDGMENTS

I would like to thank the following people for their help with this book:

Judith Strauss for her efforts, for so many years, to make my sentences clean and comprehensible; Jason Holland for his enthusiastic work tracking down facts and conducting interviews for this book; Suzanne Richardson and Charlie Byrne for their insightful comments; John Forde for his helpful suggestions; and everybody at John Wiley and Sons for their patience and support.

Alex Mandossian, Howie Jacobson, Katie Yeakle, Barbara Perriello, Julia Guth, Myles Norin, Tim Ferriss, Joe Vitale, Clayton Makepeace, Steve Leveen, Yanik Silver, Brent Jones, Rich Schefren, John Phillips, David Cross, and Bob Cox for contributing their expert knowledge.

Bob Bly, for agreeing to be interviewed and for writing the foreword to this book.

Bill Bonner, for his partnership and mentoring.

Joe Fiori, for agreeing to have his business profiled in this book.

All of my business mentors, to whom I will always be grateful.

My coauthor, MaryEllen Tribby, for her enthusiasm and for making the writing of this book an educational experience.

And, last but not least, my wife Kathy, for her constant support during this and all my other writing projects.

—Michael Masterson

I would like to thank the following people:

Jason Holland, who took the bull by the horns to make this book happen; Suzanne Richardson, who is my best editor; Charlie Byrne and Jedd Canty for running the show while I was writing; Wendy Montes de Oca and Alexis Siemon for their input; Nicole Reynolds for always helping out; Jon Herring, Andy Gordon, and Charles Delvalle for their comments; Judith Strauss for her refinement of the manuscript; and the entire Early to Rise team for their support.

Clayton Makepeace, Martin Weiss, and Larry Edelson, for their years of mentorship.

Bob Bly, for always coming through.

Rich Schefren and David Cross, my "go-to" friends and colleagues.

And, most importantly, Michael Masterson, who not only taught me to be a more prolific writer but a more concise thinker, as well.

—MaryEllen Tribby

INTRODUCTION

SHOPPING FOR HOMES

Easier, Faster, Cheaper

By MaryEllen Tribby

My parents bought their first home in 1957—51 years ago. Back then, the only way to buy a home was to look up a real estate agent in the phone book and call them. The real estate agent would come to you and tell you about homes on the market (homebuyers didn't even have the advantage of browsing through listings). And if a property that the agent knew about sounded close to what you were looking for, you took a ride together on a Sunday afternoon to check it out.

My dad loved to tell me his story about going through this process. He'd told his real estate agent, Margaret, that he wanted a three-bedroom ranch-style home in a nice neighborhood. A good public school system was a must. And he wanted at least one nice park nearby and easy access to shopping. The last thing on his list was very important to him: He did not want his family to be near any type of apartment building.

My father had grown up in a rough neighborhood, near a big apartment complex and with no parks and no convenient shopping. He attended a public school where little girls got shaken down for their lunch money, and he didn't want that to happen to his daughters.

My parents went house shopping with Margaret. She told them she had found "the perfect house" in a neighborhood they would "love." Imagine my father's surprise when Margaret drove them to his old neighborhood! He made her turn around before they even got to the place she had in mind.

When my father asked Margaret what she was thinking, she confessed that she had not actually seen the house or the neighborhood. She had trusted the owner's word that it met my parent's criteria.

Since Margaret was the only real estate agent in town, my parents continued to rely on her. These Sunday afternoon debacles went on for months.

Finally, 11 months after their search had started, we moved into a house that my parents were confident they could raise their family in. And their family had already been started. During the house-hunting nightmare, my older sister was born. My parents have always said that it was easier to have a baby than to find the perfect home.

I heard this story dozens of times growing up. So when it was time for my husband and me to buy our first home in 1996, I didn't want to leave anything to chance.

THE NEXT GENERATION BUYS A HOME

We determined the town we wanted to live in by:

- Using the Internet to research schools in the areas we were interested in, and then visiting the ones that looked promising.
- Researching the neighborhood amenities of our target areas. This meant scouring the Internet for parks, shopping, cultural opportunities, and restaurants.
- Driving around the various towns.
- Speaking to friends about what they liked in those towns.

Once we determined the town we wanted to live in, it was time to focus on a specific community. We did this by:

- Going online and plugging in the zip code of each community, along with criteria for the kind of house we wanted.

- Watching local television advertisements for new homes.
- Listening to the radio to find out about local events in the various neighborhoods.

It wasn't until we'd narrowed down our search to three neighborhoods that I even called a real estate agent. And I found her by:

- Asking friends and colleagues for referrals (word of mouth).
- Researching online to find out which agents had sold the most homes in the communities I was interested in. (I figured they knew those neighborhoods inside and out.)
- Reading the local newspaper.

After selecting Barb as our agent, we worked with her to draw up a list of homes we might want to see. From that, Barb got a good sense of our expectations. After doing some of her own research, she narrowed down our list to several options. We were able to view all of them online. With two of them, we took "virtual" tours.

Exactly 19 days after we started our research, we made an offer on our home.

THE MULTI-CHANNEL APPROACH

For my parents and my husband and me, buying a home was the biggest, most important purchase of our lives. It took my parents 11 months. My husband and I did it in less than three weeks.

The ultimate outcome was the same. We found a dream house in which we could raise our families. But the channels we took to get there were entirely different.

Because my husband and I were house-hunting at the beginning of the Internet Age, we were able to take a multi-channel approach to making our life-changing purchase.

Our multi-channel approach didn't end when we selected the home we wanted to buy. We used it for almost all aspects of the home-buying process, including finding the right mortgage company, insurance plan, moving company, and furniture.

But unlike the house search, we weren't doing all the work ourselves to get the information we needed. All sorts of companies were finding us. Furniture companies were e-mailing us about furniture sales. Mortgage companies were sending us mortgage offers in the mail. Insurance agencies were calling us about insurance. And moving companies were hoping to get our attention by placing big ads in our local newspaper.

All these marketing efforts—including the strongest sales pitches—were welcomed by us because we were emotionally, financially, and rationally predisposed to buy what those companies were selling. We were the perfect customers for most of them. We were motivated. We had money. We were prepared to buy. And receiving information about products and services we needed through so many channels made it easier and quicker for us to compare options and make decisions.

The businesses that did the most business with us were those that were relentless, contacting us through various marketing channels. They were smart enough to realize that if we weren't responsive to a space ad or postal sales letter, we might react to an e-mail promotion. And if an e-mail promotion didn't work, they could get through to us via the Internet when we did a search by typing in certain keywords. And if that failed, they could try to contact us by phone.

Your best customers are those who are motivated, financially capable of buying from you, and prepared to buy. If you don't locate and convert those customers through a multi-channel, direct-response advertising campaign, then you are leaving dollars—perhaps millions of dollars—on the table.

There is no reason to do that in this day and age, when there are so many ways to get access to the ideal buyers for your product or service. This book will teach you about the many channels you can use to reach your customers.

CHAPTER ONE

MARKETING IN THE TWENTY-FIRST CENTURY

How Quickly Things Have Changed

Sherwin Cody had a problem. He was a low-paid English teacher, but he harbored a secret desire to become a wealthy man.

Teaching people how to speak English, Cody knew, wasn't likely to make him lots of money. Yet he found a way to do just that.

Cody's first step was to write down everything he knew in a book called *The Art of Writing and Speaking the English Language*. To sell the book, he hired a copywriter named Maxwell Sackheim. After discussing various approaches, Cody and Sackheim decided they would market the book by taking out display ads in magazines and newspapers.

They tossed around dozens of possible advertising angles. They finally settled on one that became one of the most successful marketing promotions of all time. If you are a student of marketing history, you will recognize it. The headline reads DO YOU MAKE THESE MISTAKES IN ENGLISH? The ad made both Cody and Sackheim wealthy. More important, it launched them on dual careers in an industry that was just being born. The industry was direct-response marketing. The year was 1919.

Writing about direct response in the early 1900s, Cody observed that, with the advent of paved roads and a rail system, businesspeople had the ability to sell their products nationwide and deliver them quickly. And because direct-response ads in national publications could reach so many potential customers for those products across the country, it had a big advantage over local marketing by retailers, which had been the main form of advertising in the nineteenth century. As a result, he predicted, direct response would dominate marketing in the twentieth century.

He was right. During every decade of the twentieth century, direct-response marketing grew at double-digit rates. Today, at an estimated $2 trillion a year in the United States alone,[1] it is the largest single form of advertising by a mile. Countless fortunes have been made by small and large businesses that took advantage of it. And it is still extremely viable today.

Sherwin Cody went on to publish more than 200 books before he died in 1959. He made fortunes for himself and many others. And he did it by mastering the fastest-growing advertising trend of his century.

THE WAY THE WORLD OF MARKETING LOOKS TODAY

A similar opportunity exists for marketers today. As we look forward into the twenty-first century, 100 years after the birth of direct marketing, we can see another huge trend that has taken shape and is moving fast.

That trend is multi-channel marketing—an integrated form of advertising that takes advantage of everything we learned about direct marketing in the twentieth century, plus some astonishing new things we have been learning since the rise of Internet marketing in the 1990s.

Multi-channel marketing is based on new, twenty-first century technology that has radically reduced the costs of communicating with prospective buyers and existing customers. In 1980, for example, it cost about 50 cents to send a direct-response sales letter through the mail to a customer. Today, that same transaction, via the Internet, costs less than a penny.

WHY DIRECT MARKETING IS STILL KING

Direct marketing continues to be a growth industry because it offers so many advantages to entrepreneurs: low cost of entry, plenty of niche markets, and the ability to accurately measure the impact of their marketing efforts on sales.

To appreciate the size of the industry, it helps to understand its scope. It includes radio, television, magazine and newspaper ads, catalogs, sales letters sent through the mail, and now, in addition, advertising via the Internet.

Through direct marketing, sales are made by evoking a direct response from the customer. That response ranges from making a purchase to returning a free-trial postcard to making a phone call to providing information on the advertiser's web site.

The Internet has completely and permanently changed the way that marketing—and business—works.

Everything moves faster and farther. And everything is interconnected—companies with their customers, customers with the media, the media with companies, and customers with other customers.

To ignore these changes is utter foolishness. To understand and embrace them is the way to succeed in business today.

This book is about that new trend in advertising—a trend that will continue to grow at double-digit rates for decades and decades. If you embrace multi-channel marketing, you will see improvements in your business almost immediately. And those improvements will continue at lightning speed, transforming your business into something much greater than it is now. How big and how fast it grows is up to you.

The trend is huge. The time is right. Your future is unlimited.

WELCOME TO ADVERTISING IN THE TWENTY-FIRST CENTURY: THE AGE OF MULTI-CHANNEL MARKETING

To appreciate what can happen to your company when you implement a multi-channel marketing approach, let's look at how it changed the

A BRIEF HISTORY OF A BRIEF EVOLUTION

During the 1990s, there was a great deal of debate among direct marketers about how much impact the Internet would have on the industry.

Some argued that it would change the way that marketing worked—eliminating the selling part of the commercial transaction, because consumers would use the Internet to research and purchase exactly what they needed. "Pull" marketing (web site advertising) would flourish. "Push" marketing (direct-response advertising) would disappear.

Lots of brave predictions were made, but the truth is that nobody had any idea what was going to happen. The Internet, as an advertising medium, was in its infancy. Between 1995 and 2000, nearly $60 billion was invested in Internet companies.* Just about every marketing idea that could be imagined was tested during that period. And most of them—as futuristic ideas tend to do—failed miserably.

But some techniques and strategies did work. And some businesses did grow. Amazon.com and Buy.com, for example, grew rapidly because they managed to establish themselves as effective "pull" web sites. Others, such as Google, Microsoft's MSN, and Yahoo, grew from servicing both web advertising and web research. And still others grew because they refused to listen to the doomsayers who had predicted the demise of direct marketing. The Internet, it turned out, was the ideal medium for direct response.

Looking back at this very short 10-year history, we can see that most of the early strategies and ventures imploded and then were replaced by other, more effective, strategies, leading to the growth of a new generation of Internet-savvy direct-response marketers.

With lightning speed, the industry had reorganized itself and was growing again. There was, it turned out, a whole new world of opportunity out there.

*Bruce Kogut, *The Global Internet Economy* (Cambridge: MIT Press, 2003). Figure 3.2 p. 90.

business we work for: Agora, Inc., a private publishing company based in Baltimore, Maryland.

In 1998, Agora was a 20-year-old business that sold information products—mostly books and newsletters—by mailing out sales letters to lists of prospects. Its revenues were in the $90 million range. Its product lines included investment, business, and health advice. Its audience was end users—individual investors, entrepreneurs, and people interested in natural health.

Motivated by all the excitement about the Internet, marketing directors at Agora began experimenting with web sites and the methods that were being trumpeted at the time to drive prospects to those sites.

The success of those early efforts was disappointing. Money was spent and site visitors came, but revenues didn't rise and profits went down.

Never comfortable with the new concept of pull advertising, Bill Bonner, Agora's founder, initiated an old-fashioned push program that was based on the company's expertise: direct-mail marketing. And it worked well. Buyers who responded to the direct-response advertisements that were posted on Agora's investment web sites were given a free e-newsletter, *The Daily Reckoning*. They read it. They liked it. And they began buying the information products that were advertised on its pages.

As soon as this approach started showing increased sales, other Agora divisions quickly followed suit. Early to Rise (ETR), the business that employs the authors of this book, was initiated in 1999 (although it didn't start publishing its Early to Rise ezine until 2000). It sells information products in its business- and success-oriented web sites, and sends purchasers an e-newsletter that provides pragmatic advice on wealth-building, health issues, and entrepreneurship.

Within two years, no fewer than a dozen Agora publishing divisions were using this same marketing method. The growth of sales was encouraging. But what really excited everyone was the spending pattern of the new Agora buyers.

LEARNING WHAT MAKES INTERNET CUSTOMERS "DIFFERENT"

In the past, Agora customers would spend the most money on purchases they made in the first few weeks and months after their introduction to the offers. We saw this as a normal response from information enthusiasts. They started strongly, were deeply involved in a particular subject, and then moved on to other interests. There is even a term for this pattern: the "buying frenzy."

To take advantage of the buying frenzy, Agora marketers loaded up the direct-mail advertising sent to new buyers in the early weeks of the relationship, when their impulse to buy again was at its most intense. As customers "aged" on the "house files," fewer mail pieces were sent. After a year or two, only "reactivation" packages, aimed at restarting the relationship, were sent. If customers didn't respond to those efforts, they were "dropped."

The new Internet buyers had a very different pattern. They began making purchases tentatively, and then bought more frequently and invested more money with Agora as time went by. The top of their buying arc was no longer within an initial several weeks, but instead in the time period of six months to a year. And then they continued to buy from us for months and months afterward. They were more loyal, more motivated, and much more valuable over time. It was a pleasing development. It encouraged us to start more online marketing programs and roll out the ones we'd been doing more aggressively.

We eventually figured out that our new buyers were buying more from us for two reasons:

1. The large amount of valuable free information we offered
2. The increased frequency of the sales messages we were sending them

In his best-selling book *The Long Tail*, Chris Anderson talks about how the minimal cost of storing and delivering digital information products via the Internet made information publishing extremely profitable. Instead of carrying an inventory of several thousand books, for example, an Internet bookseller such as Amazon could carry several hundred thousand. Customers could browse through a much larger catalog. And they could buy more . . . which extended the tail of buying, thus increasing sales.

That was true for Agora, but the increased loyalty of customers who bought from us via the Internet was the result of another drastic cost reduction: The cost of communicating with our customers had dropped from 50 cents (what it had cost us to send them mailings) to a fraction of a penny. Instead of sending mailings to a customer 25 times a year, he or she could be contacted by e-mail hundreds of times!

We were communicating with our customers more frequently and in more depth than ever before. We were asking them questions, teaching them about our products, and offering to help them solve their problems and achieve their goals. All this "talking" created a stronger bond. And this change was paying dividends . . . substantial dividends.

The lifetime value of customers for our investment advisory products, for example, increased almost tenfold in 10 years, in some cases, from $50 per person to almost $500. This allowed us to invest more heavily in new promotions. Because when lifetime value goes up, the cost of acquiring new customers can go up too.

EXPANDING FROM ONE MARKETING CHANNEL TO TWO . . . THREE . . . AND A DOZEN

Customer loyalty and increased sales were among the first big changes we noticed. Something else was going on, however, and it meant a widely expanded way to acquire customers and increase their lifetime value.

What we noticed was that our direct-mail marketing efforts were improving at the same time. At first, this seemed counterintuitive; then we realized that our Internet marketing efforts were being seen by many of the same people who were receiving our sales letters in the mail. Increased exposure gave us greater credibility . . . and greater credibility was leading to better sales.

Our new channel of marketing was boosting our old one. Agora had changed from a one-channel marketing business to one that had two channels.

We began mentioning our web site in our direct-mail efforts, and also sending direct-mail promotions to Internet buyers who gave us their postal addresses. Again, responses increased. We asked ourselves: "What other marketing channels can we put into play?"

The next channel we tried was telemarketing. Though Agora had never had much success selling by telephone, some early efforts by The Oxford Club, one of Agora's most profitable divisions, had done well. So, based on their experience, we gave it a shot. And, as it turned out, customers who had been reading our e-mails and getting our promotions in the mail were open to receiving phone calls from us. Within two years, we had a substantial telemarketing department, handling customer service inquiries and selling high-priced products at a rate that astonished almost everyone.

Today, Agora divisions employ no fewer than 12 marketing channels to acquire new customers and communicate with existing ones. We are using all of the proven Internet channels, including search engine optimization (SEO) and pay-per-click (PPC) advertising. And we are successfully employing channels that we had failed to make work in the past.

Direct-response television and radio advertising is starting to work for Agora. And we are learning about Internet video marketing as well. Event marketing used to be a very minor, ancillary channel for us. Now it is responsible for revenues in excess of $10 million a year, and is growing fast.

THERE'S NO TURNING BACK

We believe that marketing in the twenty-first century is different from and better than it was in the twentieth century. Businesses that take advantage of these changes can expect to grow more quickly and more profitably than ever before.

The landscape of twenty-first century marketing is dominated by the Internet. But the Internet includes at least a dozen viable channels, many of which can be exploited by marketers who have traditionally kept to a single channel in the past.

The Internet has made it possible for local companies to market nationally, and for national companies to sell to the whole, wide world. The radically cheaper cost of digital storage and delivery has permanently altered almost every business in the information industry, from record and book sellers to legal services to investment advice, medical research, and entertainment. The ease and low cost of investigating businesses and products through Google and other search engines has made customers feel more comfortable about doing business online. Bad businesses are easier to identify and avoid. Good businesses get free publicity as a result of discussions about them and their products among their customers and prospective customers.

Today, the old argument, alluded to earlier, about pull (traditional direct response) versus push (Internet) marketing is moot. Most smart marketers do both. The pull vehicles are becoming more sophisticated and more prominent. The successful ones are attracting huge numbers of prospects, multiples of what they could manage 10 or 20 years ago. The push vehicles—in particular, e-mail marketing—have radically deepened the relationship between marketers and their customers. This is probably the most significant change we've witnessed, because it has increased the customer's lifetime value so dramatically.

To achieve your company's maximum potential, it is no longer enough to be good at just one type of marketing. Yes, you need to continue to do what you are already doing. But you must also expand into several additional channels, especially on the Internet. When you do, you will see how it all works together, giving a boost to every effort you make to reach your buyers.

And that brings us to the title of this book: *Changing the Channel: 12 Easy Ways to Make Millions for Your Business.*

In the chapters that follow, we will explore 12 marketing channels that you should consider for your business. We will deal at some length with direct-mail marketing, because it is so fundamental to its Internet twin, direct e-mail marketing. We will also cover social media, public relations, radio and television advertising, direct space ads, event marketing, telesales, telemarketing, joint ventures, and affiliate marketing.

In our discussions, we will include a simple explanation of how each channel works and give you an idea of its unique possibilities, as well as the challenges you will face should you choose to venture into it.

We will talk about how to analyze test results and roll out with successful campaigns. We will explain our preference for marketing campaigns that begin by picking the low-hanging fruit, while never forgetting to market most often and most strongly to those loyal customers who buy almost any product you offer them.

You will learn how to use low-cost or free media channels. And you'll discover the secrets of making Web-based products successful.

We will make an argument for making your "front-end" customer acquisition promotions outstanding—even if the cost is very high. And we'll tell you why you can spend less on promotions for "back-end" products—even though they are generally much more profitable.

You will learn why it is easier than ever before to get higher retention rates, and how successful marketing companies today are doubling theirs. We will show you how to build customer relationships by using direct mail, e-mail, and other media. And we'll help you avoid the temptation of trying to sell your customers every time you contact them—a mistake that will hurt you in the long run.

You will learn how to retain more customers by learning more about them, including suggestions for tracking customer buying-habits with a database that covers all marketing channels. We'll advise you on how to use the information you collect to segment your house list, and then send those segments offers that will appeal directly to each of them. And we will prove to you that many customers need to see the same offer from several channels before they will buy, which is why it is important to maintain a consistent sales message.

You will not learn everything you need to know about every one of the 12 channels that we cover in this book. But you will have a very good introduction to each—with advice about where to go for further advice and information—so that you can make millions for your business.

Well-known marketing expert Jay Abraham points out that there are essentially three ways to grow any business:

1. You can increase the number of customers.
2. You can increase the number of purchases they make.
3. You can increase the average amount they spend on each purchase.

Multi-channel marketing will make it possible for you to achieve all three of those objectives in a dramatic way. If you start exploring different channels as soon as you finish this book, you will see how powerful this approach can be in a relatively short time. In fact, by this time next year, you will have a much bigger and better business, and you will be on your way to making millions or even billions for your business.

CHAPTER TWO

———

"DRM" AND "MCM"

The Two Most Important Acronyms
in Advertising Today

For a business to be successful in the twenty-first century, it must be a direct marketer.

Martin Edelston doesn't have to be convinced of that. When Edelston began his business over 35 years ago, he wanted to sell his books through a variety of media, but a lack of cash flow prevented him from doing it all at once. He produced inserts and sent limited direct mail when he could afford it; built up the brand; and gradually added other channels to his marketing platform, including, over the past few years, direct-response television and such Internet-based programs as pay-per-click (PPC) advertising and SEO marketing. He also made a huge commitment to database marketing techniques to increase efficiency.

Today, Martin Edelston's Boardroom, Inc., is an industry leader with more than $100 million in yearly sales and approximately 85 employees.

"A big part of our success," Edelston says, "comes from our growing expertise in direct-response marketing and the addition of new channels of marketing to our traditional repertoire."

Retailers like Wal-Mart, IKEA, and J.Crew reach customers with print catalogs, TV advertising, online ads, and web sites. Insurance companies use telemarketing, TV and radio ads, various online channels, direct mail, and print ads. Car dealerships can be found online, in newspapers, through direct mail, and on TV.

To be sure, there are still many successful businesses that practice only one type of marketing. But it is our belief that those companies are an endangered species. Relying on one marketing method to build your business today is like swimming upstream with one hand tied behind your back. It can be done, but it is very difficult... and completely unnecessary.

To be at the top of your game, you need to continue to do what you do so well—the kind of marketing that is now working for you—but you must gradually add new arrows to your quiver. Like Boardroom, Inc., you will notice a sudden and substantial improvement in sales and profits if you do.

The mistake of sticking to one channel is not made by only old-school advertisers. Many new entrepreneurs believe they can start and build a business with one advertising method. A few years ago, for example, pop-up ads on the Internet were the way to go. And, in

---

BOB BLY'S STORY

Bob Bly is the go-to copywriter in the direct-response industry. He's worked with more than 100 clients, including AARP, *Harvard Business Review*, and McGraw-Hill, among many others. He's also an author and frequently booked speaker on the topics of copywriting and marketing. He specializes in creating powerful, effective landing pages (the landing page is the page a person lands on after clicking on an online advertisement) for many clients with online businesses.

Like most people, Bly's first exposure to direct marketing was as a customer. But he wasn't the type of customer most companies want.

"I was a big responder to direct-response offers when I was a teenager. I didn't know it at the time, but I was a premium bandit. That's the term direct marketers use for customers who respond to all the offers with free bonus gifts (premiums) and then don't buy the product. I would send for all this great stuff, and then I would just write 'cancel' on my invoice. God knows why I needed six leather-bound copies of *Moby-Dick*," recounted Bly, laughing.

Bly graduated with a degree in chemistry, but his first jobs out of college involved writing and marketing for manufacturing companies. A

BOB BLY'S STORY (*Continued*)

couple of years later, he had the opportunity to oversee a direct-mail campaign to generate leads for a new product. It was a big success, and he was hooked. He soon struck out on his own and started his career as a freelance copywriter and marketing consultant.

Bly says that although the Internet has changed marketing dramatically, it is still fundamentally the same. Direct-marketing principles apply across all channels, no matter what technology is used.

Marketers forget this at their peril, says Bly. In the rush to get online, many companies forget about the tried and true methods for making money.

"Here is the most common, number-one mistake: letting people leave your web site or landing page—if they don't buy—without at least capturing their e-mail address. It's as if they opened your direct-mail sales letter, read it, and then threw it away," says Bly.

Bly also takes issue with many "marketing gurus" who look to the future and see the death of traditional direct marketing in the next couple of decades. These so-called experts believe that marketers should just have "conversations" with their potential customers via the Internet.

"I talked about that on my blog a while ago," says Bly. "One of my readers wrote back and said, 'I'm a sales rep, and if I came back at the end of the day and told my boss I had a lot of conversations with prospects, he would fire me. I have to bring back signed contracts.'

"Direct marketers bring back 'signed contracts,'" says Bly, "and that is never going to go out of style. A lot of people are enamored with the warm and fuzzy side of the Internet—blogging, social networking sites, bulletin boards, forums—and that is all well and good. But at the end of the day, you've got to sell something or you are just wasting your time.

"You have to drive Internet traffic to some page where you can convert it into leads or sales," adds Bly. "If you are trying to build your e-mail list of names, conversion means getting people to opt in to receive e-mail from you. If you are trying to sell a product, it means getting people to order. And for that, you have to have both squeeze pages (which are intended to capture e-mail addresses) and landing pages. If you don't, you are going to get a lot of traffic and no sales."

fact, they were making tons of money for companies large and small, persuading many to base their marketing entirely on pop-up ads. Some even abandoned other marketing channels to focus exclusively on pop-ups because the money was so easy.

When one pop-up ad showed signs of fatigue, they swiftly posted the next ad. And if the next ad was not quite ready, no cash came in the door for a while. These companies were like hamsters on a wheel, always scurrying for the next buck.

What they didn't realize was that within 18 months, pop-up blockers would essentially annihilate their businesses. They were left with dwindling cash flow and growing overhead: a death blow.

Relying on one marketing channel is simply foolish. Even if you choose a lucrative channel, there is no telling when, like pop-up ads, it will change to a mere trickle. You can make temporary adjustments by using marketing tricks—special offers and over-the-top promises. But those gimmicks will not sustain sales for long.

Marketers must keep in mind that technology is changing fast. And as technology changes, so do the opportunities for growth.

DIRECT MARKETING 101

If you're not familiar with direct-marketing methods, here are a few good books to start with:

- Eugene M. Schwartz's *Breakthrough Advertising*, originally published in 1966
- Dick Benson's *Secrets of Successful Direct Mail*, originally published in 1987
- Claude C. Hopkins' *My Life in Advertising* and *Scientific Advertising*, originally published in 1927 and 1923, respectively

The authors of these books understood the profound impact that direct-response marketing can have on any business. It was their mission to teach the fundamentals—the rules and principles that apply to all businesses at all times.

To be successful today, you need to be skillful in several marketing channels. More important than that, you must be able to apply direct-marketing principles to every one of your advertising campaigns.

WHAT, EXACTLY, IS DIRECT-RESPONSE MARKETING (DRM)?

Although direct-marketing techniques have been used since the advent of the printing press, the definition that was set 84 years ago holds true today: Direct-response marketing is a form of marketing designed to solicit an immediate response that is specific and quantifiable.

You see this at work in every DRM channel. Online newsletter promotions ask you to "click here." Magazine promotions ask you to place a "yes" sticker on a postcard to renew your subscription. TV ads ask you to call an 800 number to learn more about the latest vacuum-cleaner technology. All of these channels then add urgency by stating that if you are among the first 25 or 50 or 100 to respond, you will be rewarded with extra bonuses.

They all ask customers to take action immediately. They all ask customers to follow specific instructions. And smart companies track and quantify the results.

Keep in mind that DRM is not branding. The end goals of direct-response marketing and brand marketing are entirely different. DRM wants to get the customer to provide information or open his wallet. Branding, on the other hand, wants to get the customer to remember the product.

Direct-Response Marketing	Branding
Customer opens wallet	Customer remembers
Informational	Image-building
Highly targeted	Broad reach
Explicit interest or intent	No conscious intent

Today, with the power of the Internet behind them, branding and DRM work more closely together . . . closer than they ever have in the history of advertising. The Internet allows companies to create campaigns that are nearly hybrids of traditional branding and traditional DRM.

Think about all the e-newsletters being published today. There are tens of thousands of them out there on every subject imaginable, from gardening to politics to rock music, and thousands more are created each week.

Agora, Inc.'s *Early to Rise* (ETR) is just one of those e-newsletters. Because ETR is a true daily—delivered seven days a week and reaching over 300,000 people—it has developed a certain brand presence.

By "brand presence," we mean that *Early to Rise* has a specific look and feel. It has a strong mission statement and specific core values. These are aspects of our "brand" that have been with us since ETR's inception.

All of the products we produce carry our logo. So when you see banner ads on other web sites and text ads in other newsletters, you know by the logo that the ads come from ETR.

But at its heart, ETR is not a brand marketer. ETR is a direct-response e-newsletter. That's how we've developed our subscriber list. That's how we've grown our business. And because we've been consistent with our message, our values, and our product quality, we've been able to create a brand presence that other people recognize. A brand can develop organically from good DRM.

For most small businesses (the non-Cokes and non-Nikes of the world), this is the best way to grow. Spend your money on great multi-channel direct-response campaigns and let your brand develop while you make money.

Now that you've got a handle on direct-response marketing, let's get back to multi-channel marketing.

WHAT ARE CHANNELS?

Channels are simply the method or form in which you communicate or ask your customers or potential customers to buy.

First, let's identify some of the channels of a multi-channel campaign.

As you read through the charts that follow, check off the channels you have used by themselves or in combination with other channels to execute a multi-channel marketing campaign.

Direct E-Mail Marketing

Channel	Used by Itself	MCC (Multi-Channel Campaign)	Used in Combination With
Dedicated Lists			
Inserts			
Advertising			
Sponsorships			
Joint Ventures			
Squeeze Pages			
Banner Ads			
Polls			
Co-Registration			

Social Media

Channel	Used by Itself	MCC	Used in Combination With
Word of Mouth			
Web 2.0			
Blogs			
Social Networks			
Videos			

Search Engine Marketing (SEM)

Channel	Used by Itself	MCC	Used in Combination With
Search Engine Optimization (SEO)			
Link Building			
Tagging			
Pay-Per-Click (PPC)			
RSS/Syndication			

Print

Channel	Used by Itself	MCC	Used in Combination With
Direct Mail			
Inserts			
Magazine Advertising			
Catalog Advertising			

Radio

Channel	Used by Itself	MCC	Used in Combination With
Short-Form Ads			
Long-Form Ads			
Infomercials			
Sponsorships			

Television

Channel	Used by Itself	MCC	Used in Combination With
Short-Form Ads			
Long-Form Ads			
Infomercials			

Telephone

Channel	Used by Itself	MCC	Used in Combination With
Teleconferences (free and paid)			
Inbound Sales			
Outbound Sales			

Event Marketing

Channel	Used by Itself	MCC	Used in Combination With
Platform Selling			
Break-Out Sessions			

Public Relations

Channel	Used by Itself	MCC	Used in Combination With
Paid			
Free			

If you have not tested or used many of the above channels, or if you left the last two columns of the charts blank, don't worry. We are going to identify the core of multi-channel marketing. Then, later in the book, we'll discuss each individual channel, and we'll show you how to combine them to get the biggest profits from every marketing campaign.

CLAYTON MAKEPEACE'S STORY

Clayton Makepeace is from the old school, a veteran copywriter who has been in direct marketing since the early 1970s.

Unlike many of his contemporaries from back in the day, Makepeace has adapted to changes in technology. From direct mail and print ads, he has moved online with web sites, e-mail, search engine optimization (SEO), pay-per-click (PPC) ads, and more. But each of these modern

CLAYTON MAKEPEACE'S STORY (Continued)

marketing channels is just another medium, says Makepeace, and he has not abandoned his roots.

"The medium doesn't make the sale," he explains, "the message does. And because 100 percent of the prospects who'll be getting your message are, well, *people*—and because human nature never changes—the things you must do to persuade people to buy never change."

Essentially, basic direct-mail principles are evergreen and work in every marketing channel, says Makepeace. They have always worked and will in the future. You can measure exactly how your marketing message has been received (by looking at sales) and make changes very quickly if necessary. And you don't need a multimillion-dollar budget to do it. This is what keeps Makepeace in the business.

"It's the scientific aspect. You can test everything. You can test small, roll out huge. This almost infinite, almost instant scalability makes it possible to create explosive growth even for the smallest entrepreneurs," says Makepeace. "I also love the fact that direct-response marketing is proactive. You identify a market niche. You buy the media that can take your sales message to that niche. You test, you count the money, you roll out. You are in control."

That said, copywriting and marketing in the online world is different.

"Used to be, all sales copy was pretty much the same," says Makepeace. "You grabbed the prospect with a benefit-oriented headline, presented your benefits and your credibility elements, trivialized your price, and asked for the sale. Today, online sales copy is more about gradual bonding and building to an eventual sale. You have to provide value to lift yourself above your competition and to establish credibility with your prospects. That requires an entirely different tone. And the copy itself must deliver value—give the prospect reasons to open your e-mails and read your e-newsletters or blogs."

Not all the changes have been welcomed by Makepeace, especially when they stray from core direct-marketing standards.

"Being able to contact prospects and customers for free through e-mail has created an entirely new direct-response business model. Relying on

(continues)

> **CLAYTON MAKEPEACE'S STORY** (Continued)
>
> PPC and SEO have required us to become somewhat more passive—to wait for folks to find us and to wait again, sometimes for months, before prospects make a first purchase and before we can calculate return on investment on our PPC and SEO costs," says Makepeace. "That hasn't been easy for me. Although we have clients who are using paid online advertising—who spend $300,000 or more every month online—I still prefer more proactive media like direct mail and print."
>
> He points out that the media you use should be determined by the product, market niche, and the prospect. Inexpensive household gadgets are tailor-made for 60-second direct TV ads, for example, while smaller niches do better with direct mail and the various Internet channels.
>
> "Marketers today are focusing too much on one medium at a time," says Makepeace. "And too often, their media choices are dictated almost entirely by the wrong criteria. Your customers are your friends. Would you confine all communication with your best friend just to e-mail? No way! You use every form of communication available to you to talk with your friends. You send them e-mails. You text-message them. You send them snail mail. You call them on the phone. Heck, you even talk to them in person."

WHAT IS MULTI-CHANNEL MARKETING (MCM)?

Multi-channel marketing is simply offering customers more than one way to buy.

Think about the way people you know buy things. Now try to answer the questions below.

Question #1: Do you think an 80-year-old grandmother in Stamford, Connecticut, who has a passion for gardening buys through the same channel as a 21-year-old man who loves to surf in Venice Beach, California?

Question #2: Do you think that they are both good prospects for, or have responded to, a multi-channel marketing campaign?

If you said "no" to question #1, you are correct. And if you said "yes" to question #2, you are correct.

Let's say the grandmother in our example wants a new pair of gardening gloves. She receives a direct-mail offer showing a beautiful picture of the gloves at a reasonable price. The offer comes from the same company that sold her a new shovel a year ago. The good price, the picture, the timeliness of the ad, and her comfort with the company all combine to make her interested in buying the gloves. But part of Granny still thinks she can get one more year out of her old gloves.

The very next day, she sees a TV commercial for the very same gloves. And the commercial features an 800 number that makes it easy to order. So she picks up the phone and orders. Five days later, she is enjoying her new gloves.

And let's say our 21-year-old surfer wants a new surfboard. He's already gotten numerous sales calls via telephone from the same company that sold him his first board. But he is not ready to buy a new one without seeing it first. It doesn't matter that he's familiar with the company. It doesn't matter that they are offering a convenient payment plan. He refuses to buy a new board without first seeing it with his own eyes.

As luck (or good marketing) would have it, a couple of days later he receives an e-mail from the same company offering the same board with the same payment plan. But the e-mail includes a 90-second video of the board that showcases its benefits. He orders it immediately online.

These examples show how important it is to market your products through multiple channels. Different people respond to advertising in different ways. And very often your customers or potential customers need to see offers more than once before they make the decision to buy.

In both of the cases above, the customers needed to have the same message delivered via a different channel in order to make the purchase.

Had the companies in question marketed through only a single channel, both sales would have been lost. Plus, both companies now have customers who have purchased through two different channels—and studies have shown that there is a direct correlation between the number of channels a buyer has responded to and his lifetime value to the company. (Note: A recent study by the Direct Marketing Association [DMA] found that customers who buy from two channels rather than one are between 20 and 60 percent more valuable to a company over time. Customers who buy from three channels rather than one are 60 to 125 percent more valuable. Another benefit: Multi-channel buyers purchase a wider range of products.)

WHAT IS LIFETIME VALUE (LTV)?

There are numerous ways to calculate a customer's lifetime value (LTV). And most of them are daunting. But let's see if we can make it less complicated.

Lifetime value is the contribution a customer makes to your bottom line over the period of time they continue to buy from you. You need to know your customers' average LTV for two very simple reasons.

1. Lifetime value will help you determine exactly how much you can spend to *acquire a new customer*.
2. Lifetime value will help you determine how much you need to spend to *retain an existing customer*.

Knowing the LTV of your customers will be a deciding factor when incorporating various multi-channel marketing campaigns into your business model.

If calculating LTV is new to you, we suggest you use the Harvard Business School Toolkit—Lifetime Customer Value Calculator, Basic Model. It's available for free download at hbswk.hbs.edu/archive/1436.html. Here's a quick peek at the way it works (you will, of course, substitute your own assumed values when using the software).

Assumptions

Time between Purchases (years)	3
Retention Rate per Period	80%
Average Purchase Value	$50.00
Profit Margin	25%
Profit per Purchase	$12.50
Discount Rate per Year	12%
Product Inflation per Year	3%

Cost of Reaching Potential Customer	$0.50
Response Rate	10%
Cost of Attracting a Customer	$5.00
Coupon or Other Discount Costs	$8.00
Total Customer Acquisition Cost	$13.00

Calculations

Years per Period	3
Retention Rate	80%
Inflation per Year	3%
Discount Rate per Year	12%
Change in Value of Customer Purchase Period	−13%
Discount Rate per Period	40%
Net Present Value of Customer Purchase Stream	$23.55
Cost of Acquiring a Customer	$13.00
Net Present Value of Acquiring a Customer	$10.55

There are more complex models from the Harvard Business School and other sources. But keep in mind that you are a marketer, not a bean counter. Get your numbers and move on to bringing in more revenues through multi-channel campaigns.

At Agora, Inc., several of the more successful divisions have been implementing a multi-channel marketing strategy. One division has documented that customers acquired through multi-channel marketing are five times more valuable to them over time than customers acquired through one channel.

Even within Agora, some divisions are still afraid to experiment with multi-channel marketing. They market through only a single channel, the channel that they are most comfortable with.

This is a common mistake. And companies that insist on pursuing a single marketing channel remain indefinitely in the infancy stage of business growth.

Remember how the hypersuccessful pop-up ads of the early 2000s took a huge dive in popularity and efficacy? Marketing is cyclical. You need to position yourself to reach your customers the way that *they* want you to reach them.

In the remainder of this book, we will not only discuss how to become an expert in any and all channels of marketing, we will also teach you how to determine which channels to combine for the most effective and profitable campaigns. For instance, you will learn that using four, five, or six marketing channels does not mean you are running six separate marketing campaigns. Instead, you are combining these channels into one cohesive campaign with a unified message.

We will also show you how to make your communications with your customers as profitable as possible. And we'll uncover the biggest mistakes marketers make when planning and launching a multi-channel marketing campaign.

Once you understand and apply the secrets of multi-channel marketing, you will discover that your customers are happier. And having happier customers means a healthier business.

If you're ready to find more customers, create bigger profits, and expand your business, turn the page.

CHAPTER THREE

DIRECT-RESPONSE ONLINE MARKETING

Squeezing the Juice Out of the Low-Hanging Fruit

Whether you have a plumbing business, a gardening business, or are a restaurateur, e-mail marketing is a necessity, not an option.

That is exactly what one former family-practice physician, David Keller, learned in 2005. He had spent years consulting for a health publisher that used snail mail to send out all of their products and marketing efforts. But Dr. Keller believed that to truly help the buyers of their health products, they needed to be able to communicate with them more often, answer their questions more quickly, and do so in a manner that would not bankrupt the company. In other words, they needed a way to contact their customers and prospective customers better, faster, and cheaper.

E-mail seemed like the logical solution to Keller, so he began with the names of the company's existing customers and gradually built an e-mail list through joint ventures and pay-per-click (PPC) advertising.

He soon found that by communicating with people directly, the company was gathering information about the things customers were interested in that they would never have learned otherwise. And as the list grew, so did the company's revenues.

Because of the negligible cost of e-mail, the company was able to send sales letters not every quarter or every month, but every week or even every day. And instead of receiving complaints, as Keller initially feared, he found that people enjoyed hearing from them much more frequently!

Eventually, Keller left the health publisher and went out on his own, putting his online marketing efforts to work for himself. Today, he has a multimillion-dollar business that grows larger and larger each year . . . as a result of e-mail marketing.

More multimillion-dollar businesses have sprung up in the past 10 years than in the past 50 years because of e-mail marketing. It is the single most powerful marketing channel today.

Doing business faster, cheaper, and better than your competitors is a fundamental business strategy—and the Internet multiplies its relevance. In this chapter, you will see just how relevant this strategy is.

THE INTERNET MYTH

Before we explain how to optimize e-mail marketing in your advertising mix, we need to clear up a common misperception.

Most people associate direct e-mail (endorsed or dedicated) marketing with direct-mail marketing (mailing advertising promotions to customers that elicit a *direct* response). But they are very different.

For one thing, direct e-mail is much cheaper than direct-mail marketing. The cost of sending an e-mail is virtually nothing. Compare that to the cost of a first-class stamp, especially when you're mailing thousands of pieces at a time.

This low cost of delivery means that you can communicate with your customers almost as much as you want to through e-mail. At Early to Rise, we "talk" to our customers this way hundreds of times a year. With traditional direct mail, we would be limited to sending them perhaps two dozen sales letters annually. The return on investment (ROI) simply wouldn't justify sending more.

Another difference is that with an e-mail campaign you can often monitor, in detail, customer reaction to your ad. You can, for example, find out if they clicked on a link in the e-mail to read the full promotion. You can also see the results (sales) immediately.

This brings us to another difference: Speed.

E-mail gives you the ability to test your offers, see what's working, and quickly make changes to generate more sales. (We'll talk more about testing later in the book.) And if a major news event takes place, you can incorporate it into your sales message that same day.

Direct e-mail is different from direct mail in another important respect. Because of anti-spamming laws, it is illegal to send e-mail promotions to people who have not "opted in" to receive them. In the direct-mail world, businesses routinely send solicitations to people without first getting their permission. Mailing lists—both compiled from public sources and rented from third-party businesses—are the primary source of customer acquisition.

THE CAN-SPAM ACT

In 2003, the United States enacted the first law regulating unsolicited commercial e-mail. The Controlling the Assault of Non-Solicited Pornography and Marketing Act, better known by the clever acronym CAN-SPAM, also lays down several rules for sending marketing e-mails. Some of the basics:

- All e-mails should have an unsubscribe option, and recipients who opt out should be taken off the list within 10 days.
- You must include a full postal address at the foot of your e-mail, and any removal request sent by postal mail to that address must be honored.
- The addresses of people who opted out of your list shouldn't be sold to other marketers.
- "Subject" and "From" lines should accurately describe the message content and the sender and not be deceptive in any way.

Within five years after the act came into effect, hundreds of violators were charged and convicted of spamming, with sentences ranging from fines to jail sentences. However, Internet experts disagree as to whether the law has had any real impact on the amount of spam in e-mail inboxes. As a legitimate e-mail marketer, it is nevertheless very important that you follow the rules of the CAN-SPAM Act.

But in the Internet world, you cannot do that without getting into trouble. This means, for one thing, that although traditional direct-mail promotions are routinely sent to prospects through the mail, e-mail promotions can be sent only to existing customers.

Let's take a look at how that difference plays out in advertising.

If you are in the plumbing supply business and you want to become the world's biggest seller of left-handed monkey wrenches, you cannot simply e-mail your best monkey-wrench advertising piece to people who have bought other plumbing supplies before. Instead, you would have to develop a two- or three-step program that avoids the spamming process.

You might, for example, buy an *insert ad* (also known as an "e-newsletter ad" or "e-news sponsorship") in an Internet newsletter on plumbing. You might buy a *banner ad* on some sort of plumbing web site or on a banner ad network that has a home improvement channel. Or you might make an affiliate deal with another plumbing supply business in which they would send an *endorsed* or *dedicated* promotion about your product to their list of buyers. Or you might pay Google or some other search engine or display ad network to list an ad for you based on "keywords" that relate to plumbing.

The purpose of such efforts might be to direct responders to a *landing page* in which the monkey wrench was directly sold (a sales effort). Or it could be to direct them to a site where they could sign up for a free gift—some sort of plumbing information package or home repair publication that they would receive in return for their permission to let you send them advertising promotions in the future (a name collection effort).

Only after you have created a list of thousands or tens of thousands of willing prospects would you be able to send out an e-mail sales letter that would elicit the kind of response that you could get with a one-step sales letter in the mail.

Welcome to the world of direct e-mail advertising—a more complicated version of direct-mail marketing that relies on the same basic principles but can deliver much greater selling power.

In this chapter, we will examine all of the major aspects of direct online marketing and advertising, including text ads, sponsorships, insert ads, banner ads, endorsed (or dedicated) promotions, co-registration, and polls.

But before we discuss these techniques individually, let's point out some of the major characteristics of the Internet as a direct-response advertising medium.

- There are two ways you can contact prospective customers. You can post an ad on a web site, e-newsletter, blog, or portal page and wait for the prospect to come to you. Or you can send a promotion directly to your prospect's e-mail address. The first way is sometimes called *pull* marketing; the latter, *push* marketing.
- Because, as we have said, you can't send advertising via e-mail to people who have not agreed to let you do so, Internet marketers often give away free products or information in exchange for that permission. This is called *permission marketing*.
- Because of the requirement to get permission before you send advertising to people via e-mail (which doesn't exist with postal mail), direct e-mail marketing has become a two-step process. The first step is to develop a list of people who will accept your advertising. This list is built through the use of banner ads, insert ads, and so on. The second step is to send them your direct-response promotions. These are usually longer pieces, similar to direct-mail sales letters. It is useful to think of these two functions separately, and even to designate them as separate marketing processes within your company.
- Because of the two-step aspect of direct online marketing, short-form advertising copy is now just as important as long-form copy, which has traditionally dominated direct-mail marketing.
- To be successful at direct online marketing, a company must be skillful with both push and pull advertising, as well as long- and short-form copy.

Yes, there are several basic differences between direct-mail and online marketing. But the similarities are much greater. Direct-mail advertising is based on psychological principles that have not changed with the rise of the Internet. To be effective, direct e-mail advertising must follow these same principles.

SIMILARITIES BETWEEN DIRECT E-MAIL AND DIRECT-MAIL ADVERTISING

To get a ready handle on e-mail advertising forms, it helps to compare them with older, more traditional ones. Let's take a quick look:

Banner and Pay-per-Click Ads: These are like roadside billboards or small newspaper display ads. You don't have much time to catch the prospect's attention. The advertisement is competing against all sorts of distractions. The trick to making banner and pay-per-click ads work is similar to what is needed for billboards or small display ads. You need a strong hook, something that is almost impossible to overlook. It sometimes helps if it is indirect, surprising, or odd in some way. Remember, you have only seconds to get someone's attention and have them take action (click), so a powerful or controversial headline, leading question, or strong visual image usually works.

Insert Ads or E-News Sponsorships: Insert ads are little ads placed in e-newsletters. They are like small display ads in the editorial pages of magazines. Insert ads are longer than banner ads but still relatively short—usually 20 to 50 words in length. The secret to writing effective insert ads is to craft provocative, emotionally stimulating propositions.

Endorsed Ads: Endorsed ads are sent as standalone promotions to lists of qualified customers. Because they are sent separately, they are usually long, like direct-mail sales letters. The way to make endorsed ads work for you is to treat them the same way as direct-mail promotions—which means giving them a great deal of your time, attention, and creativity.

PRINCIPLES OF DIRECT E-MAIL ADVERTISING

In no specific order, here are 10 important principles that govern direct-mail marketing.

1. **Copy is King.** There are three components that govern the success of any promotion: the quality of the list you mail to, the

offer you present to the prospect, and the copy you use. Of these three, the list is the most important, the offer is next, and the copy is third. The right offer with great copy mailed to a bad list will produce zero results. Mediocre copy with a mediocre offer mailed to a great list can produce good results. That said, selecting qualified lists and framing attractive offers is less difficult than crafting great copy. That is why in direct e-mail, as in direct mail, *copy is king*.

2. **Long copy out-pulls short copy.** This principle is highly controversial. Many Internet copywriters believe that the nature of the Internet—which makes it necessary for prospects to read copy on a screen—favors short copy. Although short copy can sometimes work very well, hundreds of tests that we have seen prove the old direct-mail maxim to be true: Other things being equal, longer copy is usually better.

3. **When it comes to long copy, the lead is 80 percent of the game.** A typical direct-mail or e-mail promotion has three parts: the lead, the body, and the close. The lead is usually less than 20 percent of the whole, but it carries the responsibility of conveying the "big idea" of the sales message and provoking an appropriate emotion in the reader. If you can do that consistently in your e-mail promotions, you will have a great deal of success.

4. **In crafting a lead, stick with the proven six.** There are dozens of ways to begin a long-form sales letter, but in the history of direct mail, six have dominated. These are: offer/promise, invitation, problem/solution, secret, story, and prediction. If you can figure out which of these six leads works best for the offer you are making, your chances of success will skyrocket.

5. **All leads range from being very direct to very indirect.** Direct leads are those that are obviously sales pitches. Indirect leads appear to be doing something else. Each approach has its strengths and weaknesses. Effective e-mail marketers make wise use of both.

6. **Given two packages with equally strong leads, the one that is well-balanced will do better.** A well-balanced promotion has four aspects: idea, benefit, credibility, and track record. We call this "the secret of the four-legged stool," because if your

promotion has all four of these "legs," it will be well balanced and it won't topple over.

7. **When composing headlines and bullets, details matter.** At Agora, we teach our copywriters to make their headlines and bullets more powerful by focusing on what we call "the four U's": uniqueness, usefulness, urgency, and ultra-specificity.

8. **Every product needs a unique selling proposition (USP).** Essentially, the USP is what makes your product stand out from the competition and gives your prospect a good reason to buy from you. Ignore this principle at your peril.

9. **Benefits are better than features—and deeper benefits are better than superficial benefits.** For example, don't tell a prospect that the car you are selling has good tires and suspension. Those are features. Instead, describe how, because of those features, they'll be able to maneuver easily through rush-hour traffic and avoid accidents with dangerous drivers. If you understand the deeper benefits your product offers, suggest them (indirectly, not directly) in the copy.

10. **Write to one person at a time in the language you would use if you were talking to that person face-to-face.** That doesn't always mean informal language. But it does mean conversational language.

Those are not the only principles that govern direct mail and e-mail marketing, but they are 10 of the most important.

NOT ALL LISTS ARE CREATED EQUAL

Perhaps the most important part of any marketing campaign is to target the right audience. In the old direct-mail days, it was called list selection. Today, depending on the specific marketing channel we're using, we sometimes refer to it as media buying—but it's the same thing.

There are basically two kinds of lists that you can market to:

1. Your house list
2. Outside lists

House Lists

Your house list in the e-marketing world comprises names you have received permission to market to. They can be divided up as follows:

- **Hot Leads**—people who have opted in to receive e-mails from you but have not yet made a purchase. They have taken the first step by saying they want information from you. The more valuable the information that you supply them for free, the more they trust you, and the sooner you can turn them into buyers.
- **Buyers**—people who have opted in and have purchased one product from you. Even though they have made their first purchase, you should continue to supply them with valuable free information. The next step is to turn them into multibuyers.
- **Multibuyers**—people who have opted in and have purchased more than one product from you. You should continue to supply these people with valuable free information as well. Your job at this point is to keep these customers and turn them into advocates for you.
- **Cancels and Expires**—former customers who canceled/returned/did not renew a service, product, or subscription they had purchased from you. Because they did not opt out of your free information list, you should continue to provide them with valuable free information as well as your promotional information. Your job is to get these former buyers to become current buyers.

Outside Lists

Outside lists are names that you do not yet have permission to market to; however, the people on these lists have agreed to receive third-party advertising. They can be divided up as follows:

- **Hot Prospects**—people who have purchased a similar product from your competitor. Let's say you are selling subscriptions to an e-newsletter on the subject of anti-aging. A hot prospect is someone who has purchased one or more anti-aging e-newsletters from other publishers.

- **Good Prospects**—people who have purchased a related product from your competitor. Again, let's say you are selling an anti-aging e-newsletter. A good prospect is someone who has purchased a book or DVD about anti-aging.
- **Okay Prospects**—people on a compiled list of names taken from directories, newspapers, or public records that have something in common or meet a certain criteria. Many people on compiled lists are not buyers. For our example, they could have simply filled out a survey, stating that they are interested in anti-aging. Don't make the mistake of using compiled lists because they are less expensive to rent.

CIRQUE DU SOLEIL AND ITS E-MAIL MARKETING ACROBATICS

Cirque du Soleil is known for amazing acrobatics and whimsical themes, but did you know that they also have a few tricks up their sleeves when it comes to e-mail marketing?

For more than two decades, this Montreal-based troupe has been touring and setting up shop in permanent performance venues all over the world. With every show, they try to forge a personal connection with every audience member. And they have the same goal for their e-mail marketing campaigns, which started in 2000, according to a case study by Marketing Sherpa.

Cirque doesn't want its relationships with its customers to end when the curtain falls. They send six to eight messages per week with news, upcoming show announcements, and product offers. But they don't want to fill their fans' inboxes with messages they don't want, so they've put together a pretty strong opt-in process. As a result, they know that everybody on their list is truly interested in their e-mails and will respond to offers of tickets and merchandise.

First of all, there is no actual Cirque du Soleil "list" that you can sign up for. There is a fan club, Cirque Club, that sends out the regular updates. The company's web site heavily promotes this club with a prominently displayed e-mail form and various related links. And they promote the club at shows, giving club members preferred seating and surprise upgrades—in full view of other audience members.

CIRQUE DU SOLEIL AND ITS E-MAIL MARKETING ACROBATICS
(Continued)

The Cirque e-mail team also heavily segmented the club names so they can send very detailed messages unique to each individual member. They do this by collecting specific information during the opt-in process, including where each person wants to see touring shows, if they want news of permanent shows (and which ones), whether they're interested in merchandise offers, and (because Cirque's founders are from Canada) if they prefer their e-mails to be in French or English. They strictly stick to these preferences, and almost never send out mass e-mails to the entire list.

They make sure each new club member "whitelists" the Cirque Club e-mails *before* they finish signing up. And they require double opt-in, meaning each new member has to reply to an e-mail from Cirque before they start receiving the updates.

As for the e-mails themselves, they are simple and mostly text. Written in the voice of characters from certain shows (depending on the member's selected preferences), they are conversational and informal. They heat up when a touring show is in town, with a series of updates in the weeks before the show urging members to attend.

The result is a very "clean" list that Cirque says responds at a very high conversion rate to offers, especially when news of an upcoming show hits.

Source: MarketingSherpa—Practical Cases and Know How: How Cirque du Soleil Uses Email to Sell Out Shows at Local Cities. www.marketingsherpa.com/article.php?ident=27496#

ANATOMY OF AN ENDORSED AD

Endorsed ads are the heart of direct e-mail marketing. They require a great deal of time and creativity for two main reasons:

1. **Endorsed ads are sent as standalone promotions.** This is a key point. The endorsed ad is the only direct online tactic that does not compete with other ads or editorial copy. A banner ad may have five other ads on the same page, as well as a gripping editorial headline, all fighting for the prospect's attention. A PPC

ad may be competing with 20 other PPC ads on the same page. You are up against the same thing with polls, co-registration, and insert ads.

2. **Endorsed ads are the foundation of your entire campaign.** If the ad is based on a "big idea" that is expressed clearly and concisely, you can leverage the time and effort you put into it by using pieces of the copy for *all* of your other tactics and channels. If your headline is a winner, it can be used as your banner ad or PPC ad. If your lead has performed well, you can turn that into your insert ad or a squeeze page.

Now, let's break down an endorsed ad for *The Healing Prescription*, a report offered by Total Health Breakthroughs (a division of Early to Rise), and show you how we leveraged the copy to create a squeeze page . . . a banner ad . . . a dedicated ad . . . an e-news sponsorship ad . . . a co-registration ad . . . an online poll . . . and a PPC ad.

The Squeeze Page

The squeeze page is the first page to page and a half of the complete endorsed e-mail ad. The headline and the lead are the most important part of any promotion. You make the beginning so compelling that the prospect is actually willing to give you his e-mail address for the privilege of reading the rest of the promotion.

The end of the promotion will ask for the sale.

- **Primary purpose**: Name collection
- **Secondary purpose**: Upsell (conversion to a sale)

In order to illustrate the anatomy of an ad, please take a look at the excerpt from the promotion shown. (Although we have included some of the elements of the ads here, we strongly encourage you to refer to the Appendix, which displays the entire promotion. This ad will serve as a valuable resource for you, as you implement or improve your multi-channel marketing campaign.)

"6 months ago, I was constantly fatigued, overweight, and heading toward diabetes. Today, I'm healthy, energetic, and can fit into jeans I wore before I gave birth to three kids...."

Ex-Supermarket Employee Reveals the Secrets of How to Reprogram
Your Body's "Metabolic Code"
for Optimal Health

Record Numbers of Patients Avoid Cancer, Arthritis, Diabetes, Alzheimer's, and Other Devastating Illness ... for Decades ...

The Banner Ad

Banner ads come in various sizes. Some popular sizes (noted in pixels) include 300 × 250 (medium rectangle), 468 × 60 (full banner), 728 × 90 (leader boards), 120 × 600 (skyscraper), 125 × 125 (square), 120 × 60 (button), and 120 × 240 (vertical). The ads can be flat (no animation), animated, or flash.

- **Primary purpose**: Upsell (conversion to a sale)—if customer is sent to a landing page, which is done very often. (For the purposes of this exercise, the landing page and dedicated e-mail are the same.)
- **Secondary purpose**: Name collection—if customer is sent to a special or free report

Note that the placement and audience you're targeting will determine the primary purpose of the banner ad. If the banner ad is running on your own web site, your primary goal would be sales conversion. If your banner ad is running on a third-party web site, blog, or banner ad network, your prospects may not be familiar with your company, publication, products, or services. In that case, you would want to focus on name collection, and then upsell those prospects later with a series of targeted conversion e-mails.

The Dedicated E-Mail Ad

The dedicated e-mail ad is dedicated to a single sales letter—the full promotion.

- **Primary purpose**: Selling the product
- **Secondary purpose**: Generateing leads

(Refer to the Appendix to see the dedicated e-mail ad for *The Healing Prescription*. The beginning of the ad is similar to the squeeze page, yet its scope extends beyond that.)

The E-News Sponsorship Ad

The e-news sponsorship ad is placed in an e-newsletter or e-zine. The placement is usually in a top, middle, or bottom position, and can be in text or HTML format. You can buy the space or approach others for swaps.

- **Primary purpose**: Upsell (conversion to a sale)
- **Secondary purpose**: Building a hot list and generating leads

Below are two examples of what an e-news sponsorship ad looked like for *The Healing Prescription*.

Are You Waking Up to Pee at Night?
David, a 56-year-old executive, had an enlarged prostate that was causing him to get up to urinate three or four times a night. He desperately wanted to avoid prostate surgery, which could potentially leave him impotent. The treatment? A bioactive compound that blocks production of DHT, a hormone causing the body to overproduce its normal amount of prostate cells. David avoided surgery, shrank his prostate naturally, and today sleeps through the night without waking to use the bathroom. Now you can learn about the same healthy prostate treatment without leaving your home. Click here for details: [URL to our landing page inserted]

Lower Cholesterol Safely and Naturally
More than 2,600 Americans die from cardiovascular disease daily.
The two most common dietary factors putting you at risk? Fat and
cholesterol. Our free report is your guide to foods that lower your
cholesterol and risk of heart disease as well as foods to avoid. Get
the straight talk on olive oil . . . omega-3 . . . salt . . . alcohol . . . folic
acid . . . potassium . . . garlic . . . green tea . . . l-Carnitine . . . and more.
For more information and to download your free cholesterol-fighting
report, click here now: [URL to our landing page inserted]

Note that since the above e-news ads were inserted into our own
Early to Rise e-newsletter, the redirect landing page was for a straight
sale. The target audience was already familiar with our publication and
services. They didn't necessarily need to "buy into" our philosophy. If
this same ad were going into an outside e-newsletter, the landing page
would likely be the squeeze page—as the primary goal would be to
collect names and add those prospects into our sales cycle, giving them
time to bond with us. The secondary goal would have been immediate
sales conversion after we collected the names.

The Co-Registration Ad

With co-registration, your ad goes on someone else's web site, generally
after a transaction on that web site (such as a newsletter signup or an
order) has been completed. Your ad is usually limited to about 200
characters. And you typically get to put a small graphic image next
to it.

- **Primary purpose**: Name collection
- **Secondary purpose**: Upsell (conversion to a sale)

Again, because these leads are coming from a third-party source,
your primary goal should be name collection via your squeeze page,
and then an upsell via a targeted series of promotions.

Following is a sample of what our co-registration ads looked like
for *The Healing Prescription*.

Special Report: Alternative Health Doctor Seeking to Shake the Medical Establishment and Find Life Altering Cures for Chronic and Serious Illnesses Ready to Help You. Are You Ready to Change Your Life Forever? Click Here to Find Out How. [URL to our squeeze page]

The Online Poll

The goal of an online poll is to collect names as well as to engage your prospects. The poll can be in the form of a banner ad that redirects to a name collection source (your squeeze page). The answers that prospects give to your poll question also give you a way to qualify them. "Very interested" may be redirected to your landing page for sales, whereas "somewhat interested" may just get a "thank you" page. Both types of prospects, however, should receive a free incentive, such as a report, for their time. It's also important to mention your privacy policy when you're doing an online poll. Prospects want to make sure their e-mail address is safe with you.

- **Primary purpose**: Name collection
- **Secondary purpose**: Upsell (conversion to a sale)

Here's an example of an online poll for *The Healing Prescription*:

Special Report: Alternative Health Guru Spills His Secrets... Interested in overcoming chronic conditions and serious illness and dispelling the myths about nutrition that could radically change your health . . . and the rest of your life?

I just met a doctor who can do all that. He's an expert in alternative health. He isn't beholden to the drug companies. And his systematic research and years of experience have yielded a proven method for balancing the nutrients and hormones in your body. The result could be the best health you've had in years, if not decades.

I'm going to tell you about this system in just a minute in a free report.

Here's just some of what you'll learn:

* 5 amazingly effective natural remedies that can clear up your children's ear infections faster than they can say "Mommy and Daddy, my ear hurts!"

* 12 natural remedies that can relieve tenderness, stiffness, aches, pains, and other symptoms associated with fibromyalgia

* A common vitamin you find in grapefruit that can speed your recovery after injury—and help wounds heal up to 50% faster

* The awful truth about canola oil...energy bars...farm-raised salmon...soy...frozen yogurt...and other popular "health foods" that are anything but

You'll also receive a complimentary subscription to the Total Health Breakthroughs e-mail newsletter—the number one source on the Web for natural health and wellness information.

Please answer the following questions and then enter your first name and e-mail below to get your free copy of this special report.

How interested are you in learning natural solutions to your diet and health problems?

[ ] Very Interested
[ ] Somewhat Interested
[ ] Slightly Interested
[ ] Not At All Interested

Your First Name:

Your E-mail:

Take Me to My Free Report!

The Pay-per-Click (PPC) or Display Ad

The pay-per-click or display ad is an online advertising tactic in which payment is based on how often Internet users click on your link.

- **Primary purpose**: Name collection—with a redirect to your squeeze page
- **Secondary purpose**: Upsell (conversion to a sale)

Note that the names we collected with our PPC ads for *The Healing Prescription* were added to the sales cycle, with targeted conversion efforts over a number of months. Typical conversion rates for "cold" prospects can vary from 30 to 90 days.

With PPC ads, you have limited space. The typical ad has about 15 words or 123 characters. So you want to take your strongest headline and call-to-action statement and use that. Your success in this platform will also be based on the keywords and keyword strings you've selected.

Look at the four examples below to see how we did it.

Fight Metabolic Syndrome
What You Need Now to Restore &
Protect Metabolic Function!
www.TotalHealthBreakthroughs.com

Do You Have Syndrome X?
Signs of Syndrome X That Could Be
Affecting You. Free Health Alert!
www.TotalHealthBreakthroughs.com

Underactive Thyroid?
You Could Have "Syndrome X". Learn
the Signs & Treatment. Free Report!
www.TotalHealthBreakthroughs.com

Underactive Thyroid?
Low Thyroid? High Insulin? Could be
"Syndrome X". Free Health Alert!
www.TotalHealthBreakthroughs.com

Do you see how we took this one endorsed e-mail ad and created an entire campaign using several other tactics? And this was for only one marketing channel.

IT'S TIME TO APPLY

Before we move on, consider your own business. Take your most successful endorsed ad and see if you can create the following from it:

- Two Banner Ads
- Two PPC Ads
- Two Insert Ads
- Two Poll Questions
- Two Insert Ads

Why did we ask you to come up with two of each one? Because that will come in very handy when you find out what we have to say about testing later in this book.

Meanwhile, let's get to Chapter 4.

CHAPTER FOUR

SOCIAL MEDIA

Informal Communication, Powerful Profits

Tim Ferriss had a challenge. He'd never written a book before, but he wanted to have a best-seller with his first one, *The 4-Hour Workweek*. He had an idea how to do it. He knew something about the Internet, and it didn't involve an expensive marketing campaign. In fact, his marketing didn't cost a dime.

Ferriss generated online buzz for his book with a clever two-part strategy. First, he developed relationships with influential bloggers in the months leading up to the book's launch. Then, when the book was ready to be promoted, he sent those people copies—and it got an enthusiastically positive response from all of them.

Blogs are like online diaries—personal web sites—that are updated regularly and available for others to see. Some blogs have become widely read, attracting thousands or even millions of readers. Some blogs focus on particular topics, such as gardening or sports or basketball. Ferriss talked up his book in both business and mainstream blogs.

Blog by blog, Ferriss chatted his way through the online community. Through links to other sites, his and others' comments about his book traveled with increasing speed. Soon he had hundreds of blogs, online communities, and other web sites talking about his book.

Online buzz often leads to offline publicity. Eventually, Ferriss was being invited to speak on network morning shows and at other high-profile venues.

The key to Ferriss's success, he thinks, is that he never pitched his book to the bloggers directly. Instead, he familiarized himself with their blogs and views on business and life, sent them messages about past posts of theirs that he liked or disagreed with, and met them in person at blogger conferences.

"The trick is to have a real dialogue," he says. "To really get to know them. Sending them a hypey marketing/PR message doesn't work. They see right through it."

Ferriss admits that this is a time-consuming approach to marketing a book. But, he says, it's a zero-cost way to promote yourself or your product on the Internet. And being known on the Internet can propel you into the national limelight, from which point publicity becomes almost self-perpetuating—a phenomenon known as "viral marketing." (Ferriss's book is still on many best-seller lists more than a year after it was published.)

THE PERFECT MARKETING CHANNEL FOR ENTREPRENEURS WHO HAVE MORE TIME THAN MONEY

Kimbo Slice is probably the best-known mixed–martial artist in the world today. A back-alley Miami brawler, he became famous on the Internet when his managers videotaped him boxing street toughs in backyards of Dade County. Slice became a legend among martial arts enthusiasts, and within a year after starting a social media campaign, his managers had him booked on network TV.

In order to drive traffic to his new web site, Mrfire.com, author and speaker Joe Vitale was looking for a gimmick that would generate lots of conversation on the Internet. He settled on selling an "Elvis Mermaid" on eBay.

What is an Elvis Mermaid? Nothing more than a photo of Elvis Photoshopped onto the image of a mermaid, both of which Vitale collected online.

Vitale had a feeling that the gimmick would attract a lot of interest, and although it was pretty silly, it worked.

The Elvis Mermaid went up on eBay and within seconds—seconds, not minutes—hundreds of people were checking it out and then going to Vitale's web site to see his Photoshopped masterpiece.

That "silly idea" gave Vitale the traffic he needed to launch his site.

Investor's Daily Edge (IDE), an investment advisory publisher, was puttering along with about 150 hits per day on its web site from its pay-per-click (PPC) ad campaign through Google. Then one day, one of IDE's writers noticed that Digg (an online social news site where readers contribute content) was getting a lot of postings about Ron Paul, the perpetual Libertarian candidate for president. He wrote a provocative article about perceived media bias against Paul and his supporters, posted it to Digg, and it was an immediate success. It drove a 400 percent spike in traffic to IDE's web site the day it was published, and then a one- to two-week period of increased traffic after the initial jump.

Gary Vaynerchuk was an anonymous wine lover and liquor-store owner when he came up with the idea of creating an Internet site devoted to his particular take on wine. His personal blend of enthusiasm, irreverence, and humor attracted fans by the thousands to his web site. Today, WineLibraryTV.com is a certified online hit, with 90,000 visitors a day. Vaynerchuk has become a mainstream wine celebrity and is frequently featured on TV talk shows and radio, and in newspapers and magazines.

As you can see from the above examples, social media marketing has changed the nature of promotion and publicity for small-time entrepreneurs and wannabe celebrities. Anybody who has the time to devote to this marketing channel can become a recognized author, movie director, pop singer, artist, or expert on any subject.

You still need to be good at what you do, but you no longer need luck or money to get the word out about yourself or your business to the rest of the world.

SOCIAL MEDIA AND ITS MANY DIMENSIONS

Social media advertising takes many forms, from online forums to message boards to blogs to video-, photo-, and music-sharing sites to social networks and comment sections on web sites. The list goes on and on.

The primary method of taking advantage of social media is through viral marketing—essentially, word-of-mouth advertising.

Social media giants such as Facebook, YouTube (purchased by Google for $1.65 billion), and MySpace (acquired by Rupert Murdoch for $580 million) have received a great deal of coverage in the press. But just as significant for the small- and medium-sized business is the rise of hundreds of less-sizeable social media sites that together have a huge audience—millions and millions of prospective customers.

FORMS OF SOCIAL MEDIA

- **Internet forum/Message board**—an online community that allows users to post messages and content, and have "discussions."
- **Weblog ("blog")**—an online diary of sorts, updated regularly, that can be maintained by one person or several. A blog can include text, pictures, video, and links to other web sites.
- **Videolog ("vlog")**—a weblog consisting mostly of embedded videos or links to videos.
- **Wiki/Group creation**—a web site that is created and modified by a community of users who generate its content.
- **Podcast**—a syndicated digital file (video or audio) that can be downloaded and played on a home computer, or, more popularly, a portable MP3 player.
- **Photo-sharing**—an online database of photos and pictures that can be viewed or even used by others, sometimes for a fee.
- **Comment posting/Wall posting**—leaving a message on a user profile in social networking sites like MySpace or Facebook.

The term "social media" applies to many different models of communication. But most of them can be put into one of two groups.

First, there are the social media sites such as YouTube and Facebook. These sites primarily feature user content. In other words, they publish videos or text submitted by users and ask other users to rate that content. Such sites have become very popular because they give ordinary people a zero-cost way of getting their message out to the world and claiming their stake of celebrity.

Then there are blogs. Blogs work very differently. With blogs, the content is generated by the publisher of the blog and user content is secondary. When blogs are very good, they can become popular very fast. When they are mediocre, they are unlikely to attract any attention at all.

To take full advantage of the potential of social media advertising, you can do two things. You can create outbound campaigns to blogs and forums and chat rooms, as Tim Ferriss did to promote his book. And you can start your own blog, as Gary Vaynerchuk did with his wine web site.

You can stimulate conversation on social media sites about you, your business, and/or your products by publishing special reports or covering news or sending out targeted surveys or questionnaires. But to ensure that the "buzz" is positive, you have to promote yourself gradually and organically, as Tim Ferriss did, by developing genuine relationships with the social media sites you have targeted.

If you have an active business, in all likelihood you have a customer service site or user network that you can go to. To ignore your own customers on your own site is an unforgivable mistake in today's interconnected world. You must always be answering your customers' questions, responding to their complaints, explaining problems and opportunities, announcing new products and services, listing upcoming events, reminding customers of upcoming deadlines, and so on.

If you have a social media site and are not involved in the ongoing conversation, you're missing out on an important chance to lengthen, deepen, and strengthen the relationship you have with your customers.

THE BARE MINIMUM

Every business should have, at the very least, an active, Internet-based customer forum.

A forum is a site where your customers and potential customers talk about you, your business, and your products. In the twentieth century, business owners liked to control what was said about them and their companies. In the twenty-first century, that's no longer possible. Smart business leaders have realized that, rather than controlling the conversation, they are better off participating in it.

Customer forums give you an excellent opportunity to find out what your customers are thinking and feeling. They have made customer surveys and focus groups obsolete. Forums will tell you what you are doing right and what you are doing wrong. They will give you clues about what your customers need and/or want and what other products they are buying.

Why pay tens of thousands of dollars for an outside marketing company to conduct a customer survey or run a focus group for you? You can learn loads more about what's really important by spending just a few hours on a forum.

The challenge of social media advertising is to get customers, prospects, colleagues, and competitors to talk about you *in a structured way*. They will talk about you whether you like it or not. But when they do so through a forum that you control, you can take full advantage of those conversations.

If your business is devoted to developing good products, the conversations on your forum will be generally positive. You will get slammed from time to time, but the naysayers will be drowned out by customers who have bought products from you and are happy with them and the service they have received. When your customers come to your rescue and defend you and promote you, that is the best publicity you could ask for. And you don't have to pay for it. It is given to you free of charge!

Amazon.com allows customers to rate and review everything they sell on its site, from books to leaf blowers. If you're in the hospitality business, online forums and message boards can be especially powerful. Sites such as Chowhound.com allow diners and travelers to rate your hotel or restaurant. They talk about the noise level, customer service, food, cleanliness, and location. Savvy web surfers check these sites before booking trips or planning evenings out.

ADVANTAGES AND DISADVANTAGES
OF SOCIAL MEDIA

The first and most notable advantage of social media advertising is its low cost.

Once your site is built and running, it costs very little to get your customers and prospects to go to it. They will do it on their own almost every time you put an advertisement in front of them and every time they consider buying one of your products. If you have established e-mail contact with your customers, stimulating them to use your social media site costs you nothing more than the expense of composing the message. Expensive list or space fees do not apply.

The next thing that should be said about social media is its wide reach. When a social message catches fire, it can travel around the world, to millions of people, in a matter of weeks or even days. The main reason for this is the Internet. But other media are often involved too. It is not unusual for a hot Internet message or video to be picked up by radio, television, magazines, or newspapers. Sometimes, all of these media jump on the subject at one time.

Social media is also, as we've said, a superb way to gather information about your customers, their wants and desires, and to deal with any business problems you may be encountering. Social media advertising is the most effective way to establish, defend, and boost your company's credibility.

Social marketing has many potential benefits. But there are drawbacks too. Of all the advertising channels, social marketing is the one that offers the longest odds. For every Joe Vitale and Tim Ferriss who was successful with their social campaigns, there are hundreds if not thousands of people whose efforts were fruitless. The reason social marketing is so difficult is because of the channel itself. It is big and it is powerful, but it is not controllable by the marketer. In some cases, it can backfire by turning into negative publicity.

This is especially true if you try to use social media dishonestly. If you misrepresent yourself online, you will most likely get caught and suffer the consequences. The online world will quickly turn against you with a wave of very bad buzz across cyberspace. This will result in lost sales, public outrage, and more.

So how do you use social media dishonestly? Shady marketers have created fake profiles of "fans" on social networking sites like MySpace in order to promote their products. They've also created "consumer" blogs that were written by their company's PR department.

In one widely publicized recent case, Whole Foods' CEO John Mackey was caught posting negative comments about a competitor on Yahoo Finance message boards. He used a pseudonym during the entire eight-year run of trash talk. Many believe his goal was to drive down the stock price of the competitor so that Whole Foods could easily take it over. That allegation was enough to get the SEC involved.

In another case, Wal-Mart's PR firm hired two journalists to travel across the United States in an RV, visiting stores along the way. Posing as ordinary people, the reporters collected overwhelmingly pro–Wal-Mart interviews with employees and customers and posted them on their blog. Around the same time, the same PR firm created a fake grassroots campaign in which a mom, part of a working-class family, sang the praises of the retail giant. Savvy Internet surfers soon realized the "bloggers" in both cases were hired guns, and spread the news online.

Honesty is a key asset with social media, not only because of the consequences if you get caught "faking it," but because of the creative strengths you enjoy when you figure out how to promote the core values and qualities of your company and products through this channel.

These are the main principles that apply to social media advertising:

- **The Message Is for the Medium.** When creating an event, writing a press release, or crafting a video for viral marketing, think about what people are interested in, not what you want to show them. Nobody in the major social media is likely to be interested in a new product you create or a new development in your company. But if you can reposition your news so that it will be interesting to the greater public, you have a good chance of getting coverage. The trick to writing good press releases and/or informational videos is to study the media beforehand. Figure out what types of stories/videos they like to run, and tailor your piece to match.

- **Audacity Is Everything.** When developing a news story or event, be aggressive in your conception. Big stories are generally better than small ones. Crazy events are more interesting than sane ones. Odd or funny videos get more play than conventional ones. But when thinking audaciously, be calculating. Study the media's preferences. Determine what kind of odd, crazy, and/or funny messages they like to feature.
- **Respect the Priorities.** Records are more interesting than lists. Lists are more interesting than facts. Social media loves world records, even world records for obscure and silly things. Next to world records, social media loves lists, especially top-10 lists: forecasts, trends, favorite picks, and so on. The best movies of the year, the best albums of the year, the best electronic gadgets, and the best travel destinations are examples of lists that are popular in social media. People have strong opinions about these subjects, and such lists can generate a lot of discussion among those who disagree with the ratings. Think of how your business can generate its own world records and top-10 lists.
- **Give Them Something to Talk About.** Everyone likes a scandal and controversy. If you can figure out how to sex up your message, try it.
- **Simplicity Is a Virtue.** When announcing your news, express it in the simplest possible language. Simple language gives you two big advantages. First, it is easier to comprehend. Second, it is easier for people to remember and repeat, like a catchy sound bite that you may hear on TV. Think of how quickly catchphrases from the sitcom *Seinfeld* ("yada, yada, yada," "not that there's anything wrong with that," or "no soup for you") passed into everyday usage.
- **Make It Brief.** The core concept of the message—the part you want people to remember—should be short enough to print on the subject line of an e-mail or in the headline of a magazine article.

Early to Rise incorporated in December of 1999 and has had a forum since June of 2000. During that time, we have had many interesting online conversations. We have also had a few dissatisfied customers post their experiences with us—and those postings were helpful. They made us aware of problems or perceived problems, and helped us improve our business.

ANATOMY OF A SUCCESSFUL BLOG PROMOTION

As we mentioned before, the main difference between a forum and a blog is a matter of who dominates the conversation. In a forum, the customers do. In a blog, the blogger (company representative, business owner, or expert) does.

For a business owner, a forum is like an auditorium full of customers that are talking about your company. You can walk in and talk any time you like, but you are always walking into a conversation that is already taking place. You can interject your comments, but you can't control the crowd.

A blog is much more like a soapbox in a public park. The business owner stands in the passing crowd and talks and talks, hoping he can get some of them to stop and listen. Some who stop will ask him questions. Some will shout out their own opinions, even criticize him on occasion. In a blog, it is the business owner or his representative who starts the conversation and does most (or much) of the talking. He has much more control over what people hear (because he can edit out any feedback he doesn't want publicized). And if he does a good job, he can create a larger and larger group of loyal listeners.

Rich Schefren has had great success using his blog to promote his business, StrategicProfits.com, and his business-development products. "When I post to my blog," Schefren says, "I am posting content for my readers. But my readers can also add their comments to my post, and other blogs can link to mine. Suddenly, my content has morphed into communication: A new dialogue between my readers and me . . . and between my fellow bloggers and their readers!"

Schefren says he has found that the key to success in blogging is "transparency." "Your readers want to know what is really going on inside your company and inside your head. The more honest and direct you can be with them, the better they will like it."

Here's an example of what Schefren means. In October of 2006, Strategic Profits and ETR came to a standstill about a planned series of teleconferences for our combined readerships. Schefren wanted the level to be fairly sophisticated, but ETR wanted to gear it toward beginners. When we couldn't agree in time to produce the first call of the series, we cancelled it temporarily. When we came to a compromise—to provide a combination of introductory and more advanced information—Schefren got on his web site to explain the decision to his readers:

> My call with ETR was cancelled because we could not decide on whether or not people were ready for (or capable of) implementing the extremely powerful strategies in use by our offices.
>
> Should we make the program just for beginners? Or should we unlock every door and leave no stone unturned, throwing in every advanced marketing technique we know?
>
> ETR made the point that many people are just starting out.
>
> I countered with NUMEROUS examples from my coaching program of clients who have gone from a one-man shop to a small virtual team doing millions of dollars per year in revenue.
>
> So I know you guys can do it.
>
> That argument led us to a compromise. The Internet Wealth Alliance will be for BOTH groups. Beginners and advanced marketers.

Schefren's posting on his web site produced a rush of responses. Everyone seemed to have an opinion, including those listed below:

- "I was encouraged that you have structured the IMA to benefit beginners like myself. I am concerned that the pricing will be such that 'true' beginners will not have a seat at the feast."
- "This thing does sound exciting. And I am very grateful you decided to break it into two groups . . . still not sure I'll be able to pay my way in but at least that sector is available and those that can will have a shot."
- "You just said in an e-mail two minutes ago 'Yep this is open to newbies as well as seasoned pros.' Well mate, not many newbies could afford the $800 per month price tag on Brad and Andy's program. . . . I'm not saying that their program isn't worth it (It probably is!) but many of us and especially 'Newbies' would have to stop feeding their kids to pay out this kind of cash."

Remarks like these weren't limited to the comments section of Schefren's blog. Many e-mails were sent in to his office by customers and potential customers as well. For several months following the "incident," both ETR and Strategic Profits readers kept writing in, wondering if Schefren and ETR were still "feuding." The reason this one posting got so much attention, Schefren believes, is because it was entirely organic. "It stemmed from a real conversation to a group of readers who were excited about the original call. They were truly disappointed when the call was cancelled, and human curiosity took over."

Because of its transparency, the Internet has brought people together like no other technology.

SOCIAL NETWORKS, SOCIAL BOOKMARKS, AND SOCIAL NEWS WEB SITES

Most people consider social networks, social bookmarks, and social news sites to have the greatest influence in social media marketing. These web sites encourage visitors to post personal content and—usually—have it rated by other visitors. Generally speaking, the higher-rated content gets the best exposure on the site.

The external goal of a social network is to link people with similar interests. The internal goal is to make money through general advertising by exposing visitors to display ads.

In many cases, users post profiles filled with personal details, likes and dislikes, pictures, blogs, and more. Each user is provided with a separate location on the network where he or she can keep in touch with friends, spread the word about movies and music they're into, and meet new people.

In recent years, some businesses have gotten into the act by posting "profiles" for their products.

The major social media networks are MySpace.com, currently the third most popular web site in the United States, and FaceBook.com. Smaller, less-general, sites include LinkedIn.com, which provides networking opportunities for business professionals, and MeetUp.com, which serves community groups and associations.

In social bookmarking, users save links to web pages they stumble across on the Internet in a publicly viewable forum. The bookmarking allows the user to remember where they found an interesting web page and find it again. But because others can see what they bookmarked, the most interesting pages are quickly bookmarked by users with similar interests. A web page that generates a lot of social bookmarking interest can become very popular very quickly and will be highly ranked on the bookmarking site.

The biggest social bookmarking sites are StumbleUpon.com and Del.icio.us.

Social news sites are a bit different. Users nominate news articles, blog posts, and any other written online content that they feel deserves wider attention. They post a review or summary of the material on the social news site with a link to the original. The community of users decides how prominent the article will be on the site by voting. One thing to keep in mind: Obvious advertising messages are summarily rejected.

Digg.com, Newsvine.com, and Reddit.com are major social news sites.

These sites are becoming more and more popular by the day. Some of them are even attracting more traffic than the almighty Google!

GENERAL ADVERTISING AND DIRECT MARKETING IN SOCIAL MEDIA

In the beginning of this book, we made the argument that the Internet is tailor-made for direct-response marketing. This has proven to be true in every area of Internet advertising, but especially when it comes to social media.

Let's start by pointing out that Internet traffic is absolutely useless if you don't do anything with it—in other words, if you don't monetize it. And, in fact, at the Webmasters World Conference in Las Vegas in 2007, the top search engine marketers in the world had a panel discussion entitled "Monetizing Social Media Traffic."

Most of the panelists admitted that it was difficult to monetize this kind of traffic. Social media users, they said, were less interested in advertising content than other web site users, and less likely to linger on social media sites to look at the advertising content posted there.

It appeared, they thought, that one of the only ways to monetize this traffic would be to use a CPM (cost per thousand) advertising model, selling advertising and charging by the number of people who visited the social media site. For a direct-response Internet marketer, this is not helpful. Getting traffic to your blog or your forum does you no commercial good unless you find a way to convert those visitors to customers.

But here's an example of how we tried—and ultimately (we think) succeeded—to make social media traffic work for the industry that ETR is in: information publishing.

Early to Rise's sister division, Total Health Breakthroughs, published an informative and controversial article on processed meats in its e-newsletter. To give the article traction, it was distributed to several social media outlets, including StumbleUpon. This article gained momentum through viral buzz within the StumbleUpon community—and before we knew it, more than 27,000 visitors came from StumpleUpon to the article itself posted on the Total Health Breakthroughs web site. Great, right? Well, sort of. . . .

Turns out the traffic was going to an article web page that didn't have an e-mail sign-up box. So, although the page received loads of traffic, it wasn't possible to harness that traffic via e-mail addresses.

The upside is that the branding, syndication opportunities, and back-links garnered from that effort were extremely helpful in terms of Total Health Breakthroughs's search engine marketing and the web site's increasing organic traffic ranking. And (though this is an assumption) some of those leads *may* have gone from the article page to the home page, where the sign-up box was located.

Of course, now an e-mail sign-up box appears on every page of the Total Health Breakthroughs web site, including the article pages, so there is no longer the potential for missed e-mail addresses from social media efforts.

Even if you think this particular marketing channel is not appropriate for your business, we encourage you to try it out. And make a good effort: The rewards can be huge. And because social media marketing is, for the most part, free, your cost is nothing more than your time.

CHAPTER FIVE

SEARCH ENGINE MARKETING

Busting Myths and Driving Sales

Have you ever wondered how companies end up at the top of the Google search results?

Search engine marketing (SEM) is what businesses do to get prospective customers to "land" on their web sites and landing pages. It is a way of drumming up business that might otherwise never take place. Search engine marketing is technical and somewhat complicated, because it involves the Internet, which is, well, technical and complicated. It is also ever-changing, because the Internet continues to evolve.

Prior to 2000, the fundamental marketing philosophy of the Internet was "Build it and they will come." The idea was that if you built a truly great web site, millions of viewers would flock to it, which would allow you to make millions of dollars by selling display ads on your site to hundreds of general advertisers.

This did, in fact, happen for a while. But then, right around 2000, many of those advertising programs started falling apart. Most of the billions of dollars that Wall Street had invested in companies that were practicing the build-it-and-they-will-come model disappeared as the companies themselves disappeared.

Remember Pets.com? The pet supplies online store had a memorable mascot, an award-winning web site, a huge warehouse and shipping infrastructure, and an expensive advertising campaign. But they couldn't attract enough customers to pay for all these costs (apparently not enough people were buying cat litter online), so the company fell apart soon after it went public.

After the dot-com bubble burst, some companies continued to overpay for fancy web sites, hoping the bells and whistles they were buying would attract potential buyers. But although some of these web sites attracted lots of viewers, few of them were able to generate enough sales to satisfy advertisers—especially direct-response advertisers, who were more scientific in their approach to measuring advertising response.

Since 2000, almost everybody has become much more sophisticated about the Internet. The idea that you can attract millions of viewers to a web site by making it clever is still out there—supported by the exceptions that prove the rule (e.g., Facebook and YouTube)—but most businesses realize that the key to having a profitable web site is search engine marketing.

Search engine marketing is a very efficient form of marketing. It allows you to get your web site in front of the right people at the right moment—when they are looking for it. The way this is done is relatively simple: The marketer pays to have his advertisement placed in front of users when they are online searching for specific information. Travel agents, for example, can place their travel promotions in front of Internet users who are searching keywords such as "Caribbean Vacations" or "European Holidays" or "Discount Travel."

By getting your site to the top of the results page on one of the major search engines, you can count on targeted traffic that is looking for what you have to offer. And that means a higher chance that this traffic will sign up for your e-newsletter, buy your products, and keep coming back for more.

SEM is something that every online businessperson needs to get involved in. For one thing, you can do a lot of it for free. But the main reason SEM is so great is that it helps you find your ideal customers. Instead of attracting a crowd of web surfers who may or may not care about what you have to offer, you're reaching out to people who are already interested. Even better, you're reaching out to them at the same time as they are looking for you.

Before you get started with search engine marketing, you need to decide on the purpose of your web site.

THE WEB SITE THAT'S RIGHT FOR YOU

There are basically three marketing reasons for a web site:

1. **Information**: To provide information about a product or company that establishes credibility for it and establishes its presence on the World Wide Web
2. **Direct-Response Marketing**: To stimulate sales through direct marketing
3. **List-Building**: To develop a list of prospective buyers

Each of these reasons is valid. Each dictates a different sort of web site.

- **The Informative Site:** A site built for information and validation purposes must be comprehensive, informative, beneficial, and easy to navigate. It should be rich in useful, free content.

   Three examples of informative web sites are RealSimple.com, CNN.com, and Slate.com. These sites offer articles, photos, video, and advice.
- **The Direct-Response-Driven Site:** A web site built for marketing purposes must have all the most important elements of direct-response marketing: a call to action, a strongly defined "look" and "message" unique to the company, free content, and a prominent e-mail sign-up box. It should also be constructed to gain high rankings on search engines like Google.

   EarlytoRise.com and StrategicProfits.com are two direct-response-style web sites. You can see an e-mail sign-up field on each page of both sites. On the homepage of each site, you'll also see a strong call to action, recommending that visitors sign up for free e-newsletters.

- **The List-Building Site:** A web site built for the purpose of developing a list of prospective buyers must be engaging, interactive, ever-changing, and easy to subscribe to. (Again, this means a prominent e-mail sign-up box.) A free bonus, such as an e-report or e-book, should be provided to those who sign up.

  You can see examples of list-building web sites at Bly.com and RobertRinger.com. Both of their homepages have copy directing you to sign up for their e-newsletter. In return, you'll get a free bonus.

  Each type of web site is different. Each requires different copy, graphics, and technology. All sites should load quickly (which means no crazy animation or videos) and be accessible to people with older computers and slower Internet connections. And all sites should have plenty of free, useful content.

GETTING STARTED WITH SEM

Once you decide on the goal you have for your web site (Will it provide information to your visitors? Will it build your e-mail list? Will it help you to sell your products?), you can start marketing it to the Internet's various search engines.

Search engine marketing includes three key techniques or operations:

1. Organic search
2. Paid search
3. RSS/Syndication

Let's review each of these and see how you can apply them to your business and your multi-channel marketing campaigns.

How Is Organic Search Like Organic Food?

Search engine optimization (SEO) can help you maximize the visibility of your web site by making its listings appear more frequently and more prominently in organic (also called "natural," "pure," or "algorithmic") search results. Some businesses—such as Early to Rise, Investor's Daily Edge, and Total Health Breakthroughs—base their

SEO strategies on the successful insertion of their web site listings into organic search results for various popular keywords.

For example, organic search tactics helped increase traffic rank and visits to TotalHealthBreakthroughs.com by 31.60 percent and 81.5 percent respectively, in only a three-month period. In that same three-month period, the site had a 62.01 percent organic search conversion rate. That's about 16,000 organic names at virtually no cost.

Many people do not use search engine optimization to its fullest potential, perhaps because it sounds daunting. The results, however, show that it is a quite simple and effective process. SEO helps you increase the number of people who visit your site from a search engine. More important, it helps you improve the quality of those visitors. For instance, if you run an online pet-accessories business, SEO helps you attract people who are looking for pet accessories.

Like many forms of online advertising, SEO doesn't cost a whole lot. You pay an expert to optimize your site, but you don't pay the search engines a dime. That's because SEO deals with organic search results.

Think about the process you use when searching for something online. Let's say you use Google. You're looking for ski equipment, so you type "Rossignol skis" into the search field on Google's homepage.

What pops up on the search results page are two types of results. On the right-hand side and sometimes at the top of the page, you'll see a clearly marked list of advertisements. These are arranged according to how much money the advertisers paid to be featured whenever someone keyed in "Rossignol skis."

Below or beside the paid advertising, you will find the "organic results." These are free listings of articles posted about the keyword or phrase—in this case, "Rossignol skis." The listings are organized according to their popularity and usefulness. So, in our example, you'll see Rossignol.com at or near the top of the organic search results. And right under that, you'll find ski equipment stores such as ColoradoSki Shop.com and ColoradoSkiOutlet.com.

Most people give organic listings more credit than paid-for advertising. Thus organic listings tend to get more productive responses. If you can get your web site to the top of the organic results (when a Web user types in a keyword that's specific to your site), you have a good chance of attracting new potential customers.

Some people shy away from search engine marketing because it seems more technical than other marketing channels. This is unfortunate. SEO marketing generally produces very qualified prospects. You will find that customers who come to you via organic search will be your highest dollar per name for e- and web marketing.

The Advantages of Organic Search

- **Superior Click-Throughs:** People trust "organically grown" search results more than they do sponsored results. According to a recent survey by Jupiter Research, 80 percent of Web users get information from organic search results. While the search engines are supported by paid ads, many consumers prefer the organic search results. The listings have more credibility, can be more relevant, and offer a greater depth of choices. While paid ads can and should play an important part in your marketing strategy, organic SEO marketing will bring you greater click-through rates and higher-yielding customers.

- **Branding Power:** In Chapter 2, we talked about how the Internet is providing brand marketers with an opportunity to take advantage of direct-response marketing. The same is true for SEO marketing. More and more large corporations are investing resources into organic search to gain the marketing benefits of promoting their brand. If your company does not show up for the keyword results in which you'd expect to appear, it can reduce your credibility with many prospective and current customers. Inserting your brand in the top search results can convey the impression that your company is important. That is why many new and smaller companies have begun to use SEO marketing to promote their brands. Sometimes they can secure better positioning than their bigger, better financed industry rivals.

- **Higher Level of Trust Equals Higher Conversions:** When prospective customers see a paid-for ad posted on top of a keyword search result, they view it with a healthy degree of skepticism. Organic results are usually viewed more benignly. You don't have to know a lot about the Internet to understand that the most prominent ad came from the company that paid the most for the space. That may give some prospects some confidence—knowing that the advertised product has a business with money behind it—but not nearly the confidence that they have when they see an organic listing. A highly placed organic listing is there because other online search engines found it relevant (i.e., useful). Thus it carries a popular imprimatur that paid advertising can't hope to have. On the whole, you should see more visitors from organic search converting to sales, assuming your rankings were for targeted, relevant keywords, not a bait and switch. In the business world, ROI (return on investment) is everything. And organic search can give you the high ROI you're looking for.

- **Organic Is Free:** After all these years, it's still free to submit to Google, the most popular of the organic search engines. Google has always been adamant about not charging for inclusion in its index of 4.2 billion pages. Most other organic engines will also index you for free, although some—like Yahoo—do have paid-inclusion options.

Usually when you have a list of advantages, a list of disadvantages is right behind it. Not in this case.

There's no doubt about it. Organic search is critical to the success of your business. And to make sure you're at the top of the organic search game, you need to practice good search engine optimization strategies.

Here are three SEO tactics you should employ right now:

Tactic #1: Keywords, Relevance, and Search Results

Search engines compile their indexes by running computer programs called "spiders" that "crawl" through millions of web pages and gather content into an index. Then an algorithm (a mathematical process) determines the relevance of the information in the index.

Relevance is generally defined by how close the content of the web page is to the keyword that people are inputting for a search. Most search engines assign a relevance score to results brought by a search query. They use these scores to determine the order in which the results are returned.

Keywords and keyword phrases are crucial to getting your site to the top of the organic search results. If, for example, a prospective customer is looking for a rhinestone dog collar for his poodle, she'll likely type in the keyword phrase "rhinestone dog collar" and wait to see what comes up. If you have a business that sells pet supplies and you have good search engine optimization, it's likely that your entry will be on the list results that appear.

If your site sells ski equipment, keywords might be "ski poles," "snow goggles," or "Alpine ski bindings." Make sure that you include these keywords—and more—in the free, useful content on your web site. Perhaps you could write a review of the best types of snow goggles, or an article about where to find the best cross-country ski trails.

The search engine spiders will be looking for your site's keywords and phrases. To make those keywords easy for the search engines

---

WHAT KEYWORDS ARE YOUR CUSTOMERS SEARCHING FOR?

Search engine marketing expert John Phillips has an easy way for you to track down the keywords that your potential customers are using right now. Here's what he has to say:

> Keywords are the cornerstone and starting point of every search marketing strategy. Understand that keyword research is never a one-and-done deal. Rather, it's an ongoing process of finding every possible permutation of your core keywords, as well as your "long tail" keywords... each of them an opportunity for a sale or a conversion.
>
> Here's how to go about doing keyword research for your site....
>
> Go to Wordtracker.com. For about $30 a week, or a yearly $299 subscription, you can discover the keywords people are using to find web sites in your industry. Simply type in the keywords that come to mind, and the software returns a series of related keywords, along with estimates of how many times per day searches for those keywords occur.
>
> Wordtracker offers a complimentary trial run of its keyword service, too. You can find the same free (yet limited) results with it, plus additional keyword results from Yahoo/Overture's pay-per-click database (on Digitalpoint.com/tools) via the Keyword Suggestion link.

Learning which keywords to use will help you soar to the top of the search engines' results pages. What are you waiting for?

to recognize, you need to define them as keywords in your html tags.

The following are critical tagging components of a web page:

- **Meta tags:** These are bits of html code that webmasters or search engine specialists use to describe content on a web page. These codes are invisible to human visitors (although you can see them in the "page source"), but are easy for search engine spiders to read.
- **Title tags:** These are similar to meta tags, but are more effective. The title tag is the first thing the search engine spiders look at when they crawl your site. Optimizing your title tags is a powerful way of increasing page ranking. Your title tag should be relevant, specific, and should contain the keyword phrase you are targeting. The contents of your title tag appear across the top of your browser window.

  If you haven't yet given your title tags a thorough review, here's what you should do:
  - Visit each page of your web site and look at the blue bar at the top of your browser. If the text in the blue bar (such as the name of your company or web site) is the same on every page, you've got some work to do.
  - You want to make sure that each page of your site has unique, keyword-rich text in the title that adequately describes what the page is about. To do this, look at the source code of each page and find this code: <title>Your Title Here</title>. Then write your new keyword-dense title tag between the >< symbols.
- **ALT tags:** Surprisingly, many web sites overlook this simple yet effective element of optimization. ALT text is a description of your web site's graphics or pictures. ALT text should be a complete sentence—again, one that is relevant, specific, and keyword-rich. Spiders calculate the number of times your keywords appear within your tags and content, which boosts organic rankings. So it's important to tag images as well as content.
- **Header tags:** Html header tags are used to define your page's organizational structure. Using header tags informs both site visitors and search engines what the important elements of your

page are. H1, H2, and H3 tags should be used appropriately throughout your web site.

- **Anchor text:** The use of anchor text is a bit more involved and takes some more work, but is well worth it.

  What is anchor text? Anchor text is the visible, clickable text in a hyperlink.

  Let's say you want to link one article on your site about Internet marketing to another article on your site about Internet marketing. Search through your article for a keyword or keyword phrase that matches the content of the article you are linking to. You might choose the phrase "increase online sales." Then, you'd hyperlink that phrase to the relevant article on your site.

  As the search engine spiders crawl your site, they are looking for (a) text they can use to determine what your page is about and (b) links they can use to access other pages of your site. Using anchor text links to connect similar pages of content through a particular keyword gives more weight to that keyword and tells the search engines that your site is a relevant resource for that search term.

  The more relevant the search engines think your site is for your targeted keyword, the more likely it is that your site will turn up at or near the top of their search results pages.

  The mistake that many web site owners make is to link their content strictly by using call-to-action links like "click here" or "read more." While it's important to use a call to action in your ads and when trying to generate sales or sign-ups, it's also important to remember that no one ever searches for the latest "click here" product or service.

- **Keyword density:** Within your body text should be content that contains relevant keyword phrases. Because spiders typically crawl a page from top to bottom, your keywords should appear most often in that same order—headlines, subheads, then paragraphs. It's also helpful to bold, italicize, or bullet your keywords for greater emphasis for the reader (as well as for search engine spiders). Content should *not* be the same keywords used over and over again or hidden in code. This is known as "keyword stuffing," and is the equivalent of spamming. Search engines frown upon it. Instead, keywords should be repurposed and rephrased in logical sentences.

Tactic #2: The Links That Make the Difference

Another tactic to help improve your organic ranking is link building, or "back-linking." Link building refers to the practice of acquiring links to your web site from other relevant web sites around the Internet. This builds your "link popularity." Links to your site from other relevant sites act as endorsements in the eyes of the search engines. They help validate your web site content—leading to high rankings and increased web traffic.

Therefore, in addition to having optimized web site pages, having a variety of news aggregators, social networks, forums, blogs, and directories linking to your site helps give your site more weight when it comes to organic listings.

The key in external links is relevancy. You can easily get hundreds or even thousands of links to your site through a "link farm," but such a strategy will get you in trouble with search engines that disapprove of such techniques because they push irrelevant links to your site. This can even have an adverse effect on your organic listing.

The best link-building practice is to acquire links from—and links to—your own neighborhood: a group of related, complementary, or like-minded sites on the Internet, each linked to other relevant sites. Niche directories, respected organizations, and well-known bloggers in your field are all examples of good links that will associate your site with good link neighborhoods.

If you ran a women's health web site, for instance, a link from the National Breast Cancer Foundation web site to your site would be a great link. Acquiring such a link would be a good first step to building a pattern of good linking behavior. In the eyes of the search engines, your site would be situated in a quality (i.e., relevant) link neighborhood.

You should also submit your site to staple directories such as Dmoz.org and Dir.yahoo.com.

In addition to external links, don't forget to link relevant pages within your site. (See "Anchor text" above for a reminder of how to do that.)

Tactic #3: Don't Wait for the Search Engines to Come to You

Search engine spiders may eventually pick up a web page on their own. But it's always a good idea for your search engine marketing specialist or webmaster to manually submit your web site to all major search engines. The top four search engines are: Google.com, Search.Yahoo.com, Search.MSN.com, and Ask.com. These garner about 64 percent, 23 percent, 8 percent, and 4 percent of Internet searches, respectively.

Now you know how important search engine optimization is to get your site to the top of those organic search results. And you know how to start implementing SEO tactics for your site. But keep in mind that SEO and organic search should not be your only forms of search engine marketing.

Pay-per-click advertising should also be a part of your marketing mix. It will build your customer list and business quickly and easily. But—unlike organic search—it is going to cost you.

Pay per What?

Pay-per-click (PPC) (also known as cost-per-click, or CPC) is an advertising model used on search engines, banner and display advertising networks, and content web sites/blogs. In this type of ad, advertisers pay only when a user clicks on an ad to visit the advertiser's web site. (This is different from the cost-per-thousand, or CPM, model, in which advertisers pay "per impression" served.)

Here's how you can take advantage of PPC advertising.

You would bid on keywords or keyword strings that you predict your target market will use as search terms when they are looking for a product or service. When a user types a keyword query matching your keyword list, your ad may show up.

These ads are called "sponsored links" or "sponsored ads," and appear next to or above the organic results on search engine results pages, or anywhere a webmaster/blogger chooses on a content page.

Let's say you own a gardening store. You bid on the search term "wrought iron planters." Then, when someone types that keyword phrase into a search engine, your site would show up as one of the paid results on the right side or top of the results page.

For most major search engines, how high your ad is placed on the search engine results page is determined by several variables. The most important consideration is usually how much you bid for it. Other considerations include your daily budget, the popularity of your ad (how many daily clicks it gets), and the relevance of the landing page your ad goes to.

Google AdWords, the PPC service hosted by Google, ranks your PPC ad based on what is called a Quality Score. As defined by Google: "Quality Score is a dynamic variable assigned to each of your keywords. It's calculated using a variety of factors and measures how relevant your keyword is to your ad text and to a user's search query."

PPC ads may also appear on content network web sites. Here's how it works: Ad networks such as Google AdSense send ads to web sites, blogs, web pages, and so on that agree to host ads relevant to their own content. They get paid whenever someone clicks on those ads. For instance, your ad for wrought iron planters might show up when customers visit a web site with an article about container gardening.

Google AdWords, Yahoo! Search Marketing, and Microsoft AdCenter are currently the largest PPC network operators. The minimum price per click can be as little as one cent. But popular search terms cost much more.

Click fraud can be a concern with PPC ads, but the major ad networks have safeguards in place. (Click fraud is when someone organizes an effort—through hundreds of people in different locations or through software—to repeatedly click on a PPC ad with no intention of buying the product. This can drive up the price of the keywords to the point where the advertiser is no longer able to pay for them.)

You decide how much you are willing to pay each time a person clicks on your ad. The more you are willing to pay per click, the higher your site will appear in the results for the keywords you choose.

The Power of PPC

A very important point to keep in mind with PPC is that you must test, test, and test some more. This is where many marketers go wrong.

WRITING YOUR PAY-PER-CLICK AD

Because this is a very technical channel and marketing tactic, many business owners and even marketing directors leave it up to their "techies" to put together their PPC campaign. This is a big, big mistake.

Think of it this way: Would you have your computer guy write your direct e-mail advertising? Of course not. You'd hire a professional copywriter, someone who knows how to write copy, to write the ad. The copywriter would send his copy to your e-mail manager, who would send it out. But the copy itself would have been written by someone who knows how to sell, not someone who knows how to send out bulk e-mails.

Don't ask a technical person to write your PPC ad. Even if he's happy to do it, he doesn't have the expertise to do a great job. Remember, when it comes to marketing, success is determined at the margins. Good copywriters give you the edge you need to run a profitable business. Don't shortchange your marketing efforts. You can't afford to.

Pay-per-click ads are typically small. On Google, they are usually limited to four lines of text: a headline, two lines of body copy, and your URL.

Generally speaking, it's a good idea to create a URL that describes your product. If your web site sells discontinued dishware, your URL should say so. It could be something like ReplacementChina.com or DiscontinuedDishes.com. That way, if people type your URL directly into their browser, they have an idea of what to expect.

The body of your PPC ad should offer an enticing and, if possible, immediate benefit to the reader. It might say something like "Millions of discontinued plates," "Find your pattern fast," or "Biggest savings on china replacements."

Your headline should grab your prospective customer's attention. Unusual or newsworthy headlines can do that. A headline like "Designer China Rip-Offs" or "Is Your Dishware Safe?" can convince your prospect to click on your ad rather than another one that has a more ordinary headline.

Brainstorming headlines is worth the time you invest in doing it, because good headlines can double or even triple the response rates that ordinary headlines will give you. One way to initiate a headline

WRITING YOUR PAY-PER-CLICK AD (*Continued*)

brainstorming session is to take a look at headlines that are working well for your competitors. Hint: The ones that are working well are those that you see repeated over and over. If there is one thing that the Internet hasn't changed about marketing it is this: Marketers love to rerun ads that work.

Here are six quick tips for making your PPC ads stand out and pull better:

1. **Use your keywords in the ad text—especially in your headline.** Keywords in your ad text that match what was searched for show up as bold in your ad and boost your relevancy.
2. **Offer something free or promote a sale.** Everyone likes free stuff and bargains. But make your free and discounted offers stand out by making them unusual in some way. Get your creative people in on the process.
3. **Use symbols or vary your punctuation where applicable.** Odd punctuation can catch a searcher's eye and make them click your ad over your competitors' ads.
4. **Specificity helps.** You don't have much space in this kind of advertising, but it's still better to be as specific as you can. "127 Ways to Boost Your Bottom Line" is better than "How to Boost Your Bottom Line."
5. **Make your offer unique.** Good products have unique qualities that make them stand out from the competition. Mention those unique selling points when you can.
6. **Make your offer urgent.** Giving prospects a reason to reply now rather than later will increase response rates.

Play with these techniques to find what works best. Test like crazy. And since you can write several versions of your text ads for each ad group when you use Google AdWords, let Google rotate them and optimize the best ads for the best results.

Remember, relevancy is the most important factor in search engine marketing. Whatever you do, make sure your ad text speaks to the keywords you're bidding on.

Howie Jacobson, Ph.D., author of *AdWords for Dummies*, points out that PPC ads are the epitome of direct-response marketing. And he calls Google AdWords a revolution in advertising.

Like Jacobson, we like to compare AdWords to Yellow Pages ads. The process of placing a Yellow Pages ad goes something like this:

- You (or your best copywriter) write the best ad you can with very minimum copy.
- You submit the ad to the printer about three months before the Yellow Pages are distributed.
- You wake up in a panic at two o'clock in the morning because you suddenly realize you did not include a very important item in your ad: the telephone number, or days of operation, or price, and so on.
- The directory comes out and you have to live with the ad for a full year, regardless of whether your ad produces one order or 10,000 orders in the first month.

PPC advertising has opened up a new world of possibilities. If you want to incorporate it into your marketing mix, you can set up an AdWords account in five minutes. You don't have to wait three months for the Yellow Pages to come out. Plus, you can start seeing results immediately. And—best of all—if your ad isn't working, you can replace it with something new.

Pay-per-click allows you to test ads quickly and easily and at a much lower cost than you could in the "old days" of Yellow Pages advertising.

Another benefit of PPC is that you can narrow its reach. You can show your ad to everyone on the Internet . . . or you can target it to specific countries, regions, states, and even cities. You can change your copy anytime you choose. And through multivariate (MV) testing, you can put as many versions of your ad on the Internet as you want.

You don't need to start off with a major investment. Start with the minimum. See how the search engine performs in terms of the traffic it delivers and how well that traffic converts into paying customers. Then alter your marketing tactics accordingly.

PAY-PER-CLICK PAST, PRESENT, AND FUTURE

Howie Jacobson, AdWords consultant and an expert direct marketer, has been involved with PPC marketing since the early days, before Google came to dominate the industry with AdWords.

"I first encountered pay-per-click marketing at a talk at a systems seminar that I attended in September 2002," says Jacobson. "Google AdWords was a few months old at that point. So it wasn't on our radar. But we were all into Overture, which was the first pay-per-click search engine."

It quickly became apparent that this new type of marketing was a way to run direct-response ads, pay only for performance, and measure results like never before.

Jacobson explains that soon, Google AdWords pushed Overture (which was bought by Yahoo!) out of the top spot.

"You get instant gratification. You run your ad and 15 minutes later you're getting traffic, as opposed to Overture, which typically took five days to a week to approve your ad," says Jacobson.

These days, in addition to list building and optimization work for clients, Jacobson uses AdWords mostly to test ad messages that he will later roll out in other marketing channels.

He points out that another innovative use for AdWords is to help design a web site. The key, again, is testing. You create identical ads and send half of the prospects to one web page, and the other half to a redesigned page (with different copy, graphics, order form, etc.) page. Whichever site brings in more sales is kept.

Jacobson predicts some changes on the horizon for pay-per-click marketing.

He sees ads becoming more local—targeted to Web surfers in a smaller, well-defined geographic area. And these ads won't be going just to PCs, but to mobile devices, in-car computers, and screens at gas pumps, among other platforms.

He sees the payment model changing, too. Pay-per-click might be discarded in favor of cost-per-action. That way, the advertiser pays when a prospect clicks on his ad and actually buys something.

(continues)

PAY-PER-CLICK PAST, PRESENT, AND FUTURE (*Continued*)

He also says that the dominance of Google AdWords is being challenged by niche search engines serving specialized markets.

AdWords isn't for every business, says Jacobson, but "if you're in a market where people are looking online for your product and services, then you should be using AdWords, because it has the biggest reach. If you want people to see your ads, you should be using Google AdWords."

Playing around with AdWords and discovering its capabilities when he first encountered it strengthened Jacobson's belief that using AdWords was a powerful way to market on the Internet. The key was—and is—testing: seeing what works and what doesn't, tweaking and changing keywords and content, and then running with the winners. Testing allowed Jacobson to steadily improve the results from his AdWords marketing campaigns.

"Over the course of about 11 months, I went from a 0.7 percent click-through rate, which means seven out of a thousand people were clicking on my ad, to 2.8 percent, which meant I increased my business by four times," says Jacobson. "I didn't know what I was doing. I was just testing this and that, running this ad, changing that word, changing the order, making something capitalized. I didn't have a huge background in copywriting and nobody knew what this medium was. We were just playing around. And I found that by sort of random testing and just keeping with the winner, I was able to quadruple my results. I thought, 'Wow, that's a powerful medium! Imagine if I knew what I was doing.' So then I set about to really learn it."

Source: AdWords.com

Pay-per-click advertising is also entirely trackable. Having a method in place that allows you to track your return on the money invested should be an essential part of your testing. If you do not track your results, not only are you wasting your money, you are missing out on valuable data that will allow you to expand (roll out) your marketing campaigns and grow your business.

Pay-per-click allows you to tailor your tracking to your particular marketing goal. Let's say your goal is to bring in new subscribers to

THE TRAVELING SALESMAN PROBLEM

You may have heard of the "traveling salesman" problem. It poses the question that if a traveling salesman has to visit a number of cities in the most efficient manner, and then return to his starting point, what would be the best route? Mathematicians call this a problem of "combinatorial optimization"—how to combine the available elements to end up with the best result. Baking a really good cake presents the same type of problem. Do you use two eggs or three? Three cups of flour or four? And so on. Years of testing have produced the best recipes.

Marketers use "A/B" testing to determine the best performing of two different elements or content variations of an ad. They might, for example, test two different headlines on a web page by creating two identical web pages, changing only the headline, and sending half their traffic to one and half to the other. This is a quick way to get a test result, but becomes onerous if you want to test many different variations of headlines, body copy, images, and so on, all at the same time, You'd have to create a single copy of every web page for every version you wanted to test, and divide up your traffic equally by that number of versions.

Multivariate testing allows you to test many different components of a web page (or web site or promotional e-mail) all at the same time, by creating a single template and inserting "placeholders" where you want the headline, body copy, images—anything you want to test—to appear. As people visit that web page, these placeholders are replaced sequentially by the different headlines and other entries that you have created.

Multivariate testing is rather like doing all of your individual A/B tests at the same time. It can, in theory, test the best performing version of limitless combinations. The only limit on the number of combinations and dynamic variables in multivariate tests is the length of time it would take to get enough visitors to generate a statistically valid result.

a newsletter you are publishing. In this case, you could direct visitors arriving from your PPC link to a subscription form set up just for them. You can then monitor how many clicks actually result in a new subscription. That way, you would know exactly how much you are paying for each new subscriber.

Pay-per-Click Search Engine Tracking Reports

We recommend that you start your PPC efforts with Google. For now, Google occupies the lion's share of search engine traffic. Plus, the reporting is easy to use.

It's best to break your ads into campaigns by topic. That will help organize the reporting. Within each campaign are your ad groups. Overall, these ad groups have a common theme, but the ads themselves may have different focuses. For example, if your campaign is called "investing," your ad groups may be "stocks," "options," "gold," and "silver." Then, within each ad group, you locate the specific ads targeting those related keywords.

This can all be viewed in the "Campaign Summary" or "Campaign Management" tool with the Google reporting system. You can also change your daily budget, as well as monitor clicks, impressions, ad position, costs, and conversions. After you launch a campaign, it may take a week or two to optimize it by monitoring the aforementioned stats and adjusting keywords and bids accordingly.

When you start seeing positive results in clicks, conversions, and page position, all at a reasonable cost-per-click, you have a winning ad.

The average Google search page displays eight ads along the right side of the page and three ads at the top. A desirable page position would be among the first five right-hand ads or the three at the top. These ads are "above the fold" (no need for a viewer to scroll down to see them). As a rule of thumb, you can figure that a CPC of under $5 would be something you could work with. That number will be influenced by your total cost and the amount of leads you bring in.

If AdWords is new to you, we highly recommend picking up Howie Jacobson's book *AdWords for Dummies*. It is by far the most comprehensive resource on this subject. By the time you have read it, you will have a full understanding of how to set up and monitor all your AdWords campaigns.

There's one more thing you need to consider before you get started with your PPC campaign. . . .

Are All Pay-per-Click Search Engines Created Equal?

We've talked a lot about Google, mainly because Google is the search engine king right now. But Google isn't the only search engine. As we mentioned before, Yahoo, MSN, and Ask.com all receive significant search traffic that you can tap into. And those are just the Big Four. There are dozens of smaller search engines that could potentially bring you new traffic and new customers.

So how do you choose which search engines to advertise with?

According to Pay Per Click Tools, "an effective pay-per-click search engine efficiently connects consumers and producers of information, products, and services—thereby benefiting both web surfers and advertisers."

For *web surfers*, a search engine should offer:

- Fast, relevant, unique search results
- A fast-loading homepage, free of advertising clutter
- No horizontal scroll bar at 800 × 600 resolution
- Minimal advertising clutter on search results pages

For *advertisers*, a search engine should offer:

- A prepaid advertising account
- An efficient, user-friendly bid management interface
- Reasonable numbers of targeted web site visitors
- Editorial review for submitted search listings[1]

Before spending any money with a pay-per-click search engine, be sure you can answer the following questions:

- How many searches a month are performed at the search engine?
- What major search partners or affiliates does the search engine have?
- How many searches are generated each month by the search partners or affiliates?
- Is it possible to opt out of having your listing appear in the results of the affiliate sites?
- What fraud prevention mechanisms are in place?
- What is the procedure for filing a "fraudulent clicks" report?
- Will an account be credited for fraudulent clicks discovered?
- Is it possible to opt out of having a listing appear for searches originating from specific countries?
- Is there a posted term of service for search partners or affiliates?

Look for search engines that have very strict guidelines for dealing with their search affiliates. This is important, because you want to be sure that the search engine is working hard to prevent fraud among its affiliates.

A Really Simple Secret to Online Success

As mentioned earlier, your search engine marketing strategies should incorporate three major tactics: organic search, PPC, and RSS.

Many online businesspeople know about search engine optimization and pay-per-click advertising. But most overlook RSS. You shouldn't. Combining SEO, PPC, and RSS gives you a powerful advantage. You will be far more advanced than your competitors who use only one or two of these methods.

What Is RSS?

Some people call it "really simple syndication," while others call it "rich site summary." Call it what you will, but understand that RSS is a format for syndicating news and the content of newslike sites— including major news sites such as Wired, news-oriented community sites such as Slashdot, and personal blogs.

RSS automatically notifies Internet users when, for example, their favorite blog has a new entry, or when the content on a favorite site has been updated.

And RSS is not just for newshounds and bloggers. Pretty much anything that can be broken down into discrete items can be syndicated via RSS: the "recent changes" page of a wiki, a changelog of CVS check-ins, even the revision history of a book. Once information about each item is in RSS format, an RSS-aware program can check the feed for changes and react to the changes in an appropriate way.

RSS-aware programs—called "news aggregators"—are popular in the blogging community. Many blogs make content available in RSS. A news aggregator can help a web user keep up with all her favorite blogs. The aggregator checks her RSS feeds and displays new items from each of them.

RSS solves a problem for people who regularly use the web. It allows web users to easily stay informed by retrieving the latest content from the sites they are interested in. They save time by not needing to visit each site individually. They ensure their privacy by not needing to subscribe to each site's e-mail newsletter.

Like SEO, RSS is valuable to both the user and the online business.

With RSS, you can inform the entire Internet—including sites with content similar or related to yours—that you're posting a new article. You just register the address of your RSS feed with a service like FeedBurner. Then your content will be automatically distributed—for free—to content syndication services all over the Web.

Whenever you submit an article for RSS, you should be sure to include your web site's URL. That way, people who read your article and want to learn more can easily visit your site.

One major advantage of RSS is that it allows you to share your content in relevant ways. For example, let's say you write an article for your Ontario travel site about the best bed and breakfasts in Toronto. RSS will syndicate the content to similar sites, such as Toronto Hotels.com or VisitOntario.com. Your article will also be syndicated to sites where the topic is relevant, such as VacationsMagazine.com or Travel2Canada.com.

By adding RSS to your marketing efforts, you can put your name and ideas in front of potential customers automatically. And you can reach a market that is increasingly wary of overt marketing. One of the benefits of RSS is that it allows readers to pick and choose exactly what content they want to read. And by offering your content via RSS, you're proving that you care about their privacy. You're not a devious spammer, trying to force ads and articles on them without their permission. And since your readers must sign up to get your RSS feeds, you know right away that they are interested.

Besides giving your readers another way to access your content, RSS can help improve your search engine rankings.

It doesn't matter whether people actually subscribe to your RSS content feed using RSS reader software. It can still benefit your position with the search engines. When search engines and syndication sites such as FeedBurner are able to access your RSS feed, your site will benefit. You can register your feed with these sites in the same manner that you would register your web site with Google or Yahoo. (You can watch a short video on FeedBurner.com about how to register your RSS feed.)

Syndication sites will index your RSS feed and make it available for searching. Certain services—including FeedBurner—will further syndicate your RSS feed across the Internet to other sites, search engines, and syndication services.

Let's say your RSS feed is about investing in gold. FeedBurner would syndicate that RSS feed. And any sites that pull data from FeedBurner via RSS on the topic of investing in gold will likely see, display, and further syndicate your article on investing in gold. Generally, proper attribution and a link to you as the originator of the content is given.

From a search engine perspective, these all count as more incoming links to your site.

Another good way to use RSS is to display RSS feeds from other web sites on your web site. This allows you to add fresh content to your web site—for example, news topics that relate to the subject matter on your web site. And search engines love fresh content.

Like other direct-response marketing methods, RSS is measurable. Phil Gomes, vice president of Edelman's Interactive Solutions, points out that advanced RSS tools can help you determine who is reading what content. He recommends that you consider segmenting your RSS feeds. If your site is about interior design, for example, you might offer RSS feeds about the overall site. Or you could offer feeds about bathroom design or kitchen design or bedroom design. These would give you ideas about which subtopics get the most attention from your readers.

The number of sites offering RSS feeds is growing rapidly, and includes big names such as Yahoo News, CNN, and *The New York Times*. It's time that you added it to your marketing strategies.

GETTING YOUR SITE SEEN

Once you start optimizing your site for organic search, using pay-per-click advertising and spreading your content around the Web with RSS, you'll start to see more traffic and more customers. This means more money for your bottom line.

Don't fool yourself into thinking that these marketing methods are unimportant. They are critical to the success of your site. By using them together, you'll put your name, ideas, web site, and products in front of people who want what you're offering. That means that you'll have a much higher chance of converting them into paying customers.

And isn't that what marketing is all about?

CHAPTER SIX

TELECONFERENCES

All You Need Is a Phone and Good Ideas

Jedd Canty, profit-center manager for Investor's Daily Edge (IDE), an Internet advisory service, was in a quandary. He had been asked to produce a stock report to give to IDE's best customers. But he didn't have time to print a report or even burn and ship out CDs. "To make matters worse," he said, "It was Christmastime, so all the good investment researchers I would have used were busy with deadlines. They could give me a few hours of their time, but they couldn't spare the time it would take to write a full report."

"I was stuck," he said. "But then I had an inspiration."

Canty's solution was to provide the investment advice via a teleconference instead of a printed report or a CD. "The teleconference provided me with several benefits," he said. "First, I could produce it quickly. Second, I could persuade all our best stock researchers to participate, since the time they had to contribute was only the time we spent airing the teleconference. Third, the costs were much less than they would have been with a hard product. It was the only feasible solution, and it was three times better."

The teleconference lasted about 90 minutes. It was free for IDE's VIP customers, but the call was recorded and later sold to other customers for $99.

About 750 people attended the first paid "rebroadcast." At $99 each, that initial call brought in $74,250. Then Canty produced an "encore presentation" that added another 300 people and $29,700 to the take.

Because the content of the teleconference was topical, Canty couldn't re-purpose it into a product. But he had it transcribed and created a "white paper" out of it that he used as a free gift for new customers in his pay-per-click (PPC) campaigns.

"And we're not done yet," he said. "Next month, we are holding a live wealth-building conference where we plan to focus one entire presentation around this content. This will let us give away the content in the white paper format to the attendees. It further allows us to sell the attendees a financial service to overcome their current economic fears."

Canty's decision to hold the teleconference brought in an initial $104,000. But the marketing tail of a teleconference can be very long. In Canty's case, it may eventually grow to more than a million dollars. "It was good in so many ways," Canty said. "It gave us tremendous credibility. It helped us bond with our customers. It helped us reinforce our USP (unique selling proposition). And it made us a lot of money!"

As you can see from this example, teleconferences (also known as teleseminars) can be an easy and inexpensive way to make a lot of money.

TELECONFERENCING AS A MARKETING TOOL

The first time we heard about teleconferencing as an advertising medium was in 1999. Alex Mandossian had realized its power as a marketing channel and was using it in his own businesses. He soon started advising others how to use this channel as well.

"I found that someone was much more willing to hop on a teleconference for an hour, rather than visit a web page for an hour. Most people will usually visit a web site for about a minute before moving on. With teleconferencing, I had an extra 59 minutes to build a relationship," says Mandossian.

Since then, he says, teleconferencing has become a standard promotional channel for marketers in a variety of fields. Event marketers, for example, use it to promote and sell upcoming conferences. The publishing industry uses it to host virtual book tours and sell new

CAN YOU REALLY HOST A TELECONFERENCE FROM ANYWHERE?

A great thing about teleconferences is that you can do them from almost anywhere. Just ask Alex Mandossian. He hosted one from the bathroom of a hospital room, while his wife and newborn lay in bed. Two hundred fifty CPAs listened in for information about a product called the "Tax Toolbox," and Mandossian made $13,000 in sales in just an hour.

Since then he has conducted seminars from the side of the highway (after getting a traffic ticket), during a boxing match, under the bleachers at his son's soccer match, during his daughter's ballet rehearsal, huddled in his closet as contractors worked on his house, and from hotel rooms across the country.

Mandossian's story highlights the power of teleconferencing. It's a marketing channel you can use from anywhere. All you need is a phone. Well, that and your ideas.

releases. And, of course, direct marketers use teleconferences to sell information products.

We were initially resistant to using teleconferencing as a sales tool for Early to Rise. We were afraid that subjecting our customers to a combination of information and advertising might damage our credibility with them. But thanks to Alex Mandossian, we were able to experience this new kind of seminar indirectly. When we saw how happy his customers were, we tested the waters for ourselves. Over the course of several years, we became more comfortable and more capable with the process. Today, teleconferencing is a regular channel of advertising for ETR.

We have produced more than 60 teleconferences since 2005. Tens of thousands of ETR customers have "attended" them. Most of them paid between $20 and $60 to call in. We also sponsor several free teleconferences each year. The per-person basis is lower, but the response is so much higher that it makes sense.

We also offer some calls as the main component of a coaching or educational program. These calls are regularly scheduled once or twice a month, hosted by in-house experts and an occasional guest.

The attendees get printable workbooks, DVD and CD sets, and other materials to supplement the information in the teleconference.

One of the first teleconferences we hosted promoted Early to Rise's first Internet business-building conference. More than 1,000 people signed up for the call, which helped us sell out the conference. A couple of months later, we hosted a teleseminar to promote Michael Masterson's book *Automatic Wealth: The Six Steps to Financial Independence.*

Since then, we've partnered with experts in fields such as real estate, finance, direct marketing, and even personal development. Guest hosts have included best-selling authors Robert Ringer and Brian Tracy, as well as industry experts, such as Bob Cox and Justin Ford, who bring their own following to the teleconferences. When they host or otherwise participate, we sometimes share the revenue from any admission charges or sales of back-end products offered during the call.

Attendance at these conferences has ranged from a few dozen to more than 2,000, and the subject matter has varied from formal goal-setting and personal success to how to start an online information publishing business.

PRODUCING A MONEY-MAKING TELECONFERENCE

Teleconferences are inexpensive to produce. Most of ETR's cost less than a dollar per attendee. Compare that to the cost of hosting a live conference at a hotel, where expenses typically start at $10 a day per attendee, and can easily run up to $100 and even more.

By giving your customers a first-class educational experience (about products and services they are interested in) with a teleconference, you create good will that can be monetized simply and smoothly by offering them buying opportunities during or after the information-giving session.

Teleconferencing today is sophisticated, but it's not complicated. The principles are easy to understand. And the technology is readily available.

You can establish a teleconferencing channel for your business in a matter of weeks. And you can do it for a few thousand dollars, not millions.

We couldn't have made this claim 10 years ago. Even five years ago. This channel is new. It's exciting. It's brimming with potential. And it's growing fast.

Before we look into the opportunities and applications of this emerging advertising channel, let's discuss the principles that govern it.

Successful teleconferencing programs follow the same basic pattern.

- You develop a teleconference program that provides some genuine value to your customers and/or potential customers.
- This program is usually informational and motivational.
- Using standard direct-response marketing techniques, you advertise the teleconference. You can give it away for free, or you can sell it for a modest fee. The choice here is dictated by the kind of customers you are looking for (e.g., business or consumer, high or low net worth) and the type and price of the product you intend to sell them throughout the program.
- Following one of several established protocols, you put on the teleconference at a given time, recording everything for future "republication."
- Before, during, and after the informational presentations, you ask the teleconference attendees to indicate whether they would buy a particular product if it provided them with the solution to all their problems. You record those positive answers.
- Taking advantage of such "commitments," you sell the product, giving attendees bonuses and discounts for responding to the offer immediately.
- You follow up closely with all those who responded to the offer.
- You continue to promote to those who didn't yet respond until your efforts are no longer profitable.

Successful teleconferencing of this type relies on two very fundamental psychological principles:

1. Reciprocity
2. Consistency

In his seminal book, *Influence: The Psychology of Persuasion*, Robert Cialdini has this to say about these critical principles:

Reciprocity: "The rule [of reciprocation] says that we should try to repay, in kind, what another person has provided for us. If a woman does us a favor, we should do her one in return; if a man sends us a birthday present, we should remember his birthday with a gift of our own; if a couple invites us to a party, we should be sure to invite them to one of ours. By virtue of the reciprocity rule, then, we are *obligated* to the future repayment of favors, gifts, invitations, and the like."[1]

Consistency: "It is, quite simply, our nearly obsessive desire to be (and to appear) consistent with what we have already done. Once we have made a choice or taken a stand [in this case, to pay to attend a teleconference], we will encounter personal and interpersonal pressures to behave consistently with that commitment. Those pressures will cause us to respond in ways that justify our earlier decision [i.e., by buying the product offered during the teleconference]."[2]

These principles really work.

Alex Mandossian made $5 million last year hosting teleseminars and repurposing their content into books, CDs, and preprogrammed MP3 players.

Early to Rise's record for a single teleconference is more than $330,000. It was the result of a free call about building an Internet business that was used to sell an upcoming conference on the same topic. Twelve hundred people attended, and, as you can see from the revenue generated, many of them came to the conference. As an added bonus, 98 percent of the attendees became ETR subscribers, a significant one-time addition to our list.

Another company we know of makes a little over $13,000 per teleconference. About half of that revenue comes from the $60 charge to attend. The other half is from the sale of back-end products during the call. Not bad for an hour-long phone call.

LEVERAGE IS LIKE GETTING PAID OVER
AND OVER AND OVER AGAIN

When he teaches marketers about teleconferencing, Alex Mandossian emphasizes that it provides both immediate cash flow and the potential for repurposing to generate a long tail of income afterward.

He says that anyone considering adding a teleconferencing channel to their existing marketing program should consider the following three main points:

1. **Product Development.** Every teleconference you host gives you the opportunity to expand. Your teleconference attendees will ask questions. You'll have answers. These answers will lead to new ideas, which will lead to more questions. And you can turn that exchange of ideas and information into a new product.

   This can be more monetarily beneficial than the original call. You have already done the heavy lifting. You outlined your call, you marketed your call, and you set up everything technically with the call. You did all the hard work, and now you are left with incredibly good, useful content. So it is time to turn that content into a home-study kit or a book.

   You may be asking, "How do I know if the content is good enough to make another product?" Coming up with product-worthy content should always be one of your goals going into a call. But there are a couple of ways to support your decision.

   • Make sure your teleconference offered useful content. If the call did not have useful content, any product you form out of it is unlikely to be useful. And if your product isn't useful, you will have disappointing sales. The better the content, the better the sales.

   • Send out a survey immediately after the call. Ask your customers what they liked and what they did not. Because you can edit your call, you can take the best/most liked parts of the call and add other components, such as a workbook or DVDs that you may have in stock that are related to the content you just developed. Suddenly, you have a $250 to $500 product to sell.

2. **Premium/Free Bonus.** Sometimes, you may not have the resources to turn your teleconference recording into a separate product. Sometimes, the content simply does not warrant a product, either because it is time-sensitive or is related to an upcoming conference/product launch. In this case, you can offer the unedited recording of the call as a free add-on to another, related product.

3. **Added Value.** In past chapters, we have talked about how customers and prospects want to be communicated with in their own way. Different people respond better to different channels. That is the idea behind what we call "mini teleconferences." This type of teleseminar call is used strictly for added-value purposes.

   Mini teleconferences are simply prerecorded messages. In fact, we have one for this book. One of the book's authors, MaryEllen Tribby, introduces herself and explains the best way to digest the information to get the maximum results for your business. (Call 800-959-0494 to listen to the mini teleconference.)

   Early to Rise did this for the first time with the launch of the Internet Money Club (IMC). IMC is an expensive program packed with information on how to start an online business, and we wanted to make sure our customers understood the program's potential. Callers heard a live voice, emphasizing the fact that there are real people behind the program and that they could ask any questions they had.

   We did the same interactive call for a $25 book, for the same reasons.

   This is something you can implement in your business immediately. But remember to be consistent. Keep the message and tone of the mini teleconference the same as the message and tone of your product. For example, this book is written in a very conversational tone. The prerecorded message from MaryEllen Tribby is equally informal and conversational. It would have been odd if we'd had a formal, English-accented gentleman do the recording, don't you think? If you're not consistent, your customers will feel confused . . . or worse, misled. If they get the wrong message up front, they may not even bother to use your product.

That is the purpose of the mini teleconference in a nutshell. You want people not only to buy your product, you want them to use it. You want to build lasting relationships with your customers, not merely go for one-shot deals. It is all about lifetime value. People who buy but do not use your product are usually not repeat buyers.

A mini teleconference is the fastest, easiest, and cheapest way for you to bond with your customers and add value to your relationship with them.

As a matter of fact, teleconferencing is one of the fastest, easiest, and cheapest ways for you to communicate with your customers. Even more important, teleconferencing is one of the easiest-to-use and most convenient channels for your customers.

Think about it. Who does not have access to a telephone 24 hours a day? With teleconferencing, you can reach your customers when they are shopping, sitting by the pool, waiting for a plane at the airport, or commuting to and from the office. Time is a valuable commodity these days. Give your customers more value for their time, and they will do more buying from you in return.

CHAPTER SEVEN

DIRECT MAIL

An Old Dog That Still Knows a Few Tricks

In the early 1990s, five American businessmen bought a 3,000-acre farm on the Pacific coast of Nicaragua. Their idea was to convert the property into a retirement community. They had no real estate development experience, and very little business experience outside the United States.

One was a writer; another, a publisher; another, the publisher's in-house counsel; another, a marketing expert; and the fifth one worked for a large investment banking company. All together, they had bought fewer than 10 properties. They had never created a master plan. They had never applied for environmental approvals for a development. They had never secured a construction loan. They had never sold property on a professional basis.

In short, they were completely ill-equipped to carry out the project they had undertaken. An outside business expert, if asked to assess their chances of success at the time, would have been wise to rate them on a one-to-ten point scale.

But the fact is, they were very successful. They managed to sell about 40 lots—for a total of $800,000—sight unseen, within 48 hours of signing the closing documents. That was enough to pay for the first half of the property price. Within a year—using the same selling tactic—they had paid off the second and final payment, and were cash positive to the tune of several million dollars.

How did they sell so many lots so quickly? By doing the only kind of selling they knew. They were all involved, directly or indirectly, in the direct-mail publishing industry. The writer wrote newsletters that were sold through direct mail. The publisher published them. The marketer sold them. And so on.

Because they lacked experience in selling overseas property, they ignored the traditional method: direct selling at seminars and conferences using high-quality audio-visual presentations, assisted by professional salespeople on the floor. Instead, they drafted a simple direct-mail sales letter (it was actually written by the lawyer) and sent it to a select group of investors who had enrolled in a direct-mail investment club. The letter explained the comparative value of the lots (they were selling for one-tenth the price that comparable lots were selling for in neighboring Costa Rica) and explained that the highly discounted prices would be offered for a very limited time. Within two days, they had sold all of the 20 lots set aside for that offer.

The development project went on to become very successful. More than 300 lots and homes were sold, and today it is a thriving, growing community. Some of those properties were sold through traditional methods such as seminars, but the lion's share of them were marketed using the fundamental principles of direct mail.

Since that experience, three of the investors went on to develop substantial real estate development portfolios of their own. And in each case, they have integrated direct-mail marketing into their selling channels.

WHAT EXACTLY IS DIRECT MAIL?

Direct mail is an unsolicited advertising message sent to a consumer or business through the mail asking for an immediate reply. The purpose of these mailings is customer acquisition. Direct mail comes in various formats, and you've undoubtedly seen many of them in your lifetime.

Here are some of the common forms of direct mail and a little bit about each:

- **Tabloid**—This is a mail piece designed to look like a newsstand tabloid. They are 13 × 10 in size, with eye-catching headlines and colors. They offer easy ordering access.

WHAT EXACTLY IS DIRECT MAIL? *(Continued)*

- **Catalog**—Catalogs have eye-catching photos along with product listings and make ordering simple. They come in all sizes and usually have easy ordering instructions, whether via telephone, Web, or business reply envelope.
- **#10 package**—This is the most common size of envelope used in business. A "teaser" is often printed on the envelope to convince the recipient to open it and read the enclosed letter. They are often mailed with first-class postage rates.
- **Invitation package (a.k.a. a 6 × 9)**—The look and feel of this package is warm and friendly. And it will contain a BRE (business reply envelope) for easy reply purposes.
- **Postcard**—These come in all different sizes. Most common are single, double, and triple fold. Postcards usually contain a soft offer, meaning that the mailer is asking for an immediate reply, but not immediate cash.

DIRECT MAIL CAN BE USED FOR ALMOST ANY PRODUCT

Direct-mail marketing is often thought of as an advertising vehicle for get-rich-quick schemes and used cars. In reality, it is a proven marketing channel for a host of products and services:

Appliances	Financial advice	Organic foods
Arts and crafts	Food	Perfume
Associations	Furniture	Pets and pet supplies
Automobiles	Hair products	Plants and plant products
Books	Health advice	Real estate
Building materials	Jewelry	Self-improvement advice
Business advice	Kitchen supplies	Spiritual advice
Clubs	Lighting	Surgical devices
Computers	Machine parts	Televisions
Cosmetics	Music equipment	Weight-loss formulas
DVDs	Natural supplements	Wine
Electronics	Newsletters	
Farming supplies	Office supplies	

Like other areas of advertising, the direct-mail industry has been profoundly affected by the growth of the Internet. In 2000, direct mail in the United States was a $44.7 billion industry, a 36 percent increase from just five years earlier. And it accounted for 22 percent of the advertising in the country.[1]

In the past couple of years, growth has continued, but at a slower pace. It hasn't kept up with the rapid rise of Internet advertising, which has experienced double-digit growth in recent years—at a time when many other advertising channels have declined.

But direct mail isn't out of the picture by any means. Direct-mail spending grew 5 percent in 2007. At $58.4 billion, this means traditional direct mail still accounts for 30 percent of the direct-response advertising in the United States. And the Winterberry Group, a global strategic consulting firm, expects direct mail to keep growing at that rate until at least 2011, when it should hit $72.3 billion.[2]

While direct mail is obviously still very viable, how marketers use it is changing. Like direct space, it is still a very good market for multi-channel marketers. Industry analysts agree. According to the Winterberry Group, one hot trend for the coming years is marketers using direct mail more and more as one component of their multi-channel marketing efforts.[3]

At its core, direct-mail marketing is a simple business: You acquire a list of names and mailing addresses. You write a sales letter. You mail it.

If the money you get back is greater than the cost of mailing and fulfillment, you are happy and you do it again. If you fail to cover your costs, you don't. What's wonderful about direct-response marketing generally, and direct mail in particular, is that it is the one form of advertising where you can "cut your losses and let your winners run."

DIRECT MAIL STEP-BY-STEP

The seven-step process of direct mail is as follows:

1. You have a product or service you want to sell. You contact a "list broker" who recommends a handful of mailing lists that he believes will be responsive to your offer. (A typical test might include 10 lists.) The broker's recommendations are based on

the mailing history of the lists—that is, whether they have been responsive for similar product offerings in the past. You then order a sample amount of each of the recommended lists; 5,000 names is the usual test quantity.

2. You hire a copywriter to write a sales letter. He interviews you about your product, studies the "similar product offerings" that the broker has access to, and thinks about how to position your product most effectively. He comes up with two distinct ideas. You like them both and ask him to write two letters.

3. You print the quantity of direct-mail packages that you need for the test. In a typical test of 10 lists of 5,000 names each, you would be printing 50,000 direct-mail packages—25,000 of one sales letter and 25,000 of the other. Each of these 20 groups (two sales letters going to 10 lists each) is uniquely coded (i.e., the response devices have unique code numbers printed on them) so you can track how each mailing list responds to the two different sales letters that you mail.

4. When the orders come in, you can easily determine which of the two sales letters worked better and which of the 10 lists you mailed to were most responsive.

5. You then mail the letter that performed better to a significantly larger number of names. The quantity of this second, "roll-out" mailing is determined by how responsive the "roll-out" lists were. In a typical roll-out, the quantity you mail might be two to five times the test quantity—that is, 10,000 names to 50,000 names.

6. When sending out this second mailing, you might test another variable (such as the introductory price or the guarantee). Generally speaking, you always want to be testing something when you mail. The idea is to use the test results to constantly improve the effectiveness of your direct-mail package.

7. When the results of the second mailing come in, you analyze them just as you did the first time: by list and by "split" (i.e., the variable you tested). Based on that analysis, you roll out once again—from two to five times the roll-out quantity (20,000 to 250,000 names), depending on how strongly each list "performed." All these roll-out decisions are based on statistical probabilities. When done properly, the roll-out process is only moderately risky.

By following this simple progression, it's quite possible to go from a test mailing of 50,000 pieces in January to a major roll-out of a million pieces less than 12 months later. That twenty-fold increase in mail volume will normally result in a twenty-fold increase in cash flow.

That's the beauty of direct-mail marketing. It is an amazingly fast and surprisingly safe way to build up a profitable business. It doesn't require a large capital investment. Most entrepreneurial ventures can be started with an initial marketing budget of less than $50,000. And because of the predictability of roll-outs, a successful direct-mail promotion can grow a business rapidly without significant investment risk.

WHAT IT TAKES TO SUCCEED IN DIRECT MAIL

Like direct-print advertising, direct-mail advertising is a mixture of art and science. The art is in writing sales letters that deliver. The science is in tracking responses and using statistical computations to plan future mailings.

Writing successful sales letters is a creative process—a matter of figuring out the market and devising a new promotion based on the customer's current concerns. List testing and analysis, by contrast, is a left-brain activity—tracking responses accurately and running them through statistical models to determine future mailings.

So to be successful in direct mail, an entrepreneur needs to get both sides of their brain working: the creative *and* the analytical sides. This is a challenge, but it is also a wonderful benefit. There are very few other business enterprises that require this level of holistic thinking. Developing a direct-mail channel for your business will not only add a significant flow of new customers to you, it will also provide you with an infinitely rewarding intellectual business life.

Although entrepreneurs should be comfortable with both sides of the marketing process, most tend to favor one side or the other. Those who are more mathematically inclined tend to focus on list building, while those who feel more comfortable as communicators pay attention to copy testing and development. As the business grows, this division is usually formalized. A marketing director takes on the list work, while a creative director focuses on the copy.

Sometimes these directors work side by side and both report to the CEO. Sometimes one of them assumes the position of marketing chief and runs the production schedule, which includes a track of list activities and a separate track of creative tasks. There is no hard and fast rule for deciding which type of person should be running your direct-mail marketing activities. It's a question of what kind of product you are producing and the individual personalities of the executives concerned.

If your products tend to be need-to-know products or commodities, a list-oriented marketer is usually preferable for the job. That's because those kinds of businesses tend to depend more on list development than copy. On the other hand, businesses that market publishing and other want-to-know products are usually better off having a creative person at the marketing helm. That's because those kinds of businesses depend heavily on breakthrough creative concepts. Having someone on top of marketing who can recognize such a breakthrough is a big plus.

In either case, the head marketing executive for a direct-mail business or department must be someone who is comfortable working with tight schedules and demanding hard work and attention to detail. In direct-mail marketing, perhaps more than most other forms of marketing, details and timeliness matter. Good fundamental strategies are not enough to ensure success. You need detailed planning and exacting execution to create the profitable mailings that allow the business to grow.

PRINCIPLES OF DIRECT-MAIL MARKETING

In the second part of this chapter, we will examine successful direct-mail campaigns in practice. Right now, we'd like to enunciate the most important principles of direct mail as we have come to know them during our combined 50-plus years in the business.

The List Is First

There is an old saying in the direct-mail industry: Copy is king. What that means is that creating breakthrough copy is more important than other direct-mail marketing activities, such as list development and the offer you make. This saying makes sense from a certain perspective, but it's misleading to neophytes—dangerously so.

Finding the right mailing lists to mail to is far and away the first and most important job of the direct-mail marketer. That's because of the importance of list selection in determining a mailing's response rates.

A good list will respond reasonably well to a direct-mail promotion even if the copy is mediocre and the offer is ordinary. A bad list, however, won't be responsive at all—even if both the copy and the offer are terrific.

If you recognize a similarity between the points we discussed about media buying in Chapter 3 and here, it is not a coincidence. Direct print and direct mail are twin sisters.

Whether you select your own lists or have a list broker do it, you must be the person who decides what response rates you need and determine which of the selected lists will meet your targets.

Accompanying your print-out of list choices should be a data card for each individual list.

Data cards contain standardized information on direct-mail lists. They tell you—among other things—how that particular list was developed, the number of addresses available, and the rental price. They will also give you information about what companies have mailed to the list in the past more than once, which can suggest what type of offers that list responds to.

Other information to look for on a list includes:

- **Purchase channel**—This tells you whether the list is direct-mail sold (i.e., all the names are direct-mail respondents) or compiled (i.e., the names were culled from directories). Generally speaking, direct-mail-sold lists are more responsive than compiled lists.
- **Average unit of sale (AUS)**—This is very important when selecting your list. If you are selling high-end riding lawn mowers that cost as much as $4,000 or more, you don't want a list of people who purchased only gardening gloves for $9.95. Instead, look for the list of prospects who just installed a new sprinkler system with an average unit of sale for $5,000.
- **Universe size**—This is simply how large the list is. A list's universe size is an important consideration in making roll-out decisions. If you do not have any other history and you have two lists that seem to be equal in every other respect, you should select the list with the larger universe simply because you have greater roll-out potential.

Some smaller lists cannot be subdivided. But larger lists can be. Normally, direct mailers take a random selection from the full list to create a test list. (This is called "nth selection.") But with many larger lists, it is also possible to make other selections based on a number of factors. For example, some lists are selectable by:

- Gender
- Income
- Age
- Homeowners
- College graduates
- State
- Zip code
- Home office
- Actives
- Expires
- Hotlines

To the neophyte, it might seem that the more selections you make, the better. But parsing out a list doesn't necessarily make it more responsive. It might make sense to do a gender select if the product you are selling is for women only, but it is unlikely that selecting by education will affect responsiveness if you are selling foosball machines, for example. It could have an effect, but it probably won't. Also keep in mind that for each select you request, there will be an extra charge.

Usually a mailing list will cost between $75 and $250 CPM (cost per thousand names) with a 5,000-name minimum. Some smaller lists may reduce the minimum. But for every select you add on, be prepared to pay an additional $5 per thousand names.

SELECTING A LIST FOR YOUR PRODUCT

If you are putting together a direct-mail campaign for a promotion selling high-end lawnmowers, you may think selecting men across the board is a wise decision. A male select of a garden-supply list might make sense because such a list might include many women. However, if the list you are selecting is totally vertical (i.e., a list of people who have previously bought lawnmowers), then it is foolish to do a male select because you would be deselecting female lawnmower buyers.

Hotline lists are almost always a good select. That's because they are based on recency, and recency is usually a reliable determinant of responsiveness. Customers who have recently bought pens, for example, are more likely to buy more pens than people who haven't bought pens in a while. The reasons for this are complex. But they can be boiled down to the emotional tendency that people have toward enthusiasm. (Think of the new golfer who buys every book and device and video he can in the first six months... and then buys much less as time goes on.) Hotlines are usually selectable by quarters—that is, the most recent 30, 60, and 90 days.

Here's a hypothetical data card for a high-end lawnmower called the Grass Shredder 2000.

Grass Shredder 2000 Buyers

20,400 buyers	@US$50/M
Sex:	100% male
Age:	40 (average)
Profile:	Grass Shredder buyers are independent, active men who want to effectively maintain their lawns and gardens. They purchase a variety of lawn-care products and publications on a regular basis.
Source:	100% direct mail
Restrictions:	Sample mailing pieces must be submitted for approval. Minimum order: $5,000 No free offers or positioning available. List Rental Agreement must be signed by mailer.
Maintenance:	List is updated quarterly.

PUTTING IT ALL TOGETHER

After consulting with a list broker and selecting the lists you intend to mail, it's a good idea to put them into a spreadsheet. Then you can make sure that they meet your assumptions for this direct-mail campaign. (See Table 7.1.)

The following is a format that has worked well for more than 20 years:

- **Promo Name**—the name you have given a specific DM package
- **Mail Date**—the date the DM package mailed
- **List Code**—your internal code to track each individual list
- **List/Select**—the name of the list with the select (if you have a select, put it in the spreadsheet)
- **Cat (category)**—there are three categories:
  - T = test, first time using the list
  - C = continuation, using part of the list again
  - R = roll-out, using the entire universe of a list
- **Qty (quantity)**—the amount of the list being used
- **Total Universe**—the total number of names on that list select
- **20% m/p Qty**—the count of the list after it has gone through merge/purge
- **Cum Qty**—the cumulative quantity of your campaign
- **Cost**—how much that list is costing you in total, including postage, printing, letter shop (processing facility), and royalties
- **Cum Cost**—the cumulative cost of your campaign
- **Proj Resp (project response rate)**—the percentage of people who respond to your offer
- **Proj Subs (projected subscribers or customers)**—the quantity mailed multiplied by your response rate (if you mail 1,000 direct-mail pieces and have a 1 percent response rate, the number of subscribers is 10)
- **Avg Sale (average unit of sale)**—the average purchase price from a buyer
- **Proj Rev (projected revenue)**—this is the AUS (average unit of sale) multiplied by the number of subscribers

TABLE 7.1 Mail Plan Spreadsheet

Promo Name: Grass Shredder 2000

Mail date

Avg Mail Cost—INVESTMENT

				Postage	Names	Royalties	Printing
			0.59	0.28	0.15	0.05	0.26

List/Select	Cat	Qty	Total Universe	30%m/p Qty	Cum Qty	Cost	Cum Cost	Proj Resp	Proj Subs	Avg Sale	Proj Rev	Cum Rev	Profit/ Loss	Profit/ Loss Cum	Proj ROI	Cum ROI
Real Simple	R	50,000	1,986,605	20000	120300	$19,300	$111,777	0.07%	14	$2,000	$28,000	$140,765	$8,700	$28,988	145%	126%
Better Homes and Gardens	R	75,000	7,687,533	30000	90300	$28,950	$82,827	0.07%	21	$2,000	$42,000	$102,765	$13,050	$19,938	145%	124%
Horticulture	R	50,000	202,904	20000	35950	$19,300	$33,286	0.07%	14	$2,000	$28,000	$40,100	$8,700	$6,815	145%	120%
Family Circle	C	15,000	4,011,530	10500	133000	$8,445	$122,345	0.05%	5	$2,000	$10,500	$152,365	$2,055	$30,020	124%	125%
Gardening Life	C	25,000	78,697	15000	57000	$12,600	$51,105	0.05%	8	$2,000	$15,000	$58,125	$2,400	$7,020	119%	114%
Good Housekeeping	C	25,000	4,632,531	10000	100300	$9,650	$92,477	0.05%	5	$2,000	$10,000	$112,765	$350	$20,288	104%	122%
Good Housekeeping	C	25,000	4,632,531	10000	100300	$9,650	$92,477	0.05%	5	$2,000	$10,000	$112,765	$350	$20,288	104%	122%

Canadian Gardening	T	5,500	152,234	3300	60300	$2,772	$53,877	0.04%	1	$2,000	$2,640	$60,765	−$132	$6,888	95%	113%
Gardening How To	C	25,000	588,484	13750	15950	$11,863	$13,986	0.04%	6	$2,000	$11,000	$12,100	−$863	$(1,886)	93%	87%
Ladies Home Journal	T	5,500	3,911,188	3300	136300	$2,772	$125,117	0.03%	1	$2,000	$1,980	$154,345	−$792	$29,228	71%	123%
Gardening Design	T	5,500	258,805	3850	42000	$3,097	$38,505	0.03%	1	$2,000	$1,925	$43,125	−$1,172	$4,620	62%	112%
Southern Living	T	5,500	2,802,258	2200	122500	$2,123	$113,900	0.03%	1	$2,000	$1,100	$141,865	−$1,023	$27,965	52%	125%
Organic Gardening	T	5,500	190,287	2200	38150	$2,123	$35,409	0.03%	1	$2,000	$1,100	$41,200	−$1,023	$5,792	52%	116%
Fine Gardening	T	5,500	175,585	2200	2200	$2,123	$2,123	0.03%	1	$2,000	$1,100	$1,100	−$1,023	$(1,023)	52%	52%
TOTALS		298000	26678641	136300	136300	$125,117	$125,117	0.06%	77	$2,000	$154,345	$154,345	$29,228	$29,228	52%	123%

- **Cum Rev**—cumulative revenue of your campaign
- **Profit/Loss**—how much money you have made or lost on that list
- **Profit/Loss Cum**—the cumulative amount of money made or lost on the campaign
- **Proj ROI**—the return on investment for an individual list
- **Cum ROI**—the return on investment for the campaign

Having cumulative columns is very important. They allow you to understand where you are at any given point of your campaign. Suppose your objective is to plan a campaign to 100 percent ROI, and you assumed you could mail only 10 lists. But after all your lists have been input into the spreadsheet, you see that your campaign is at 130 percent: You should keep going.

It can also work the other way around. You think you should be at 100 percent, but when everything is entered into your spreadsheet, you find you are at 75 percent ROI. In this case, you can move up the sheet and see where you need to cut off.

This process makes it easy to ensure that your direct-mail campaign will produce the results that you are looking for.

Let's move on to the offer.

THE OFFER: WHAT IS IT GOOD FOR?

Copy is king. And list selection is critical. But what about the offer? Direct-mail pundits give so little emphasis to the offer. Yet it is very important. Here's why: A good offer can easily double response rates. A bad or botched offer can easily kill a mailing that would otherwise be profitable.

What is the offer?

It is the deal you make with your customer and the terms of that deal. The offer is what he gets for what he gives you. It includes the product, the service, all the promises made about the product and service, and the guarantee.

The offer also includes the transactional details, such as how the customer can buy the product (by direct-mail reply device, 800 number, web site, etc.) and the coding (explained above).

All these details are important, and all of them should be spelled out at the end of the sales letter and in the order device. Failing to spell out these details properly and fully could be a costly mistake.

For example, let's say you invested in postage for a 24-page magalog, did all your list homework, spent more than you thought you ever would on copy, and even went as far as testing your price point online first. So you think you have a winner. But you only mention your 800 telephone number on the last page of the sales copy. It's not anywhere else—not even on the order form! This is the kind of mistake that happens all the time. It may seem small, but it can be disastrous.

THE OFFER MUST BE STRONG

Every direct-mail package you drop in the mail should contain a strong offer. The offer should be an incentive or reward that motivates prospects to respond to your mailing, either with an order or with a request for more information (depending on your goals).

To be effective, your offer must pass the "10 Tests" rules, several of which are from direct-mail copywriter Alan Sharpe:

Test 1. Is your offer specific?: Will the prospect understand exactly what they get and how to get it?

Test 2. Is your offer exclusive?: Are you making your offer only to a select few (and making them feel that they are an exclusive bunch), or are you making your offer to everyone?

Test 3. Is your offer valuable?: Will your prospects perceive your offer to be of value to them? Your offer may be inexpensive for you to make, but it must have a high perceived value to your potential customers.

Test 4. Is your offer unique?: Is the deal you're offering only available through your business?

Test 5. Is your offer useful?: Your offer can be exclusive but useless, or unique and useless. Make sure your offer helps your prospects save money, save time, do their jobs better, or is something else just as helpful.

Test 6. Is your offer relevant?: Do prospects want what you are offering?

Test 7. Is your offer plausible?: Some offers are too good to be true, and others are just plain silly. Either way, your offer needs to lend credibility.

Test 8. Is your offer easy to acquire?: The harder you make it for your prospects to obtain your offer, the lower your response rates will be. So make your order forms clear, simple, and short; your toll-free telephone number obvious on the page; and your terms and conditions of purchase concise.

Test 9. Is your offer urgent?: Are you clear about the deadline of your offer? Is it an early-bird special or are you limiting it to only the first 250 people who respond?

Test 10. Does your offer have a guarantee?: Did you strengthen your offer with a money-back guarantee? Perhaps you could even allow the subscriber to keep all bonuses and/or issues up to that point, or make sure the prospect knows that there is no risk whatsoever.

Take a moment now to go look at the offers of all your current campaigns, not only for direct mail, but for all channels of marketing.

If you are just starting out and do not have any of your own campaigns, look at offers that you have responded to, either in the mail or online. Examine each piece and circle how many of the above test rules the offer used.

Be conscious of the "10 Tests" rules while going forward—and we're certain you will find that the more often you see an offer repeated, the more of the above components it contains. That's because promotions that are getting responses and making money are the ones you see over and over again.

You can have great copy written and you can select very responsive lists . . . but if the offer is weak, you will get a much smaller response than you could get if it were strong. The right offer makes a big difference. Give the creation and execution of your offer the time and care it deserves.

LONG LIVE THE KING

We've discussed principles and practices of list selection and offers. Now it's time to look at some fundamental rules that apply to the third primary element of direct-mail marketing: advertising copy.

> **Don't proselytize. Preach to the converted.** Direct-mail marketing is a form of direct-response marketing. One of the tenets of direct-response marketing is to target the sales effort to qualified prospects: people who have already demonstrated an interest in buying products and services similar to those you are selling. Trying to sell a watch to someone who has never bought a watch before through the mail is an uphill battle at best. Most of the time, your advertising will be directed at proven buyers—enthusiasts, as it were. When writing to enthusiasts, you should write enthusiastically and remind them constantly of what they already believe—that buying your product will make them feel good, the same way it has made them feel in the past.
>
> **Start with the prospect.** Many beginning direct-mail copywriters make the mistake of spending too much ink touting the product, describing all its features at length and in detail. This is an understandable mistake when writing about a new and exciting product. But the direct-mail marketer must keep in mind that the prospect doesn't really care about the product. All he really cares about is himself and how the product might be able to help him. Keep that in mind when you write direct-mail copy. Ask: "What is my best customer thinking about? What's keeping him up at night? What is he dreaming about?" Figure out the answers to those questions, and your copy will never stray far from the mark.
>
> **The lead is 80 percent of the sale.** A bare-bones direct-mail sales letter would consist of an envelope with "teaser copy" printed on it, and a sales letter and order device inside it. The envelope teaser, the headline above the salutation, and the first several hundred words of copy after the salutation are, taken together, considered the "lead" of the sales package. Most of the rest of the letter is considered to be the sales argument, while the last few paragraphs of the letter and the order device are considered

the "close." In terms of size (i.e., number of words), the sales argument and the close constitute about 80 to 90 percent of the total.

However, the lead—at only 10 to 20 percent of the total—has the greatest impact on the eventual sale. The lead packs most of the punch, because it is what most prospects read before deciding to either continue reading or trash the sales package. If the lead is well written (i.e., makes a strong, emotional case for the product), then the rest of the selling (i.e., convincing the prospect that his desire to buy the product is a rational one) is relatively easy. When developing direct-mail copy, always focus most of your creative and critical energy on the lead.

The lead is yours to win. The body is yours to lose. As mentioned in the previous paragraph, the lead is where the emotional pitch is made. Winning over the prospect's heart is a very challenging task. He typically has all sorts of other direct-mail offers he can look at. Why should he focus on yours? Still, if you ask the right questions about what he is thinking and feeling, and then come up with the right answers, there is a good chance that the lead you write will "hook" your prospect and make him want to read the rest of the sales letter with enthusiasm. That enthusiasm makes your job of writing the sales argument much easier. The enthusiastic prospect is willing to overlook minor mistakes and omissions, because he wants to believe that what you are selling him makes sense. But you can blow the sale after a strong lead if you get too sloppy. One of the most common ways of getting too sloppy is to provide insufficient proof of all the claims you make about the value of the product. If you subject the sales argument of your sales letter to the "four-legged stool" test, you won't have to worry about losing the prospect.

Check the copy with the "four-legged stool" test. Think of your sales argument as a four-legged stool. To stand solidly, it needs all four legs in place. Take one leg away and it will stand, but it won't be stable. Take two legs away and it will certainly fall. The four legs of a good sales letter are Idea, Benefit, Track Record, and Credibility. The Idea is the one, big unifying concept that pulls the sales argument together and (usually) expresses the product's USP (unique selling proposition). The

Benefit is the promise you make to the prospect about how the product will help him. The stronger your promise, the higher the response you will get when you mail it. The Track Record refers to the history of the product and its history of performing as promised. Prospects who don't know you, your company, or your product from Adam will be interested in seeing proof of your claims. Credibility is the fourth and final element of good direct-mail copywriting. Both the product and the manufacturer of the product must be presented as credible to the prospect. Otherwise she won't have the courage to buy.

Make every offer irresistible. Close your sales copy with an irresistible offer—one that is simply too good to refuse. Most copywriters never take the time to think "How can I make this offer stronger?" Or, "How can I ratchet up the promise so that everyone who reads this will be unable to refuse it?"

HOW THE COPY PROCESS WORKS

In an ideal direct-mail world, here's how advertising copy would be developed:

Somebody in the business develops a product that is in some way better than other, similar products in the industry. This product inventor will then have several conversations with the copywriter, explaining how the product works and the many ways in which it is better than the competition.

After the copywriter has heard enough—and has had all his questions thoroughly answered—he will go back to his studio and think and read and think and read until he comes up with a killer headline and several hundred words of killer copy. He will subject that "lead" to a "peer review," in which four or five people will critique it using an objective, four-point rating system developed by Agora, Inc. and American Writers & Artists, Inc.

Based on the rating and suggestions given at the peer review, the copywriter will revise the copy and put it through another quick assessment to ensure that it merits the 3.0-plus score (the minimum passing score) it received. If it passes muster, then the copywriter would write out the rest of the sales letter, filling up the sales argument with many diverse claims and providing proof for each and every one of them.

When the sales argument is finished, the copywriter will send it out to a half dozen trusted colleagues, asking for feedback on whether the writing is clear and comprehensible—and believable, too. Where the copy is weak, he improves it. When the revisions are completed (usually within 24 hours), he sends it out to the graphic artist for formatting and then to the marketer to be mailed.

Direct-mail advertising makes more sense today than it ever has. And it has always been a sensationally effective way to sell products. Because of the low expense of direct e-mail marketing, marketers can test their headlines and leads to potential customers before going to the expense of printing and mailing it. This had led to a new idea about testing: When in doubt, test it out. And test everything. After all, it costs you practically nothing. And it can make a big difference to your bottom-line results!

CHAPTER EIGHT

DIRECT PRINT

Getting More Than Ever for Your Ad Dollar

"Serious Lighting for Serious Readers."

That's the headline of a tiny print ad (which also featured a drawing of a desk lamp, an address, and a phone number to call for a free catalog) that launched a multimillion-dollar business.

"Space ads enabled us to get started. They helped my wife, Lori, and I launch our company 20 years ago," says Steve Leveen, president of Levenger, the Delray Beach, Florida-based provider of high-end reading tools, diaries, notebooks, briefcases, and more. "At our peak, we were in 20 publications or so."

These included *The New Yorker*, *The New York Times*, *Smithsonian* magazine, *The Nation*, and *Law Journal* (many attorneys are still loyal customers), among others. Levenger included address codes unique to the magazine in which the ad appeared. This allowed the company to track and quantify the response from each one.

Levenger doesn't use print ads anymore, but Leveen believes it is still a very viable marketing channel, even in the Internet Age.

Collectible coins is one industry that still markets primarily through space ads. Look at any issue of *USA Today* or *Parade* and you will see ads from several different companies offering sets of presidential quarters or collector's editions of newly minted coins.

BRANDING VERSUS SELLING

In this chapter, we are talking about direct-marketing print ads. They are quite different than many ads you've seen in publications for perfume or consumer electronics or cars. Those types of ads seek to create an "awareness" about the product. These "branding" ads are usually eye-catching, but the advertising company has no real way of knowing exactly how much business the ad brought them.

In direct-space ads, the entire ad is directed toward convincing the customer to take action immediately. There is a phone number or web site so that the prospect can order the product right then. And because those orders can be tied to a particular ad in a particular publication, the company knows exactly what ad provoked the strongest response … and which one didn't. This testing, which allows the marketer to drop the losing ads and roll out the winner, is another key to direct response.

In fact, pick up an issue of *any* newspaper or magazine and you will see direct-print advertising at work. Everything from exotic travel to reading lamps to celebrity memorabilia to dolls to plants to time shares are routinely sold from little ads on the pages of all the most popular newspapers and magazines. Specialized periodicals—aficionado magazines and trade journals in particular—abound with direct-print advertising.

It makes sense. Direct-print advertising combines the best of two worlds: the wide reach of general advertising with the qualifying and monetizing characteristics of direct mail.

WHAT ARE YOU WAITING FOR?

If you are in the direct-mail or direct e-mail business already, it behooves you to develop a parallel channel of direct-print advertising. If you aren't currently doing direct-mail sales, print advertising is a good place to start.

Direct-print advertising has many advantages. The cost involved in testing is modest, the likelihood of success is reasonable, and the financial returns can be great.

Developing a viable print advertising channel will benefit your business in two important ways. First, you will acquire customers you couldn't get through other media. And second, you will give your brand or product widespread exposure that may one day convert to direct sales.

We have had lots of experience in direct-print advertising over the years, selling everything from jewelry to perfume to cosmetics to books to seminars and travel. We believe that there is almost nothing that can't be sold through this channel. And that's not surprising, considering the range of media—from local "penny savers" to nationals such as *The Robb Report*.

Despite the potential of direct-print advertising, most entrepreneurs are reluctant to try it. To them, as outsiders, it seems risky and expensive. But the truth is very different. Making direct-print advertising work is a pretty simple process.

Generally, magazine and newspaper publishers price their advertising space according to circulation, size, color, and location.

Circulation is the most important factor. A magazine that reaches 3 million people (such as *Time* or *People*) is going to charge much more for print space than one that reaches only 400,000 people (such as *Bicycling* or *Computer Shopper*) or 40,000 (such as a locally published periodical).

Size is the next most important factor. Bigger ads are more expensive than smaller ads. Ad sizes can range from multipage layouts to double-truck ads to full page to half page to quarter-, eighth-, and sixteenth-pages.

Then, color and position must be considered. Here, too, common sense rules. Color processing is more expensive than black and white. And better page positions carry premiums.

So how do you decide what kind of ad will work for you?

That depends on the product you want to sell. Some products work very well as small black and whites placed randomly on a space-available basis. Other products need the attention-grabbing capacity of a full-page, four-color ad, placed in a prominent position.

DIRECT-PRINT ADVERTISING IS DECLINING, BUT STILL VIABLE

According to the Newspaper Association of America, readership of newspapers has been falling since 1990. Only about 48 percent of American adults regularly read at least one newspaper during the week.[*] The decline in readership has resulted in a 20 percent drop in advertising dollars in only the past 10 years.[†] Magazine ad rates have remained about the same for the past 20 years or so.[‡]

From a direct-marketing perspective, this trend is not quite as bad as it seems. That's because some of the drop-off is due to a migration of advertising dollars from print to the Internet. At one time, for example, the back of *The New York Times* was the only place that summer camps for obese children could effectively advertise. *The New York Times* still works for such advertising, but today there are dozens of Internet sites on camping that work just as well, or better. Thus, the advertising dollars spent to sell these summer camps may be the same, but the amount going into old-fashioned print is diminishing.

That shift notwithstanding, print advertising is still a large and viable market. According to the Newspaper Association of America, print advertising in newspapers alone brought in $46.6 billion in 2006.

[*] Newspaper Association of America, "Daily Newspaper Readership Trend—Total Adults (1998–2007)," www.naa.org/docs/Research/Daily_National_Top50_1998-2007.pdf. Accessed: February 22, 2008.

[†] Newspaper Association of America, "Advertising Expenditures," www.naa.org/TrendsandNumbers/advertising-expenditures.aspx. Accessed February 22, 2008.

[‡] myadbase.com, "Magazine Advertising Rates," www.myadbase.com/cgi-bin/guide.cgi?page=magazine_advert_rates. Accessed: February 23, 2008.

SUCCESS IN DIRECT-PRINT ADVERTISING

As with all channels of advertising, your success (or lack thereof) is affected by several factors. In direct–print advertising, this includes:

Media: The most important factor is media—which particular publications you choose to advertise in. In this regard, direct-print advertising is like direct mail, where the list you mail to (rather than the offer you make or the copy you employ) has the greatest impact on response rates.

The difference between media selections can be enormous. One magazine might give you back four times the money you spent on it, while another might give you nothing back at all.

That's why it is so important to test lots of different media. Most won't work for you, but some will. To find one publication that's profitable, you may have to test half a dozen that aren't.

In direct mail, everybody understands this concept. But when it comes to direct-print advertising, most marketers have an entirely different point of view. They approach the market skeptically. And then reluctantly test one or two ads in one or two publications . . . and wait for the results.

If they get a good response, they move forward. If they don't, they back away. "We can't make print work," they say with confidence. They believe they have given it the old college try, but they haven't.

To develop a direct-print-sourced channel of customers for your business, you must commit to the process in a serious way. Serious means studying the market carefully to determine where similar products are being sold—and then committing to testing 10 to 20 different publications before you decide that direct print doesn't work.

Most entrepreneurs who got their start using direct-print advertising will tell you stories about how they struck out time and time again before they discovered the media that worked for them.

We remember coaching a friend who wanted to start a physical therapy business for pelvic ailments. She tested a dozen of the bigger, more obvious local newspapers and magazines before she found one—a local Jewish newspaper—that proved enormously responsive. Based on that one source alone, she quadrupled her business in one year. That growth of cash flow allowed her to continue to look for other media that would work. She found only two more, but the three together were enough to grow her business to a point where word-of-mouth advertising was all she needed thereafter.

Cost: After media, the next most important success factor in direct-print advertising is cost. Yes, finding a publication that works is critical. But if the cost of that advertising is greater than the profit you derive from it, you won't be happy in the long run.

Some marketers take a blanket approach to cost, refusing to pay more than a certain number of dollars per thousand readers. ("Dollars per thousand" is a standard industry measurement.) As a general rule, this is a mistake. Each publication that carries your ad is going to give you a different type of customer. Some will respond immediately, but die out quickly. Others will have a longer tail. Some will buy only very inexpensive products. Others will be responsive to higher margin promotions.

In building a profitable direct-print-based channel, you will eventually need to know the "lifetime value" of each of the publications that take your ads. As the term suggests, the lifetime value tells you what a customer is worth over his buying life with you. The lifetime value of your customers depends on how you treat them, as well as on the quality and cost of the products you sell them. But lifetime value is also influenced by where you get your customers.

Each source—each publication in which you advertise—will deliver a different lifetime value. For that reason, it's necessary to track your customers according to source. By analyzing lifetime values this way, you will be able to determine just how much to spend on each print publication in which you advertise.

When you test a new source (i.e., a new magazine or newspaper), you won't know its lifetime value for at least six months. While you are waiting, you can make decisions about continuing advertisements with that source by assuming that it will deliver an average lifetime value. If the initial response is stronger than average, you can go forward with a reasonable degree of confidence. If the response is average, you should continue, but very conservatively. If the response is below average, it's usually better to wait till you can determine the lifetime value of those customers.

Generally, the quality of customers you get from any individual source will remain constant unless something changes with the source itself. Sometimes a change of editorial policy can improve or diminish its quality. Sometimes a change in circulation—particularly a sudden increase—will signal a change in quality, one way or the other.

For this reason, it's important to pay close attention to editorial consistency, advertising practices, and response rates of sources during the testing phase. If they suddenly change, be alert. Consider curtailing or even stopping your advertising until you have reason to be optimistic again.

Offer: After media and cost, this is the most important factor in determining your success in print. The "offer" is a broad term—it consists of the product, the price you ask for it, and other variables such as premiums and guarantees. Finding the right offer takes some time and testing. When you are beginning and don't know what offer to use, look around at what your competitors are doing. If they've been running offers for any length of time, it is usually because they are working. Imitate and "test against them" by changing individual aspects of the offer (price, premium, guarantee, etc.) and seeing how such changes affect response rate.

Offering products or premiums for free will usually generate the greatest response, regardless of the source you are using. But free offers also tend to bring in less qualified customers (i.e., customers with lower lifetime values), so be careful about entirely free offers. It's usually better to incorporate some sort of price qualifier—even if that means as little as charging a small fee for postage and shipping.

Copy: The last factor that will affect the outcome of your print placements is the copy you use. Although this is the fourth most important factor, that doesn't mean you should give it short shrift. The copy can double or halve response rates, even when the source and offer are the same. For that reason, you should test copy constantly, always looking to beat the current control.

If you have direct-marketing experience, all of these principles will be second nature to you. Direct-print advertising is, like direct mail, just another aspect of direct marketing.

BUYING PRINT

In purchasing space, give priority to source—that is, test the publications in which you have the most confidence. But never forget the importance of keeping your costs down. Negotiate the best rates you can at all times.

Sales reps for print space will do their best to talk you into spending as much as you can afford (or even more!). They will try to get the highest rates possible by arguing that you should buy full-page, four-color ads in prime locations. Only you can know what kind of space works best for you. Test when you can afford to. The object is to find space ads that work well without spending top dollar.

Sales reps will also try to convince you to buy multiple placements. Most will argue that your response rates will increase with each successive placement. As far as we know, there is no evidence that this is universally true. Our own experience has been mixed. Therefore, our recommendation is to begin with a single placement only, even though this will be—on a relative basis—more "expensive" than multiple ads.

These are the standards and principles of direct-print advertising. Now let's take a look at how these operate in practice, along with some clever and useful techniques you can use to improve your results.

LEFTOVERS ARE GOOD!

Whenever possible, try to purchase remnant space. This is space in a magazine or newspaper that has not sold in time and is "left over." It is also referred to as remainder advertising or last-minute advertising space.

Unlike the Internet, print advertising has very tight deadlines. These deadlines are necessary due to the time sensitivity of the medium.

That gives sales reps only a limited amount of time to sell ad space. If the sales reps do not sell their quota in time, the very same space will be offered at a steep discount, for two reasons: (1) The reps (and publishers) would rather collect a fraction of the space price compared with no revenue at all, and (2) if the space is not sold, it will be filled with house ads or public service announcements (PSAs). If this happens too often, it sends a message to the advertisers in that publication. It essentially tells them that the publisher could not sell the allotted ad space—and it makes them think twice about advertising with that publication again.

Knowing that the publisher is motivated to offer you remnant space is good for your advertising campaigns. Make sure you are aware of the publication's deadline; then call right before that deadline and start your negotiations. If space is available and time is tight, the publication will most likely take your offer.

NEWSPAPERS: DAILY OR WEEKLY

Your chances of obtaining remnant space are even greater in newspapers. Unlike a monthly magazine, which can easily alter its page count, newspapers often have a set format and page count . . . and even tighter deadlines. And as fewer consumers are reading papers, advertising revenues are more important to them. This does not apply only to small town local newspapers.

About five years ago, we bought a full-page ad in *USA Today* for the discounted price of $1,500. We were advertising a $24 book on investing and would need only 63 orders to break even. Because the newspaper's circulation was nearly 2 million at the time, getting 63 orders (a .00315 percent response) seemed like a very reasonable expectation.

To create the ad, a 24-page sales letter written by master copywriter Clayton Makepeace was converted into the tabloid space ad format. The order form was changed to emphasize an 800 number.

The result: 217 book orders. That's an ROI of 347 percent on the $1,500 investment. That was good news. Even better news was that customers who ordered the book went on to have a lifetime value almost equal to direct-mail buyers. Plus, this test was an important breakthrough because it provided the company with a new channel of new customers.

However, had we paid the rate-card price for the ad, we would have lost almost $10,000.

Regardless of whether you are testing newspapers or magazines, be aware of that publication's rates and deadlines—and you will be well armed to get the very best deals.

START WITH YOUR ABCs

The following is an excerpt from the Audit Bureau of Circulations (ABC) web site that explains the important services they provide to direct-print advertisers:

The Audit Bureau of Circulations is a third-party circulation audit of print circulation, readership and web site activity.

That data is disseminated into reports and made available in various formats. Accurate, credible reports are issued in comparable formats. Comparability is the key.

An ABC audit is an in-depth examination of a publisher's records that assures buyers that a publication's circulation claims are accurate and verifiable.

We also maintain the world's foremost database of audited circulation and readership information. ABC's reports and services are essential for buyers and sellers of print advertising to make informed business decisions.

With more than 4,000 members in North America, ABC is a forum of the world's leading magazine and newspaper publishers, advertisers and advertising agencies. The organization provides credible, verified information essential to the media buying and selling process. ABC maintains the world's foremost electronic database of audited-circulation information and an array of verified readership, subscriber demographics and online activity data.[1]

This is a resource to be used in three ways:

1. To expand your universe to publications you may never have even heard of.
2. To verify that you are getting what you are paying for.
3. To clarify if the publication has a paid or controlled circulation base.

Once you have identified the publications you think may be worth advertising in, you need to go one step further and download their media kits. Again, the Internet has made this process so much easier and faster.

Years ago, you had to call a publication and request that a media kit be sent to you. Then, you had to wait for it to arrive. Today, you can go online and view the media kit instantly.

Here is what Canadian Heritage, Canada's cultural preservation organization, has to say about media kits:

A media kit is the opportunity to use materials to showcase the magazine's or newspaper's strengths and convey credibility to advertisers. It shows advertisers what the publication can do for them. It's a chance to tell your story. It is what you should use to assess the publication. Therefore, it must contain a clear statement about the publication and the audience it delivers to.

Credibility is crucial. This is because sales reps are selling an intangible product. They can't promise an advertiser that he'll get results—they can only rely on the experience of past and current advertisers. This is why so much of the media kit is geared towards credibility—numbers, research, audits, testimonials, etc."[2]

A good media kit will contain:

- **A mission statement**
- **An editorial profile**—a short description of the magazine's editorial content
- **An editorial calendar**—indicating publishing and advertising deadlines
- **A reader profile**—psychographic information on their likes and what they spend time doing
- **An audience profile**—demographic information such as gender, age, income, education, and occupation
- **Rate base**—the publication's readership, both newsstand buyers and subscribers, both paid and controlled

AND LET'S NOT FORGET ADVERTISING RATES!

So how do you know if you are getting a good rate for your advertising?

The best way is by figuring out how much it costs you to reach 1,000 readers. This is known as CPM, or cost per thousand. Here's the formula:

$$CPM = (Cost of Ad/Circulation) \times 1,000$$

For example, if a full-page ad in a magazine costs $2,300 and the circulation is 135,000, you divide $2,300 by 135,000, and then multiply by 1,000. This gives you 17.04. In other words, it will cost you $17.04 to reach 1,000 people.

With this handy calculation, you can compare the cost of advertising in any publication you find.

BIRDS OF A FEATHER FLOCK TOGETHER

Many marketers do not get their expected results in space advertising simply because they fail to do one thing.

They think that because they have followed all the steps described above, they're safe. But they miss the simplest step of all. Don't make the same one!

Before you sign on the dotted line for your space advertising, get the last six to twelve issues of the publication. Then go through every page and chart the following:

- How many ads are direct-response ads?
- How many similar companies are advertising?
- How many similar offers are being advertised?
- How many of the direct-response ads and the similar companies and the similar offers have been repeated in the last six to twelve issues?

When marketers are getting expected results or better, they do not stop or pull a campaign.

This is information you will not get from a media kit or sales rep. But it is crucial. You must go through this process *every time* you do a print-ad campaign.

DIRECT IS DIRECT IS DIRECT!

We talked about all the different tactics of direct e-mail marketing in Chapter 3 and about direct-mail marketing in Chapter 7. Well, the fundamental principles are the same for direct space.

If you are already having success online or in the mail, you are in a very good position to venture into direct-space marketing.

We say that because if you have a direct-mail or e-mail campaign that is working, it means you have thought about your copy concept and your offer. If your first channel of marketing is direct space, that is okay, too. However, do not try to write copy for a quarter-page ad.

Go through the same copy guidelines we discussed in Chapter 7. Brainstorm the idea and the offer. It's all right if you end up writing

10 or 12 pages of copy, even though you can only use about a quarter of it.

Once you are satisfied with that copy, it's time to peel it down to an appropriate amount. But before you send it off to the printer—test it!

Test your headline in pay-per-click (PPC) ads. Test the copy for the entire ad on your web site. If you don't have a web site, test it on a competitor's site. It will be cheaper to test it on a web site rather than in print—and you will have results within hours.

WHEN TO BEGIN YOUR DIRECT-SPACE CAMPAIGN

In any multi-channel campaign, we recommend starting with these three "directs" in this specific order:

1. Direct e-mail marketing
2. Direct-mail marketing
3. Direct-print marketing

There are several reasons for this sequence:

- You go through the same creative process for all three channels. But by approaching each channel in the above order, you are able to go through the creative process once . . . and then "slice and dice" your existing copy into direct-mail and direct-space ads. This is the best way to leverage the work of your marketing team and your copywriter.
- You can approach your customer in the way he or she is most likely to respond. Your media/lists are interchangeable. Let's say you do an endorsed e-mail campaign to Newsmax.com, and it does well. Next, you test banner ads on their web site, and that shows good results. Next, you rent their mailing names for your direct-mail campaign and, at the same time as that campaign is set to arrive in your prospects' mailboxes, you place an ad in the Newsmax magazine. These ads are all directed toward like-minded people (birds of a feather) who will choose to respond to your offer in different ways.

- This sequence gives you the biggest bang for your marketing buck. You can test your creative efforts in the most cost-effective channel first. Starting with direct e-mail allows you to get quick and inexpensive results. You can easily interchange PPC ads to find the headline that works. You can easily test two e-mail endorsements against each other to find the most effective copy. And once you get those results, you can "roll out" to direct-mail and direct-space ads.

We will go into greater detail on launching your multi-channel campaign in Chapter 15. But in the meantime, if you want to get started now, use these three "directs" and start gathering information on your possible media buys.

CHAPTER NINE

DIRECT-RESPONSE TELEVISION

Why Super Bowl Ads Don't Work

Would you ever consider forking over millions of dollars for an advertisement that barely mentions your product?

Of course not. But otherwise shrewd businesspeople do it all the time. The advertising channel we are talking about is television.

Most television advertising is rubbish. And Super Bowl commercials are the worst kind of rubbish—expensive, self-absorbed, and impotent.

Super Bowl commercials are, for the most part, elaborately produced minimovies, with action-packed plot lines and famous actors and beautiful scenery. Some are dramas. Some are action adventures. Some are comedies. We laugh at them. We cry at them. We hold our breath in anticipation. We do everything we do at the movies. But we don't run out afterward and buy the advertised products. In many cases, we don't even know what the products are.

This has been confirmed by recent studies. University of Tampa researchers, working with ad agency Brain on Brand, found that a year after watching Super Bowl commercials, most viewers couldn't remember what products had been promoted. This held true even for those much-talked-about commercials heralded at the time for their originality. In fact, in one case, many subjects thought an ad for FedEx was actually for UPS.

The best-remembered commercial studied—a Budweiser ad that was lauded by advertisers as brilliant and successful—achieved only a 46 percent recognition factor. In other words, fewer than half of those who watched it realized that it was selling beer![1]

THE SUPER BOWL COMMERCIAL THAT BROKE THE MOLD

There was one exception to these findings, however. It was a low-budget advertisement that didn't feature a movie star, had no special effects, and placed last on many of the post-game lists of "best Super Bowl commercials." It was reviled both by TV critics and advertising "experts," one of whom called it "monumentally brainless and amateurish."[2]

But what they missed was that the ad, for Vin Gupta's database marketing company infoUSA, was a huge success in terms of selling the product.

The offer—"For 100 free sales leads, go to salesgenie.com"— brought 30,000 people to the web site. More than 2,000 people called the company for additional information, and the commercial was watched by 25,000 more people on YouTube. The bottom line: infoUSA signed up more than 10,000 new subscribers to its service as a direct result of that one ugly ad.[3]

This simple commercial led directly to "the third highest market share rise among Super Bowl advertisers, after King Pharmaceuticals and Budweiser," according to Hitwise, a company that monitors Web traffic.[4]

"Gupta didn't earn accolades from the advertising industry with his commercial," said Denny Hatch, a direct-marketing expert, "but his $3 million was well spent. It brought quantifiable attention to his business, not just water cooler talk on Monday morning."[5]

We have always been delightfully dumbfounded by brand advertising in general and by television ad spending in particular.

How can these hotshot corporate executives explain their advertising budgets to their shareholders? Don't they feel obligated to produce a return on their advertising investments? Or do they think that winning an industry award for "most creative Super Bowl commercial" is a sufficient reward for all the time and talent that they invest in these micro-Hollywood wannabes?

Don't get us wrong. We believe in TV advertising. But we also believe that if you spend a dollar promoting your product, you should get back that dollar—and then some—in product sales.

When you abandon that purpose or give it second priority in order to impress the world with your cleverness, you are abandoning your fiduciary responsibility to your company or your client.

When advertisers pay agencies millions of dollars to produce commercials that don't sell product and fail to be recognized by half of those watching, then something is definitely wrong. How do these ad agencies convince their clients to pay for these boondoggles?

There is some great buying and selling that occurs in the television industry, but it's not the selling that's supposed to take place: between the advertiser and the viewing public. Instead, it's the buying and selling that occurs between the agency and the advertiser.

WHAT CAN BE DONE

But what about selling the product? Can that be effectively done on TV?

The answer is yes—but with qualifications. Over the past 20 years, we have been involved in about a dozen TV advertising campaigns, including short form (30- and 60-second commercials), long form (30- and 60-minute infomercials), and marketing on TV auction shows.

We enjoyed some notable successes (one campaign that generated $4 million in sales in under two weeks), some memorable losses (an $80,000 investment that netted less than $100 in sales), and lots of results that were somewhere in between. These experiences taught us that TV can be a viable, secondary medium for multi-channel marketers, *if* they take a careful, direct-response approach *and* avoid the lure of brand advertising and award ceremonies.

To make money using this channel today, you have to go back to what worked when television was in its infancy: strong pitches that focus on value, uniqueness, and benefit.

In considering whether you want to add television to your overall marketing program, keep in mind that it is a very unique medium. It addresses consumers when they are in a passive mood—usually sitting in a comfortable chair or lying in bed at home. Print and Internet advertising, by contrast, engage prospects actively. In fact, these consumers are usually actively searching and scanning for information that they find interesting and rewarding.

Because television advertising is passive, it has to try harder to capture interest and motivate. This is why creative advertising usually doesn't work. By disguising itself as (or fully becoming) entertainment, it further relaxes the consumer's already zoned-out brain and sends the message: "This is just for fun. You don't have to remember any of this."

ADVERTISING TO YOUR TARGET MARKET

When most people think of television advertising, they think about the commercials they see on network TV. Such advertising gives the advertiser an immense reach—sometimes to as many as hundreds of millions of people. But the greater the reach, the less targeted the audience. For every person who might be interested in your product, there will be a hundred or a thousand with absolutely zero interest.

If you're advertising Nike footwear or Coca-Cola, you want this kind of reach. But if your product is more specialized, the huge expense of TV exposure becomes an exorbitant bet.

For most businesses, television advertising should be a supplemental endeavor restricted by a limited budget. Focus on smaller audiences, especially targeted ones—TV channels and programs that concentrate on market niches such as investing, real estate, pets, home shopping, building wealth, and so on.

With the growth of cable and regional TV, it's easier to find channels and programs that cater to the prospects you want to reach. If you spend some time looking at the growth of targeted and local advertising on these new cable stations, you will understand how viable this type of market can be.

All these channels need advertising revenue to remain on the air. And because the industry is bigger and more competitive now, many stations are offering very affordable rate packages, within easy reach of even small businesses and organizations.

Creating TV advertising isn't cheap, but it doesn't have to be Hollywood-expensive either. Industry watchers say that the average production cost for a 60-second direct-response TV spot is $30,000. But that average includes big-budget national ads. Direct-response commercials designed for local and targeted audiences will generally cost a third to half of that amount.

A spokesperson for South Florida Productions Inc. (North Miami, Florida) said they regularly produce 60-second spots for less than $15,000. "We just produced a very effective commercial for a local business for just $8,000," he added. That's quite reasonable.

UNDERSTANDING TV ADVERTISING

Planning is especially essential for the businessperson approaching broadcast advertising for the first time. When you're starting out, it's important to educate yourself about the medium—and the best way to do that is to talk to a lot of people. This includes advertising representatives from TV stations, other business owners, and your customers.

But before speaking to anyone, you'll want to have a basic understanding of how TV advertising works. Like direct mail, direct-response TV ads come in various formats. The top three are:

1. Short-form ads that run 15, 30, 60, or 120 seconds. These ads can run throughout the day and night.
2. "Paid programming"—long-form ads or infomercials that run about a half-hour. The length gives the marketer more time to demonstrate and "sell" the product. These usually run late at night or on weekends.
3. Home shopping ads on channels such as the Home Shopping Network and QVC. These dedicated TV channels run ads 24/7.

In your business, you can use one format or mix them up.

It's good to know that all these ads, no matter what their length, follow the same formula. They use repetition to make viewers believe they want the item being advertised. And, of course, they all follow direct-response principles. They ask the viewer to take action immediately—usually by calling in to buy the product. And like all direct-marketing efforts, you'll know if your ad is working almost immediately after the commercial airs.

HOME SHOPPING CHANNEL SUCCESS

By David Cross

QVC (Quality Value and Choice) and HSN (Home Shopping Network) are two of the better known and well-recognized television shopping channels in the United States. They are both highly adept direct-response marketers, and it may be worthwhile to explore them as a viable advertising channel to sell your products.

Start your exploration by actually watching these stations for a while. That way, you'll be able to pitch products to them that fit well with their marketing approach. They are looking for high-quality products at the right price point. Plus, they want to offer diverse and interesting choices to their customers (people who watch and order from their TV shows).

Let's talk specifically about QVC. Initially, you'll be pitching your product to your buying contact at the station. The main thing to appreciate with QVC—indeed, with any selling—is that people are buying benefits and the way those benefits will change their life. Selling on QVC is about creating a credible lifestyle story that people will identify with and buy into.

It's probably better to start small with QVC. You'll learn and pick up tips along the way, allowing you to build up your business with them as you go. If you're a small- or medium-sized business, a few big hits on QVC can have a phenomenal impact on your profits.

To achieve this goal, you should know your product inside out, and then use your best direct-marketing tactics to create short, benefit-driven sales messages around it. Remember that you can link your product's features (what it has or does) to its benefits (what your customer gets by or from using it) with the phrase "which means that." Example: "This umbrella is made of rip-stop, waterproof nylon, *which means that* it's light and easy to carry around, it will keep you dry, and because of the rip-stop nylon, it won't get damaged even if it's blowing up a storm!"

If you're going to be appearing on QVC live, you'll definitely want to *watch* it a few times—to understand more about the channel, how products are offered, and to scope out your competition. Notice that there is always a multitude of call-in questions from prospective buyers. So be ready to answer any and all questions about your product. One way to do this: Spend a day—or two or three—answering product questions at the customer support hotline in your company.

> **HOME SHOPPING CHANNEL SUCCESS** (*Continued*)
>
> When you're on the QVC program, be sure you always answer questions in a succinct and focused (yet friendly) way . . . always draw the question back to a main benefit of your product . . . and always close your answers on a positive note.
>
> Even if you won't be appearing on QVC live, this is an excellent exercise that will help you further your marketing efforts. So take some time to run through the process.

PRINCIPLES OF EFFECTIVE TELEVISION ADVERTISING

The principles that apply to television are fundamentally the same as those that apply to other media. Good television commercials should be . . .

- **Arresting:** If you don't catch your viewers' attention, there's no way you can sell them anything.
- **Direct:** The purpose is to sell your product. To do that effectively, you must show the product, promote its benefits, and provide a good reason to buy it.
- **Benefit oriented:** Mention the features of the product when needed. Always stress the benefits, especially the USP.
- **Consistent:** The quality of the commercial's production should reflect the quality of the product itself.
- **Compelling throughout:** Grabbing attention in the beginning is crucial. Letting that interest flag later on is unforgivable.
- **Intentional:** Ultimately, the commercial must sell something. Be sure a purchase is at least implied.

To ensure you get the biggest bang for your buck, make sure you can answer "yes" to these three vital questions about your product from Entrepreneur.com:

The 1, 2, 3, Formula
1. Can its benefits be demonstrated? Without demonstration, you can't use TV effectively to make a sale. Think about

the kinds of products you see in direct-response spots, such as a hair-braiding tool, a children's paint kit, or a "revolutionary" car finish. They lend themselves to effective visual presentation.

2. **Does it have mass appeal?** When you select your target audience, there should be a high probability that the majority of those people can use your product. Whether you're buying time on cable systems or individual stations, you can save money by purchasing "broad rotators," which means your spots may run anytime during the entire day, and not only within specific, higher-rated shows.

3. **Is it unique or novel?** It's best if your product is novel enough that there's little competition for it on the retail level. In fact, once a product is widely available in retail stores, direct-response TV spots stop working.[6]

What Works

For successful direct-response TV spots, follow these important guidelines, also from Entrepreneur.com:

- **Create 60-second spots for direct sales.** While 30-second spots are the norm for most TV advertising, their primary function is lead generation. If that is what your advertising model calls for, use 30-second spots. But if you want to sell directly to viewers, then favor 60-second spots in your testing.

- **A visible call to action.** Experts say you should have your toll-free number, and possibly your Web address, onscreen for at least 40 seconds. Some advertisers display this information throughout their spots.

- **Test the magic number: $19.95.** According to several TV advertising gurus, $19.95 is the most successful price point for direct-response TV ads. But our experience has shown us that all sorts of offers (prices, terms, guarantees, etc.) can work on TV. Start with $19.95 and test "away from" that number until you find the offer that works best for your product. For expensive products, you should definitely test long-form ads. (The 30-minute infomercial is the standard.)[7]

HOME SHOPPING SUCCESS

Robert Cox is an entrepreneur and business consultant. Years ago, he was a founding partner of the Home Shopping Channel (today known as the Home Shopping Network, or HSN).

As an early practitioner, HSN had a big hand in setting many of the standard practices used by direct TV marketers around the world. But what many people don't realize is that those principles of "home shopping success," according to Cox, were put into place before the network ever went on the air.

"We knew what others didn't," says Cox. "We had it right from the beginning, and we never changed it."

First, the target market was similar to, if not the same as, people who buy from print catalogs. As Cox points out, catalog buyers tend to be people with disposable income, but without the time or ability to go to the mall to browse for items they need. Working mothers, the elderly, and those who have medical issues that prevent them from walking long distances make up most of this market.

To tap into this demographic, HSN focused on appealing to them with everything it did on air *and* off. The following is a list of what Cox considers the key elements of HSN's direct-TV success:

- Hosts were cute and friendly, but not sexy. Spouses should be comfortable watching the shows together.
- Viewers were always shown that there was a limited amount of the product. This creates a sense of urgency.
- There was no regular programming for certain specific products. Customers were never told ahead of time what would be on sale when. "You want people to think they'll miss something if they don't tune in," explains Cox.
- Both the retail price and the wholesale price were always listed. You want your customers to know how much they're saving by buying from you.
- Phone-in testimonials from happy customers were interspersed throughout the shows.

(continues)

HOME SHOPPING SUCCESS *(Continued)*

- Celebrity endorsements can boost a product's sales tremendously, especially if the celebrity had a hand in creating the product.
- "Scientific" evidence was presented whenever possible. So if it's appropriate for your product, be sure to include the results of studies that show your product does what you say it does. Of course, those results must be believable and should be from an unbiased third party.
- A 100 percent money-back guarantee. People have to know when ordering a product from TV that they can send it back if they are not satisfied.

Direct-TV marketing can be a powerful way to reach customers. The visual aspect, as well as those elements listed above, all play a part.

"What the eye sees, the heart desires," says Cox.

MAKING A GREAT COMMERCIAL

Experts say that viewers pay attention to TV marketing in the following order: graphics, headlines, bullets, and text. The headline must be the strong opening to a simple and clear message that stresses benefits. This all has to be done visually. Show rather than tell—and don't forget that call to action. Television has made the phrase "Call today!" a popular call to action in all advertising.

Remember, a TV commercial has only a few seconds to grab a viewer's attention. Wise advertisers do that with interesting headlines and marketing messages, supporting those messages with graphics and visuals.

That may sound simple. But the logistics of direct-response TV advertising are somewhat complicated. Lots of issues need to be handled by lots of different people. Some examples are:

- **Concept development**—The style and format of the commercial.
- **Marketing plans**—The goals you have for the ad (the number of sales) and how it fits into your overall multi-channel campaign.

- **Creative**—The scripts and marketing messages of your ad. These should be written by experienced direct-response copywriters, preferably with experience in writing for TV.
- **Production**—The actual creation of the ad in the studio with cameras, lights, microphones, sets, and so on. This includes post-production work (graphics and editing).
- **Media buying**—Buying airtime on TV stations. You should do your due diligence to find out which stations and times work best for your product. Of course, you have to balance that with what you can afford.
- **Tape duplication**—Once the creative is shot, you will need to send a copy (either on videotape or DVD) to every station that is going to air the ad.
- **Telemarketing and fulfillment management**—Most direct-response TV features an 800 number for customers to call. This usually means hiring a professional telemarketing company (see Chapter 11). You may also need to contact a fulfillment house to fill your orders.

When beginning, it's a good idea to hire competent service companies to do the production and placement, as well as other technical tasks you aren't already doing yourself. For instance, if you haven't incorporated telemarketing into your marketing mix, the details involved in setting up your own toll-free number may be enough to convince you to stay away from the rest of the process.

Whether calls are going to be handled in-house or by a telemarketing company, scripts must be developed to maximize sales and leads—and scripts that aren't working will need to be rewritten. If you're using a service, the operators will need to be trained so that when they answer your toll-free phone number, they're educated about you and your product. Plus, you want to be sure they understand your initial offer and your upsell offer.

Throughout your campaign, incoming calls have to be monitored to be sure they're being handled professionally. Also, call volume must be tracked during each telecast to ensure that there are enough operators to handle the load. And that's just one part of running a direct-response TV ad.

You'll also need to purchase airtime on a market-to-market, station-to-station basis—a continual process of bookings, cancellations, changes, and renegotiations. In the best-performing venues, the demand generally exceeds the amount of time available, so it's best to have a placement company working for you that has developed solid relationships with station contacts.

DIRECT TV AND YOU

TV may be the perfect venue for selling kitchen gadgets, other time- and effort-saving devices, wealth-building programs, motivational programs, and real estate programs. It's also great for exercise machines and DVDs, as well as offbeat recreational products. These are all examples of what probably comes to mind when you think of TV-based direct marketing. But you can potentially sell any product this way.

TV marketing is visual—you can see the product in action. And this means that the desire to buy is instantly strong in your prospect. The ease of ordering (all you have to do is pick up the phone), as well as a money-back guarantee, further breaks down the prospect's resistance.

We urge you to check out direct-response TV marketing for your business. If you take the time to understand how it works, it can be a vital component of your multi-channel campaign. Indeed, it has the potential to bring in more money to your business than any other channel.

CHAPTER TEN

DIRECT-RESPONSE RADIO

Music, News, Sports, and Talk = Money

After dropping out of Southeast Missouri State University in the early 1970s, one young man spent the next 15 years bouncing from job to job.

A second young man, a scraggly teenager from a rough blue-collar town in Long Island, managed to graduate college, but also spent much of the 1970s and 1980s bouncing from job to job.

Both men eventually made names for themselves and took high-profile positions in New York City.

The first man now has an audience of nearly 20 million people a week, and, in 2001, signed a contract with an annual salary of $31.25 million. His name is Rush Limbaugh.

The second man received a $500 *million* budget for his services for five years in 2004. His name is Howard Stern.

How did these two men build their incredible fortunes? *Radio.*

Radio is broadcast 24 hours a day, 365 days a year, around the world. Music, news, sports, talk shows... it's all there on the dial. And each and every one of these radio broadcasts offers you the chance to reach more potential customers.

Despite advances in technology, radio is still one of the most powerful and widespread communication and advertising mediums. In 2005, nearly 94 percent of people still listened to a radio at least once a week.[1] Plus, radio can reach potential customers in places where you may not otherwise be able to contact them. People listen to their favorite stations, music genres, and on-air talent in their cars, in their homes, in their offices, while waiting at the mechanic's shop, or waiting for the dentist. Radio is constantly with you, wherever you go. And that gives you more chances to put your message in front of millions.

Radio advertising was one of the earliest forms of mass media advertising. And it remains a popular option. However, the industry isn't exactly growing by leaps and bounds. According to the Radio Advertising Bureau, total radio industry revenue was $21.3 billion for 2007, a continuation of a relatively flat trend for the past several years. That figure includes $1.6 billion in revenue from off-air ads, such as ads on radio-station web sites, a move made to address flagging on-air advertising.[2]

Television, the Internet and, more recently, subscription-based satellite radio have been slowly eroding radio's audience—and advertisers—over the years. And the effect on the industry has been tough. But radio is still an effective way to spend your advertising dollar.

RADIO ADVERTISING EXPLODES

By 1928 advertisers were spending $10 million or more a year on radio ads.[3] Ads at that time were much the same as many you hear today: loud and repetitious. What separates radio ads from print ads is that they are spoken presentations. Therefore, actors and actresses can effectively insert emotion and drama into the pitches.

The 1929 stock market crash affected the entire economy. Advertising in all channels fell from a peak of $3.5 billion in 1929 to a little over $1 billion in 1933.[4] Radio was hit hard. But it came roaring back, eventually becoming the number-one advertising channel in the world.

That is not the case today. In 2007, for the first time, online advertising dollars surpassed radio advertising. And, according to a report by eMarketer, Inc., online advertising dollars will be double that of radio advertising dollars by 2011.[5] Projections of ad spending on the Internet and radio (in billions) are listed in Table 10.1.

TABLE 10.1 Spending on the Internet and Radio (in billions)

Year	Internet Advertising Dollars	Radio Advertising Dollars
2006 (actual)	$16.9	$20.1
2007 (actual)	$21.7	$20.4
2008 (projection)	$28.2	$21
2009 (projection)	$34	$21.5
2010 (projection)	$39	$22.1
2011 (projection)	$44	$22.6

Source: Webmetro.com

A LITTLE RADIO HISTORY

Who "invented" radio is a matter of some dispute. Many people were working on it at the same time, and subsequently claimed to be "the inventor of radio." But it is generally accepted that, in 1895, Guglielmo Marconi was the first to successfully demonstrate "wireless telegraphy," which is what they called radio at the time.

As the pioneers of radio worked to improve the technology, their efforts were somewhat divided. Some worked on setting up stations that reached many listeners at the same time. This was known as "broadcasting." Concurrently, their counterparts were developing and perfecting transmitters for communication between one sender and one receiver: ship to ship, ship to shore, or between military outposts, for example. This was known as "narrowcasting."

Because this is a book on advertising, we will focus on broadcasting.

By the 1920s, commercial radio stations, licensed by the government, had sprouted up all over the United States and the rest of the world. These stations had regular schedules. They broadcast speeches, news, readings from popular books, radio plays, music, and more. In fact, the format was very similar to what we have today.

The early radio stations struggled to find a way to pay for their equipment, performers, and other costs associated with their operations. Some station owners subsidized the cost, viewing broadcasts as great promotions for their other businesses. Some pushed for a subscription-based model, in which listeners paid to listen. Eventually, despite some government pressure to severely restrict radio ads, the advertising model won out because it was the most practical.

So does this explosion of Internet advertising mean you should not spend your time, company resources, and money on radio advertising? Absolutely not! Radio advertising is still an effective way to attract customers—and dollars—to your business. As such, it should be incorporated into your multi-channel marketing campaign.

But you don't have to take our word for it.

A CASE STUDY IN RADIO INFOMERCIALS

According to entrepreneur Brent Jones of Affinity Lifestyles, radio advertising played a very large role in getting his company off the ground and making it profitable. Although Jones has moved to a different business model in the last year, radio was his main advertising channel for nearly eight years.

Half-hour radio infomercials were his main marketing platform, although he also did significant Internet marketing. Jones had tried 30- and 60-second spots, but he could never make any money with them. That's when he found a winning formula.

Each infomercial was done interview-style, featuring a host asking Jones (and sometimes another expert) questions about the product and its benefits. Four or five testimonials were thrown in during the segment. There were three pitches during the ad, which Jones says was more like a radio program than a standard commercial.

Prior to recording, Jones worked with the interviewer to put together a rough outline of what questions would be asked, when they would cut to testimonials, and when they would pitch the product. However, because they were going for an "impromptu" feel, they made a conscious effort to stay away from sounding too scripted.

The content changed as different products were promoted, of course. But the format—which was pretty successful for Jones—stayed pretty much the same.

"They ran on various stations. During the week is where your standard advertisers buy their hour or half-hour slots, so the weekend would be free for us. Eighty-five to 90 percent of our radio programs ran on the weekend," says Jones. "We'd run all across the U.S., just finding the best deals we could get for the weekend slots."

Interested listeners were directed to an 800 number or a web site, to buy the featured products. The calls went to a telemarketing company hired by Jones. The sales were sent to Jones' office on Monday for fulfillment, and orders were sent out soon after.

Like all direct marketers, Jones constantly monitored the ROI from his infomercials. He says he broke even if there was $1.50 in sales per $1 spent on the ads. This covered production costs, media buys, telemarketing costs, and returns. Anything above breakeven was profit, of course.

Getting above breakeven was a constant challenge. Sometimes Jones could negotiate with the radio stations for free ad time to make up for a poorly performing ad. But he relied heavily on testing to improve his ROI. He'd try multiple ads, multiple tests—and when he found a combination that yielded a good rate of return, he'd run with it.

Constant vigilance was necessary, however. A well-performing ad could run out of steam at any time. "It might work for three months and then just die off. You've got to change it, tweak it," explains Jones. "That's one of the things with radio—it's so fickle. You could be doing well, then all of a sudden it just drops off. Then it takes a little while to find something else that works."

But all these problems are just part of the game. Jones found great success on the radio; for many years, it was his main marketing channel because it was the right one to reach his customers.

DON'T GET CAUGHT UP IN THE UNKNOWN

Like Brent Jones, many companies have used radio ads to transform their businesses. Unfortunately, too many entrepreneurs and marketing professionals don't try it because they think it is beyond their reach. Or they try it once . . . and if it doesn't produce the expected results that first time, they give up on the entire channel.

That's too bad. Radio advertising can be a great marketing tool. It is especially useful in helping entrepreneurs reach specific demographic segments of the general population.

The cost of advertising on the radio varies, depending on the region, the reach and popularity of the radio station (its market share), the time of day, the length of the ad, how many times a day the ad is run, and other factors. But remember that cost isn't everything. Like every other marketing channel we've discussed in this book, what matters most is return on investment—your ROI.

Therefore, you have to do your research and keep track of all the testing you do with radio advertising. Only then will you know if it is a cost-effective way to bring in customers. You also need to determine how radio fits in with your product and the other marketing channels you are using.

But before you do anything, review the checklist below to make sure you get the most out of your radio campaigns and give yourself the greatest chance of success.

Step 1. Determine Your Target Market: Figure out exactly who buys your product. What are your customers' interests and spending habits? What do they like about your product? Through which marketing channels can you reach them? This is a no-brainer, but many companies forget this step.

Step 2. Ask Your Fellow Businesspeople about Their Experiences: If you are thinking about getting involved in radio advertising, talk to some of your friends in the business about the experiences they've had. Seek out their advice. Learn from their mistakes. Build on their successes.

Step 3. Hire a Pro: If you aren't experienced in radio advertising, hire a consultant (or consultants) to walk you through the process of creating and producing an ad that will resonate with your customers. Consultants will help you write scripts, record in a professional setting, choose a proper format, and so on. Besides being money down the drain, a badly produced ad could do a lot of harm to your company image.

Step 4. The Voice of Your Product: Many times, a business owner or entrepreneur will lend their own talent and voice to their radio commercials. If the thought of being in an ad alarms you, don't worry. Just hire someone. Voice talent is easy to find. Your consultant or the radio station will be able to help you.

Step 5. Get Bids from Different Radio Stations: Once you've created an ad, don't just run it on the first radio station that pops into your head. Check out all the stations that serve your target market. Let them know you are interested in buying air-time—and then make them work to get your business. Ask for proof of their effectiveness in reaching your potential customers, a recommendation for how often your ad should run (this varies depending on your demographic), and proposed costs. All this information should help you make an informed decision.

Step 6. Check Out Sponsorships: Consider sponsoring news reports or the weather—perhaps with a short intro like this: "This Storm Tracker report brought to you by [Your Company]," followed by a quick mention of your web site or 800 number.

Step 7. Remnant Space—a Low-Cost Opportunity: Remnant space is air-time that hasn't yet been sold to advertisers. The closer they get to the air date without advertising, the more nervous radio stations get that they won't make *any* money on that time. So they start offering discounts—as high as 75 percent—to advertisers willing to step in. That's your chance to save a lot of money.

RADIO CHANGED THE WORLD

It may be hard for today's "electronic generation"—accustomed to big-screen TVs, VHS/DVD players, computers, cell phones, MP3 music players, PDAs, digital cameras, camcorders, and the like—to imagine it, but when radio was introduced to the world, it had as profound an impact as the Internet did in the 1990s.

Communication changed. The relationships between countries and cultures changed. People and places were linked. The spread of information was not limited by the speed of a boat or train. News traveled at the speed of sound. Physical barriers and large distances no longer posed an obstacle.

And don't forget, many places in the world still don't have regular access to the Internet or even television. But radio is a constant presence, even in remote areas. For many people, it is their lifeline to the world and, thus, radio advertisers have a captive audience.

That's why, even today, radio is a vital part of many companies' multi-channel marketing approach, as viable as any other format or channel. With radio, you will reach those customers who may never turn on a computer and who don't read newspapers or magazines. That said, radio is not appropriate for every business, just as e-mail marketing or direct mail might not work for everyone.

But that's the beauty of multi-channel marketing. You do your research and testing . . . find the mix of advertising formats that works for you . . . and go with it!

CHAPTER ELEVEN

TELEMARKETING

Inbound, Outbound, Money-Bound

When most people think of telemarketing, they think of regional bucket shops full of middle-aged men soliciting police-fund contributions or first-year stockbrokers pumping high-risk investments.

In fact, telemarketing is a diversified business ranging from nonprofit companies promoting political or environmental causes to Fortune 500 companies selling high-priced business products to qualified customers all over the world.

Cold-calling prospects using trade journals or telephone books is the most troublesome, and least interesting, part of this business. In this chapter, we will focus on a more respectable and more profitable form of telemarketing: establishing quality relationships with your best customers by providing, via the telephone, additional services and benefits that they may be very interested in buying.

HOW WE'VE USED TELEMARKETING

Our own experiences with telemarketing date back to the mid-1980s. We'd had success (as we will explain in Chapter 13) in selling $500 and even $1,000 conferences to our customers via direct mail. But then we came up with the outrageous idea of selling a much more expensive conference—a very specialized asset-protection seminar—that was going to be priced at $25,000 per attendee.

We knew that most of our customers couldn't use or afford such a high-priced seminar. But we believed that a very small percentage of them—customers with a net worth in the millions of dollars—would consider the price a bargain...if we could deliver a good product.

We put together some of the world's top experts and selected a world-class venue. Then we loaded the offer with all sorts of extra benefits, which had a combined value that exceeded the high price we were asking.

Confident that we had a worthy product to sell, we set about devising a marketing strategy. We began by talking about our plans in our newsletters, explaining to all our customers exactly what we were offering, and making it feel like, because of the high price, the seminar was meant only for a select few.

We invited customers to let us know, via e-mail, if they could benefit from the seminar. We told them that, if they were interested, they should give us their phone numbers so that we could call them and find out if they were qualified.

We hired a small group of experienced telemarketers and explained that the first call was to be a real qualifying call. We didn't want customers who couldn't benefit from it showing up at the seminar, even if they had the money to spend and wanted to attend.

By doing that, we established a positive rapport with the people who had shown an interest in the seminar—and left them wondering if they would indeed qualify for acceptance.

Then, after reviewing the responses, we created a callback list and instructed the telemarketers to call the people on the list and "soft sell" them on the seminar. They were to explain that it was limited to 30 attendees (a necessary limitation because of the intensity of the attention they would be getting), and end the call by getting nothing more than a "Yes, I would be interested" answer.

When the next follow-up phone call was made, the telemarketer already had several significant advantages: He knew the customer would benefit from the seminar, could afford the seminar, and was genuinely interested in going. It was relatively easy at that point to close the sale. The seminar sold out in less than four weeks.

This experience taught us a bit about the art and science of telemarketing. What was even more important was that it taught us how powerful this channel of selling can be—if it is done intelligently and appropriately to a list of prospects who have been qualified in some important way.

Since then, we have incorporated telemarketing as a back-end channel in most of our businesses with good results.

TELEMARKETING FOR BACK-END SALES

Agora, Inc., for example, uses a dedicated telemarketing group to capture sales that would otherwise be lost. In the past, when a customer's credit card company declined an order online, they just let that customer go. But now the customer's contact information—including telephone number and a list of other products they have bought—is sent to a special sales team.

Every morning, this sales team gets a list of the customers whose card had been declined the day before. The average is about 50 to 60 per day. All the products involved are priced above $199, with many—especially trading advisory services—running to $2,000 or more.

Sales reps call each customer, talk to them about their credit card problem, and try to figure out what happened. Fixing the problem is the primary goal, but upselling (offering an additional similar product) is also part of the call.

So why is a card declined? Sometimes, it's simply because of a mistyped expiration date. Or because the credit card company puts a hold on large purchases. (In that case, the customer just needs to call the credit card company to authorize the transaction.) And if the customer is paying with a debit card, they might have a $400 to $500 per day limit on purchases. (In that case, the rep will arrange to distribute the payment over a couple of days.)

Whatever the solution, the sales reps "fix" the problem about 70 to 75 percent of the time, resulting in thousands of dollars of potentially lost revenue being captured. Even if it turns out that there was no problem—if, for example, the customer cancelled payment because of buyer's remorse—they aren't let off that easy. They are offered the chance to buy other products. Every call is an opportunity for a sale.

ONE OF THE SIMPLEST FORMS OF MARKETING

One of the great advantages of telemarketing—and one of the reasons we recommend it to the businesses we work with—is that it is a very simple form of marketing. It doesn't involve complicated mailing programs, Internet applications, or financial tracking systems. It is also relatively simple from a creative standpoint.

What you need to run a good telemarketing operation is a good list of names to call, a good reason to call them, and a simple script that presents the product well and makes a compelling offer. Most telemarketing scripts can be written by in-house copywriters, which obviates the need for expensive outside talent.

Making a telemarketing script work is a matter of testing various offers and wording until you find the most effective combination—and then, rolling out with it as long as the list stays responsive.

As with other channels of marketing, there are some fundamental principles that apply to telemarketing. Because telemarketing is a relatively simple affair, these principles are fairly few and easy to understand.

- The list is king. The most important element of success in telemarketing is the strength of the list of phone numbers you are calling. The best lists are in-house lists of repeat buyers—customers who have demonstrated their responsiveness by buying multiple products from you in the past. The next best names are usually buyers who have bought only once but have bought expensive products. The third tier is the rest of your customers. Expired customers come next. And then qualified prospects—direct-response buyers who have bought other, similar products either by phone or by direct mail or e-mail.
- Telemarketing to existing customers (i.e., back-end telemarketing) is usually the best way to initiate a telemarketing campaign. When you are calling people who already know you and are familiar with your products, you have good reason to expect that they will take your call and listen to your pitch, even if they aren't accustomed to buying over the phone.
- When conducting back-end telemarketing, it is usually a good idea to contact your customers beforehand—preferably by

Internet communication (because it is practically free)—and let them know that you intend to call them to give them some good news. Such "alerts" should make it very clear that these calls will be beneficial to them and risk-free. They should indicate that the call itself is a form of customer service—in this case, alerting them to some new benefit or advantage that other people won't hear about until much later, if at all.

- It's very important to establish trust in the first minute of the telemarketing call. That is best done by documenting the relationship—letting the customer know that they are not getting a cold call from a salesperson, but rather a service call from someone they do know or should know.

- Follow this by asking some questions about the customer's satisfaction and/or knowledge of prior service. This is a good way to reduce any buyer resistance and establish a rapport that will be critical to the sales pitch itself.

- Urgency is a key component of successful telemarketing promotions. The customer needs to know why he is being called rather than contacted in some other way. An urgent update or opportunity, one that is time-dated and important, is a common and effective way to do that.

- Not all products can be sold effectively on the telephone. They must provide benefits that are easy to explain quickly, before the prospect runs out of patience.

- The offer—what the customer is being sold, the price, the premiums, the reason for urgency, and the guarantee—are all critical elements of the sales pitch. Getting this right is usually a matter of intuition and experimentation. Write the best script you can and then modify it over time. Much in the way that a good comic develops a killer comedy routine, the astute telemarketing professional can take a good script and make it great simply by paying attention to where in the script the customer's attention lags, and revising it until there are no weaknesses.

The most important element of creating a successful telemarketing operation is integrity: creating an irresistible offer that is irresistible because it is really, truly good. Businesses that operate with the customer's well-being in mind will have the greatest and most lasting success with telemarketing. If you commit to developing a program with integrity as your paramount interest, you will have no problem adding this very lucrative and customer-friendly channel of marketing to your business.

THE TOP 10 TELEMARKETING MISTAKES, MISHAPS, AND BLUNDERS

In order to maintain your integrity, secure your credibility, and use telemarketing effectively, let's take a look at the top 10 mistakes many marketers make:

1. **Not figuring out what you want telemarketing to do for your company before you get started:** Telemarketing is a great form of direct marketing. That's why we dedicated an entire chapter of this book to this channel. It has a track record of success, and it can be easily coordinated with other marketing channels. As a result, many companies rush in and set up a telemarketing effort without first figuring out what they want to get out of it. But just as you would with direct mail or direct e-mail campaigns, you have to figure out your required ROI, and what sales numbers you need to reach that ROI. You need this information before you start testing telemarketing as an element of your multi-channel approach.

2. **Not realizing the potential of telemarketing:** Telemarketing is not only about cold-calling a customer, trying to make a sale and saying "Have a good day" if the prospect says they are not interested. Telemarketing can be a great way to harvest a tremendous amount of information. Every call is an opportunity to ask potential customers which marketing channels they prefer to be contacted through, or perhaps to get their e-mail or home address. All this is useful for future contacts. You can also gather demographic data.

3. **Choosing the cheapest telemarketing company you can find:** Yes, you want to keep costs down. After all, every expenditure comes off your bottom line. But you don't want to be cheap when it comes to your telemarketing services provider. A cheap rate will probably mean cheap service.

4. **Never letting your reps go off script:** With good training, your telemarketing workers should be able to respond to questions from

**THE TOP 10 TELEMARKETING MISTAKES,
MISHAPS, AND BLUNDERS** (*Continued*)

customers without reading directly off a script. Over time, they will develop their own approach. If it works (you will know if it works because you will be constantly monitoring your telemarketing team), let them run with it. Yes, the script is important and should be followed, but a cold reading can turn a customer off.

5. **Picking a telemarketing vendor simply because they are close by:** Your telemarketing company doesn't have to be in your town or state to do a good job for you. As long as they know your product and are trained correctly, they can be almost anywhere.

6. **Not making an in-person visit before choosing your provider:** A telemarketing company can look great on paper, and they can promise you the world. But, as with all aspects of business, due diligence is key before hiring anybody. So before you sign with any company, get to know them better by visiting their offices. Check out their staff. Listen in on some of their calls. Figure out if their employees are full-time professionals or just temps zoning-out between calls.

7. **Not providing your telemarketing team with the proper information and materials:** From the first day they start working for you, your telemarketing team should know as much as possible about your company, your products, and how you want your telemarketing campaign to work. We're talking specifics here.

8. **Violating (on purpose or by accident) do-not-call laws:** It is illegal to call someone on the do-not-call list. Your company can be fined thousands of dollars, depending on the state, if you call someone on that list. It sounds simple, but make it crystal clear to your telemarketing team that this is a no-no. Make sure they have the right processes in place to ensure that it doesn't happen.

9. **Not keeping up with quality control:** We've mentioned that before you ever start your telemarketing campaign, you must set goals for the campaign, as well as a best-practices model to follow. But you can't simply set all this up and leave it at that. To maintain quality,

(continues)

> **THE TOP 10 TELEMARKETING MISTAKES,**
> **MISHAPS, AND BLUNDERS** (*Continued*)
>
> you have to constantly monitor your telemarketing efforts. Are sales being made? Are leads being recorded and acted on correctly? Also, there is always room for improvement. Your telemarketers should always strive to do better: more leads, more sales, more happy (and paying) customers.
>
> 10. **Ignoring the back end:** It's tempting to look at a telemarketing program, see great front-end sales and lead-generation results, and think that everything is going great. But what about refunds? What about customers who don't convert? You have to look deeper at the numbers to see the actual results of your telemarketing.

INBOUND, OUTBOUND, AND MONEY-BOUND

Telemarketing is split into outbound, where your marketers call consumers, and inbound, where prospects call your company to buy products, ask questions about their purchases, or seek more information. You can choose to do one or the other, or a mix of both. It really depends on your company and your products. If you are not planning to keep your telemarketing operation in-house, then you have to outsource. Whether you will go the outbound or inbound route is a question that you have to answer before you start researching companies to hire. You must also decide if your telemarketing efforts will include:

- Front-end or back-end selling
- Cold calling
- Lead generation
- Surveys
- Order confirmation (contacting customers who purchased through other marketing channels)

You should also figure out how much preparation you can do on your own. Can you write the scripts? Do you have your policies and procedures sorted out?

And before you hire anybody, you have to determine how many customers you intend to reach with your telemarketing effort, and how you will measure the success of your campaign.

If all of this sounds daunting, remember this: Your telemarketing campaign, even if it is being "managed" by an outside company, should fit in with your company's mission and goals. If you stay within the bounds of what your company is all about, you'll be fine.

FIRST CONTACT WITH TELEMARKETING SERVICE PROVIDERS

Yes, you can check Google or industry publications for a list of telemarketing companies. But we recommend that you also ask your friends in business who they are using and what they've heard about certain companies. From those sources, you'll have an initial list.

Each company on that list should be reputable and experienced in telemarketing, of course, but they should also be experienced in working with companies in your industry. Then get on the phone with each one. Tell them what you need, and ask what they charge and what services they can provide to meet your requirements. This first call is a great time to get a feel for the company and the people who work there. You want to make sure they know that, as your telemarketing provider, they will be a major connection between you and your customers. You have to be able to trust them not to jeopardize that relationship.

Obviously, you won't know everything there is to know about a company from one phone call. But this first contact should allow you to cut companies you suspect won't work out from your list. You should have about three to four "possibles" at this point. Ask each for a written proposal and quote.

AN IN-DEPTH LOOK AT WHAT THEY CAN DO ... AND HOW MUCH IT WILL COST

Price should not be the only reason you choose one company over another, but it is important. You, of course, need to look at the services they provide and whether they meet your needs. You also need to know how they report the results of a campaign. Can they give you data that fits into your company's systems? And don't be afraid to ask for references from past and current clients.

Different companies will charge you in different ways. Most will charge an initial cost for set up and then by the hour for regular telemarketing work for which they were contracted. But you will find that some companies ask for a lower hourly rate in exchange for commission. In some cases, that kind of arrangement can boost sales and productivity.

Arrange an On-Site Meeting

Before you make a final decision, you absolutely must visit the potential telemarketing company. You do this to make sure everything is above board. Are the representatives professional and able to do the job? Are the managers good leaders? Are employees at all levels hardworking and committed to making your company's telemarketing campaign a success?

When MaryEllen worked at PBS's WNET/Channel 13 in the mid-1980s, she was in charge of setting up fundraising telemarketing campaigns. Those campaigns brought in millions of dollars and were responsible for the continued existence of the station.

WNET was located in New York City and was the largest PBS affiliate in the nation, but she did not take the chance of assuming that the telemarketing company was familiar enough with the organization's goals and objectives. Even though the company had been taking calls for them for eight years, she always made sure they knew the ins and outs of the whole campaign so they could better serve callers.

She flew to Salt Lake City each year to meet every single person who would be working on her two-week fundraising campaign. And there were often hundreds of them.

She brought videotapes (this was before DVDs) of what the studio in New York looked like. The tapes included the company spokespeople, the marketing people, and the president of the station explaining what the reps' hard work meant to the station, and how they were a huge part of the company.

She held daily contests for the reps, offering whoever got the highest dollar amount in pledges a prize of $50. At the end of the two-week campaign, a grand prize was awarded, and the winner received an all-expenses-paid weekend in New York City for two, which included staying at a fine hotel and dining at the best restaurants.

By taking the time to truly get to know the reps, MaryEllen not only engaged them, but was able to create a fun yet competitive environment, where each rep strived to be the best.

The Number-One Rule When Dealing with an Outside Company

Once you have hired your telemarketing provider, the real work begins. Both companies must collaborate to set up the campaign. Your marketing manager should be very hands-on at this stage, making sure that your company's vision is carried through in all aspects of the campaign. They have the technical knowledge, but your company is the boss. They work for you, so they should be willing to make changes based on your input and concerns.

But it's also important to make them feel that they are a part of your team, not hired help. Let them know that you are there not to find fault with them, but rather to help them serve your customers better.

Listen in on calls during the first few days of the campaign, so that any problems can be addressed quickly.

You will be constantly monitoring your telemarketing campaign throughout its life.

IS TELEMARKETING RIGHT FOR YOU?

As we said at the beginning of this chapter, telemarketing is a very simple form of marketing. It's easy to set up—and before you know it, you can be raking in sales. But it doesn't work for every company and every product out there. So just because it is easy doesn't mean you should do it. You have to do your research. Talk to your marketing people. Ask other companies in your industry if it works for them. Read trade publications to learn about the latest trends and news.

Then closely examine whether telemarketing will be an effective component of your multi-channel mix. Will your target market respond to offers over the phone? Can your telemarketing campaign work in conjunction with other channels? For instance, earlier in this chapter, we told you about a telemarketing campaign at Agora that is used to capture customers who unsuccessfully tried to order products online. In that case, telemarketing has been providing an extra push to bring in many customers who otherwise would have been lost.

It can do the same for your company.

CHAPTER TWELVE

JOINT VENTURES

Only Streets Should Be One-Way

In Chapter 1, we talked about how Agora, Inc. skyrocketed its growth by combining direct marketing on the Internet with multi-channel marketing. That happened in the late 1990's. But it wasn't the first time Agora dabbled in multi-channel marketing. Way back in the early 1980s, when the company was just starting out, it achieved fast growth by combining direct-mail advertising with joint-venture (JV) marketing.

From about 1980 to 1995, for example, Agora grew its investment newsletter business from $1 million to $60 million, primarily through joint-venture marketing deals. The proposition was pretty simple.

Agora was very good at direct-mail marketing, but its employees had very little investment expertise. Rather than attempt to develop financial gurus in-house, Agora went out into the media marketplace and found investment writers who had newsletters with a small number of subscribers.

Agora's proposal to them was as follows: They would form a joint venture, with both sides as 50-percent partners. The partner would continue to own his subscribers and his editorial product, and would continue to have all the fulfillment obligations. The partner would hire Agora to act as his newsletter's marketing agent. Agora would take all the risk with the marketing efforts and keep the revenue stream. The partner would get the new subscribers risk free. In turn, the partner had to ensure that the deal worked for Agora, as well.

For a financial writer with limited marketing resources, it was a no-risk, all-reward proposition—an impossible deal to refuse. For Agora, it was an efficient way to attract first-rate writing talent—some with established reputations and great track records in making stock tips. If Agora's marketing worked, both partners would be very happy. If it failed to work, the joint venture could be dissolved, and both partners would then be free to go back to what they were doing before.

Agora used this joint-venture strategy to develop more than a dozen newsletter franchises during the first 15 years of its existence. In that time, it saw revenues climb from $1 million to more than $60 million. "I don't think we could have grown that much so quickly without these partnerships," Bill Bonner, Agora's founder, said. "They allowed us to market some of the best people in the investment advisory business then, which gave us an advantage our competitors lacked.

"As our company grew, we developed in-house editorial expertise. Most of our writers nowadays are employees or freelancers under contract. So we don't use that kind of joint-venture deal anymore. But we do employ joint-venture agreements on the Internet marketing side—and these are proving very valuable in terms of growth."

In 2001, Katie Yeakle, president of American Writers and Artists Inc., decided she wanted to sell her products in Germany. One option was to set up a branch office in Bonn, and hire a local manager who would then hire translators and find service bureaus to publish AWAI's correspondence courses in that country. The other option was to locate a German publisher who was already marketing to the kind of customers AWAI favored and make a joint-venture deal.

She chose the latter option. AWAI entered a joint venture with Germany's largest direct-response publisher. Because the publisher already had an existing operation, they were able to take on the new project without adding extra personnel or office space. Costs were thus reduced. And profits were increased dramatically, because the publishing company was able to market to its own list of buyers. Perhaps most important, AWAI and its German partner could combine their skills and knowledge to take full advantage of the German market quickly, thus avoiding any concern that another enterprising business would fill the gap.

To make matters simple, the contract established AWAI as owner of its product line, established the publisher as the line's sole marketer in German and Germany, and stipulated a fixed royalty (a percentage of the sales) for AWAI.

Had Yeakle decided to make a go of the German operation herself, AWAI might have made more money, since it would have kept 100 percent of the profits. But it would surely have taken many years and would have had a greater chance of failure. By going with a joint venture, the German business was up and running in less than a year, and was very profitable in less than two years.

PERFECT FOR START-UPS AND SMALL BUSINESSES

Many small-business owners don't like joint ventures. They don't like the idea of splitting revenues. They like selling their own products because they get to keep 100 percent of the revenues.

This sort of thinking simply misses the mark. When a joint venture is executed properly, it doesn't subtract from a business, it adds to it.

Had Agora taken a "no-joint-ventures" attitude, it would have taken decades to create the quality product line that it was able to develop in only a few years.

There are many ways to do joint ventures. But for a growing small business, the most lucrative type of joint venture usually involves at least two of three key elements: a product, a promotion, and a market.

Yanik Silver, an Internet marketing specialist who regularly writes for *Early to Rise*, says that joint ventures have been "very, very good" to him. He suggests that people unfamiliar with JV marketing deals consider all the ways there are of selling products and making money that they aren't already doing:

- Pay-per-click (PPC) advertising
- Direct mail
- Direct e-mail
- Print advertising
- Web site advertising
- Telemarketing
- Search engine optimization (SEO)
- Publicity

It reads like a partial table of contents of this book. No coincidence there! One of the best ways to expand your marketing base is by adding on new marketing channels . . . and one of the fastest and most efficient ways of doing that is to form joint ventures with colleagues and competitors who have expertise that you lack.

Silver talks about one information marketer who entered a joint venture with a telemarketer. He paid the telemarketer a large percentage of the sale for events and other high-end products he was producing. This joint venture brought in millions of dollars in extra revenue, Silver says. And it did so without "the headache of babysitting and training a bunch of telemarketers."

Instead of hiring employees and running a mail shop himself, Silver gets all his direct-mail marketing done on a joint-venture basis. "My partner does all the little things necessary to get a direct-mail piece out," he explains. "He's also a good copywriter, so he writes envelope teasers, lift notes, and so on, too. I pay him based on the results of each mailing. We are both in it together. If I do well, so does he."

One of the key secrets to joint ventures, Silver says, is not to be greedy. "I give all my partners a fair percentage of the sales they help me make. It has to be significant. I want them to be happy."

He also recommends getting the joint venture agreement in writing, "even if you are best friends with your partner. Memories fail, but a simple written agreement (which could be nothing more than an e-mail outlining key points) will clarify any discrepancies or misunderstandings that might crop up in the future."

HOW TO WORK JOINT VENTURES WITH GURUS AND CELEBRITIES

We have had lots of success with joint ventures with celebrities, authors, and business leaders. This kind of arrangement is especially effective nowadays, because most of them have their own Internet lists of thousands or even hundreds of thousands of dedicated fans.

Alex Mandossian, an Internet marketing expert, has made a career out of joint ventures with business celebrities—a technique he recommends to other entrepreneurs whose businesses can benefit from the halo of a superstar.

His first celebrity joint venture was with Jack Canfield, Mandossian explains. Before he even met Canfield, he bought a domain name: AskJackCanfield.com. Then he went to Canfield's estate in Santa Barbara and said, "People want access to you. Let's give it to them for free, via teleseminars." He explained how teleseminars worked (see Chapter 6) and how Canfield would profit from them.

To make the process easier for Canfield, questions were submitted to him beforehand (on the AskJackCanfield.com web site). Then, once a week, Mandossian would pose the questions to him in a live teleseminar.

The seminars provided several benefits for both Canfield and Mandossian. They provided Canfield with ideas for new articles and books. And they provided him with some immediate income as well—because each seminar could be repurposed into products that they could sell.

Here's how it worked . . .

When people submitted a question for Canfield on the web site, they were redirected to an IPP (Intermediary Paid Page) before they could get to the page that had the call-in number for the seminar. On the IPP, Mandossian was pictured pointing to a big, clickable button that said something like, "Look, we have four times as many people who have registered for the call as we can handle. And that is the absolute truth. But if you can't get in, that's okay . . . because you can listen to this call for life for $10."

If they chose not to pay the $10 (to get unlimited access to a downloadable recording of the seminar), they had to click a small button that said, "No thanks." This, Mandossian found, raised his response rate, "because people don't like to say 'No.' So we got lots of people paying $10 for unlimited access because it's easier to say 'Yes' than 'No.'"

In addition to that immediate income, there were downstream revenues. For example, by transcribing and editing the teleseminars, they created a line of little books that they sold. Each was about 50 pages and came with a CD recorded by Canfield. Then they bundled 12 of the books together and sold them as a complete program at a higher price.

Canfield got all of that income, but that was fine with Mandossian, because his goal was not the immediate income, but the development of a relationship with Canfield. After months of working together, Canfield was so comfortable with the relationship that Mandossian had no trouble getting him to agree to a joint venture that would allow him to market his products to Canfield's list.

"You can use a similar, step-by-step strategy to show a celebrity . . . just how valuable you can be," Mandossian states. "Once you've proven you can make him money, you can ask him to market your products to his list. It's likely that his list will be much bigger than yours. That means it has the potential to make you boatloads of clams."

"This is a free-to-fee strategy," Mandossian explains. "It takes guts, because you won't be making money right away . . . but the payoff can be very big. Think of yourself as a stalk of bamboo. When it's first planted, you don't see anything above the ground for three years. After three years, a shoot germinates. Then, from the moment it sees sunlight, it's full-grown in 60 days."

THE PRINCIPLES BEHIND JOINT-VENTURE MARKETING

Joint ventures take advantage of two of the fundamental principles of wealth that Adam Smith talked about in *Wealth of Nations*: division of labor and unrestricted trade. The principle of division of labor is that wealth is produced more efficiently and in greater abundance when working people divvy up the workload according to what sort of work each worker can do best. The theory behind unrestricted trade is that wealth is not limited. Unlike a pie—which must be sliced up and shared—it is an organic thing that will grow naturally if allowed to do so freely.

These principles give rise to the following characteristics of successful joint ventures:

- Good joint ventures are those that pair up businesses with asymmetrical resources and skills.
- The stronger the resources and skills brought to the table, the stronger the potential of the joint venture.
- All other things being equal, joint-venture deals grow more quickly and strongly when there are few restrictions impeding their growth.
- Trust and respect are essential ingredients in good joint-venture relationships.

STRATEGIES FOR SUCCESSFUL JOINT VENTURES

Joint-venture marketing relationships can be extremely valuable. Every ambitious entrepreneur and marketing director should be open to them. Making them work, however, does take time and consume resources. And because you don't have unlimited time and resources, it makes sense to be strategic in selecting your joint-venture partners.

- Look for strong partners—businesses that have significant skills and/or resources that you lack
- Make sure that your contribution to the deal is equal to your partner's. An unbalanced partnership is not good for either party.
- Avoid partners whom you don't trust.
- If possible, limit the scope of the venture in the beginning and extend it as trust increases.
- Make agreements simple, but put them in writing.
- To avoid costly misunderstandings after the venture has begun, identify the value of each partner's contributions at the outset. These should include skills, intellectual resources, marketing resources, capital, and so on.
- In determining the value of those contributions, remember that fairness is not an exact number, but a range. Try to be flexible—and favor partners who demonstrate the same flexibility.
- Establish clear protocols at the beginning for amending or unwinding the relationship if it fails to meet expectations.
- Goodwill is essential for success. Goodwill means that you want your partner to benefit from the relationship as much as you do.

The idea is to develop joint-venture relationships that are easy to maintain, financially profitable, intellectually rewarding, and long-lasting. After a necessary period of negotiation and implementation, you want the relationship to grow well and quickly and painlessly.

If you pick a weak or untrustworthy partner, the joint venture will eventually fail. If your partner sees you as weak or untrustworthy, the venture will also fail.

If, on the other hand, you develop a reputation for being a good, trustworthy partner, good people will come to you and be happy with the terms that you suggest.

We have started and developed businesses that have grown entirely through joint-venture marketing arrangements. For your business, though, joint-venture marketing will probably be simply another channel that can be integrated with what you are already doing.

That being the case, you should establish clear priorities in terms of how much energy and time you will put into each of your joint ventures. As a general rule, you will want to invest more in those relationships that will return more to you. If your business is currently generating $5 million in revenues each year, for example, you might want to create three categories of joint ventures, based on potential additional revenue:

Category A: More than $1 million per year
Category B: Between $250,000 and $1 million
Category C: Between $50,000 and $250,000

In this example, you would be precluding for consideration any joint-venture marketing deals that couldn't bring in at least $50,000 a year, and you'd be giving your greatest personal attention to those that could be worth $1 million or more to you. That's as it should be.

Another recommendation: Make it easy for people to do business with you.

Although you are seeking partnerships that will benefit you, you won't be attracting many joint-venture partners by talking about what you want or need. Like all other business-building activities, creating joint-venture deals is a matter of selling—selling potential partners on the value *they* will get from doing business with you.

To attract the attention of potential partners, we like to do something nice for them, unsolicited and unilaterally. Often, for example, we will recommend one of their products to a portion of our customer base. We make sure they know that we have done them this favor (usually by sending them a copy of the recommendation). But we don't ask for any compensation and we refuse any, if offered.

We *do* pay close attention to the response of our target partners. If they offer to compensate us for our good deed, or reciprocate in some way, this tells us that they are people we want to do business with, people who understand the value of give-and-take. If, however, they come back to us asking only for more free advertising, we know that we don't want to do business with them. In either case, we've learned something very valuable at a very modest cost.

Think about the major players in your marketplace. Consider the strengths and weaknesses of each. Ask yourself how you might benefit from working with them. Make a list of potential partners and develop a strategy to approach them and show them how they could benefit from doing business with you.

Here are some of the questions you should ask yourself when considering joint-venture marketing deals:

- What are my objectives in entering this joint venture?
  - What do I want now?
  - What do I want eventually?
- Do the short- and long-term objectives of this potential partner differ from mine?
- If so, could these differences cause a conflict?
- If so, could that conflict be resolved?
- What specific qualities, skills, and resources is the partner bringing to the table?
- How valuable are these qualities, skills, and resources to me?
- Does the partner attribute roughly the same value to them?
- If not, is there some way we could resolve the difference?
- Are there other ways to get these qualities, skills, and resources?
- If so, what would they cost?
- Which one of us has more power at the outset of the relationship?
- Will that change as the joint venture moves forward?
- If it does change, could that pose a problem?
- Could that problem be serious?
- What can I do to prove my value to your potential partner?
- What do I need to make the deal work?
- How soon can we get started?

Joint ventures may be the best way to stimulate growth when, for whatever reason, you have limited resources and skills that you are willing to devote to a particular channel of marketing. Joint-venture marketing deals should be a part of the thinking of every executive who wants fast, impressive growth.

PRACTICE WHAT YOU PREACH AND OFFER TO TEACH

When we began publishing *Early to Rise* online in 2000, we didn't have a list, we didn't have products, we didn't have large internal resources or a big budget, and we weren't even sure what our target market was.

Now, eight years later, we have figured all of that out . . . and much more.

However, at the time, what we had was valuable, quality editorial content. Who in their right mind wouldn't want that? We researched other web sites and saw what they perceived as good content. We knew what we were offering was better. We had years of experience compiled into an easy-to-read e-letter.

And we knew that we could learn and develop the rest.

So we choose the JV path for four main reasons:

1. **To Find a Like-Minded E-mail List:** Let's go back to Chapter 8, where we talked about "birds of a feather." We knew that a joint venture was the cheapest way to test a list. We did not have to buy ad space on a JV partner's web site or rent their list to do it. We offered the people on their list something of value (content), and that allowed us to grow our own list at the same time.

2. **To Learn about Our Market:** By using joint ventures, we were able to assess what worked and—equally important—what did not work. We looked at the demographics and psychographics of our targeted prospect. We looked at which offers worked, and dissected the promotional copy.

    This allowed us to gain an entirely new perspective on the marketplace without spending hundreds of thousands of dollars in market research.

3. **We Had Limited Internal Resources:** We had built a decent-sized list and were sending out our e-letter several times a week. But we still did not have the resources to develop our own products. So we carefully evaluated our competitor's products to see if any of them would make sense for us. In evaluating those products, we asked ourselves two simple questions . . . the same questions we ask today when approached by a potential partner:

- Is this product good for our customers? This means that the product must keep the promises it makes—that it must fulfill a "want" and solve a problem.

  If you believe a particular product could make you tons of money, yet in your gut you know that it is not a good product, pass on it. Your customers are your lifeline. You have one chance to prove that you are ethical and care about them.

- Is this product good for our organization? This means it must meet a monetary metric. We talked about this earlier—about deciding what a joint venture is worth to you. Let's say two potential partners come to you with very similar offers. You should endorse only one. So if you are sure they have equal quality and they are both good for your customers, you need to see where your bigger payoff lies. You may want to ask yourself questions such as:

  - Who has the bigger list?
  - Who has been in business longer?
  - Who has better promotional copy?

  Ultimately, though, the decision should be based on which product is better for your company. And once the decision is made, it makes sense to agree to a joint venture with that partner.

  That way, you can test your joint-venture partner's product to your customers, using your own sales copy, without incurring any product research and development costs. (Your partner has already taken care of that.) If the product is successful with your list, you can then develop your own version of it. (Don't be afraid to take on the best if you believe you can do it better.)

4. **To Build Long-Term Relationships:** Doing one-shot deals is a waste of time, even if they make you a lot of money. Long-term relationships will yield much more in the end. Make sure your partners share your core values and missions. Ensure that you are giving more than you are getting. This may seem counterintuitive, but if you have 20 40/60 deals instead of 10 50/50 deals, you will be much better off in the long run ... and many of those partners may wind up working exclusively with you.

BEING AN AFFILIATE IS BEING A BUSINESS

One question we often hear is "Are joint ventures and affiliate marketing the same?"

The answer is "No."

We understand how one could confuse the two, because there are many similarities. However, affiliate marketing is simply the promotion of other people's products by a third party (you, the affiliate) in exchange for commission-based compensation.

Most online marketing companies nowadays have an affiliate program. When you sign up for Company XYZ's affiliate program (it's free to sign up), you are able to promote, advertise, and sell their products on your web site. When your web site generates a sale for one of those products, you make a commission.

Signing up is easy. Collecting the commissions is easy. Even building a web site is relatively easy.

Essentially, what you do is start an online business. Creating a web site is your first step. This is reasonably cheap to do. We recommend you use XSitePro software (www.xsitepro.com). You can buy it for about $300.

Once you have a web site and a list of potential customers for the products you'll be selling as an affiliate, you need to promote those products to your list so the people will want to come to your web site to make a purchase.

You can promote to your list through the various online tactics that we have already discussed. But we recommend that you start with a PPC (pay-per-click) affiliate program instead.

The reason you should start with PPC is that it's the easiest way to make money with an affiliate program. With PPC, you will be making profits based on the click-throughs that visitors to your site make to the affiliate company's site. In other words, you'll be able to profit even from site visitors who do not buy anything.

Not only that, but when people find the products and services that they want on your site, you will be building your site's recognition as a valuable resource. And visitors are likely to keep coming back to review what you're offering more closely.

Most PPC affiliate programs can also help you promote your own products, too, by allowing you to spend your click-through commissions on advertising with them instantly—and with no minimum earning requirement. This is an effective way to "exchange" your raw visitors for targeted surfers, those who will have a greater tendency to purchase your products.

PPC programs usually have ready-to-use affiliate tools that can be easily integrated into your web site. The most common tools are search boxes, banners, text links, and some 404-error pages. Most of them can enable you, by using only a few lines of code, to integrate a remotely hosted, cobranded search engine into your web site.

The key benefits? Not only is more money generated, but also some extra money on the side. Plus, you can end up with a lifetime of commissions once you have referred some webmaster friends to that search engine.

Think about it: Where else can you get all these benefits while generating quick income with your web site?

AFFILIATE-MANAGEMENT SOFTWARE

To have a successful business as an affiliate, you need the right software. It can be locally hosted, managed by a third-party affiliate- and commission-tracking network, or run by the software company itself.

Whichever route you choose, the program you end up with should have all of the following functions (recommended by TamingtheBeast.net):

- Affiliate link-generation cookie setting
- Commission calculation
- Banner/text link display
- Affiliate reporting
- Administration reporting
- Multitier calculations
- Payment processing
- Mailing functions
- Antifraud functions

(continues)

AFFILIATE-MANAGEMENT SOFTWARE *(Continued)*

Locally-Hosted Options

When you run your own software, you don't have to worry about paying a provider monthly fees to run it for you. And you can alter the program in-house anytime you want.

Third-Party Affiliate Management

An affiliate- and commission-tracking network will take a lot of the hassle out of your hands—payment processing, fraud protection, and communications with affiliate partners—but you will pay for the convenience. Depending on the network, there can be set-up charges, monthly maintenance fees, and commission fees per transaction with your affiliates.

Remotely Hosted Affiliate Management Software

With remotely hosted software, the company that created it makes it available to businesses, but keeps it on its own servers. They charge for access and usually charge set-up fees, as well. But leasing the software is often cheaper than buying your own.

Source: "Affiliate Management Software," www.tamingthebeast.net/articles3/affiliate-software-services.htm. Accessed April 22, 2008.

JOINT VENTURES AND AFFILIATE MARKETING— MORE SIMILAR THAN DIFFERENT

The reason joint ventures and affiliate marketing are in the same chapter is because the same basic seven principles will determine your success:

1. Build partnerships, not one-shot deals.
2. Don't be greedy; give more than you get.
3. Create win/win situations.
4. Sell products that are good for both partners' customers.
5. Fill a need or solve a problem.
6. Consider your long-term goals.
7. Make your partner lots of money.

CHAPTER THIRTEEN

EVENT MARKETING

Having Fun with Your Customers

In 1984, the Oxford Club was a small investment club with big ambitions. Its founders wanted to one day become the largest private business of its type. They wanted to provide expert advice on international investing from offices around the world. They thought a good way to start the ball rolling would be to sponsor an investment conference offshore. They picked Grand Cayman Island.

They didn't have much money. And they had very little experience with event marketing. Regardless, they booked a dozen expert speakers, booked every room at the Cayman Holiday Inn, and promoted the conference to their members.

The response was good. They filled up half the rooms within a week. Not sure what to do next, they asked some of their speakers—the ones who were newsletter writers and publishers in the investment world—if they would promote the conference to their subscribers. A revenue split was agreed upon, and the writers and publishers sent out their invitations. In another week's time, the conference was overbooked.

"People kept signing up week after week," says Barbara Perriello, current director of Agora Travel and the woman who ran the conference. "The tail on those invitations was so much longer than we expected. Eventually, we had 700 people signed up—about twice the number of hotel rooms that existed on Seven Mile Beach at the time.

We had to run the conference twice, back to back. It was chaotic but very profitable. And we learned so much from it."

Twenty years later, the Oxford Club has achieved its original goals. With more than 70,000 members worldwide and chapters in several countries, it is the largest and most successful club of its kind. The Oxford Club sponsors regional chapter meetings, cruises, and financial seminars, the biggest one being Investment U, held every spring in Florida (www.investmentu.com). They also host World Financial Tours around the globe with Agora Travel (www.agoratravel.com).

"Our seminars make dollars . . . and sense," says Julia Guth, executive director for the Oxford Club and Investment U. "And by sense, I mean they provide countless opportunities for us to deepen the relationship with our most active members.

For example, the seminars and tours:

- Allow Club experts and staff from around the country to meet with each other and their top customers face-to-face and get direct feedback.
- Generate valuable new investment ideas for members, and expert contacts for the editors
- Provide hours and hours of videotaped and audiotaped content that can be used in various ways, both online and in courses . . . or as added value in special reports
- Provide the editors with new insights and observations
- Provide opportunities for customers to give us real, detailed testimonials for our products and services.

"The seminar business is a time-intensive business . . . there are few shortcuts to doing it right," says Guth. "We end every event physically exhausted, but, at the same time, highly re-energized. The goodwill and ideas they generate are so valuable. We get so inspired by all the positive feedback and great suggestions from our customers. We can't wait to get back and go to work on their behalf."

Early to Rise threw its first annual conference in 2004, just four years after the business was launched. That first year, it drew only a few dozen attendees and failed to recoup its marketing costs. But the next year's attendance increased by more than 100, and it has increased by that number every year since.

"We run three very successful large-scale events every year," Charlie Byrne, ETR's associate publisher, says. "They are all very remunerative. But what's most important is how effective they are in generating ideas for new products and services . . . new ways to provide value to our customers."

As Perriello, Guth, and Byrne have observed, event marketing is a superb way to get to know your customers and create extra income. Plus, when you do it right, events are plain, old-fashioned fun.

Event marketing refers to a wide range of promotional activities— from major conferences and trade shows to smaller, more specialized seminars, contests, parties, fundraisers, and retreats. Basically any sort of one-time happening that publicizes and/or promotes your company or your product is, or should be, an advertising event.

Event marketing makes great sense for information-marketing companies, such as the Oxford Club and ETR. But what about other businesses? Does it make sense for them?

Our answer is an emphatic and enthusiastic "Yes!" Event marketing has great potential for any business that is creative and wants to know its customers on a face-to-face basis.

If you are a manufacturer of fine watches, for example, you could produce an annual event for your "best" customers, during which you bring out your new line. A lavish welcome reception might precede the showcase presentation at which attendees would have the chance to buy early editions of your best and most expensive products, with special discounts and premiums not available to later buyers. To reduce expenses and generate extra income, you might invite a prestigious wine merchant to sponsor the welcome event and let them sell their products at the showcase, too. You could do the same by planning a cigar-smoking hour. Again, the vendor would pay for it. And you would split half of their sales.

The first time you sponsor such an event, you will probably attract a limited number of attendees. But if you put on a great show and promote that show to your customer base while it is going on (by sending them on-the-scene e-letters), you'll be sure to have lots more people coming the second year . . . and lots more people after that.

Another kind of event is put on by luxury car dealers who invite high-net-worth customers to two days at a track so they can test the power and excitement of driving one of their new, very expensive sports cars.

MAKE IT FUN ... LOTS OF FUN!

The challenge in promoting events comes from the fact that they take place in a fixed location at a defined point in time. It takes time—a considerable amount of time—and money for your customers to attend them. Because top customers are usually very busy businesspeople, it's often difficult for them to find the time.

But the counterbalance to the fixed location/time problem is how your customers are likely to view a marketing event that you sponsor. If you plan and promote it right, they won't think of it as a chance for you to sell them more products. They will see it as a chance for them to be treated like VIPs and have a lot of fun.

And that brings us to the first and most important principle of event planning. First and foremost, they should be about having fun. At AWAI's annual three-day copywriting bootcamp, for example, fledgling copywriters get to enjoy all of the following:

- An opening night networking dinner where writers meet each other, staff members, and celebrity speakers at a cocktail party and poolside buffet.
- Book signings where guest speakers sign copies of their latest books.
- An ersatz TV show performed on stage in which a famous copywriter is interviewed and answers questions from the audience in the manner of James Lipton's "Inside the Actors Studio."
- A dessert buffet at the bootcamp's job fair where writers meet with companies that are looking to hire copywriters.
- A Wall of Fame awards ceremony where members are recognized for their professional accomplishments.
- A group stretch each morning led by a professional trainer.
- Occasional chair massages, set up during lunch breaks.
- A farewell cocktail reception.

At the annual ETR wealth-building bootcamp in Delray Beach, customers are treated to many similar experiences, plus:

- A "connecting" session where attendees are asked to stand up and say something interesting about themselves that links them to something said by other attendees.
- A networking party for our VIP customers in the hotel's presidential suite. We don't only eat and drink. We advise our best customers on how to improve their businesses, their copy, their marketing, and their web sites.
- An awards luncheon to celebrate the accomplishments of our friends (and competitors) in the business. Among the awards: Entrepreneur of the Year, Marketer of the Year, Affiliate of the Year, and our Lifetime Achievement Award.
- Exercise classes conducted by speakers and guests.
- Motivation and productivity tips from our emcee, Alex Mandossian, to pump up the audience before each presentation.
- Raffles, dance contests, conga lines, and so on.

Fun isn't just for entertainment value, of course. It's also about getting customers to relax and let their hair down, so you can find out what is really on their minds.

PLAN CAREFULLY TO AVOID UNEXPECTED PROBLEMS

To maximize the amount of fun your customers have, you should ask yourself this when you start to plan an event: On a scale of 1 to 10, how much fun will this be?

At the same time, you must ask yourself how much interaction the event is likely to produce. Getting your staff connected with your customers is an essential component of success.

And, third, it's critical that the event be useful to your customers. Your relationship with them is ultimately based on usefulness—the benefits that your products and services provide. So you must also take time in the planning stages to ask "How valuable will this be to our customers?"

TAKING THE BULL BY THE HORNS

The story of energy-drink-maker Red Bull is a classic tale of an event-marketing campaign. And you can still see it in action today.

The Austria-based manufacturer is an example of a corporate-events master. Based on a Thai health tonic encountered by the company's founder in the early 1980s, Red Bull was introduced to Europe in 1987 and the United States a decade later. Since then, the company has ingratiated Red Bull to young people worldwide, essentially making it the go-to energy drink of an entire generation. However, before Red Bull's PR machine kicked in, nobody even knew they needed an energy drink, especially one that costs $2 for an 8-ounce can and tastes like a melted sweet candy. How'd they do it?

Since the beginning, Red Bull has sponsored athletes—and even entire athletic events—in extreme sports such as snowboarding, motocross, and skateboarding. They sponsor hip nightclub happenings, concert tours, and similar entertainment. The signature drink, Red Bull and vodka, is nearly synonymous with a night on the town in many circles. They also put on air races for professional pilots, as well as soapbox derbies and glider competitions for amateurs.

Whatever the event, attendees know that Red Bull is the sponsor. Signs, banners, T-shirts, hats, and more are everywhere. The drink itself is free-flowing. But nobody is turned off by the blatant product placement. To the contrary, the brand is associated with the young, hip, and cool. And, despite the introduction of competitors over the past several years—including many from larger companies such as Coca-Cola—Red Bull continues to dominate the industry. The company controls half the energy-drink market in the United States, which is expected to grow to $10 billion by 2010.

Source: Research Wiki, "Energy Drinks Marketing Research," www.researchwikis.com/Energy_Drinks_Market_Research. Accessed on June 11, 2008.

Structuring your event around the answers to these three questions will ensure success and profitability. And that success and profitability will grow each year that you run a particular event. In fact, you may be amazed at how events can grow if you run them right.

In addition to asking the three big questions, you should also take steps to avoid problems. Otherwise great events can be ruined by lack of preparation. We recommend the following "Disaster Prevention" checklist, to be consulted before you put any event into action:

- How good are the speakers and speeches? Don't be afraid to ask your speakers to present their material beforehand. Avoid academic or overly technical presentations and speakers who are inexperienced or poorly rated as public speakers.
- Have you hired an excellent master of ceremonies? Don't make the mistake of thinking that anyone can do the seemingly simple job of introducing speakers and event functions. Only a skillful professional can engage the audience and put everyone in the right frame of mind.
- Do you have a superstar running the event? Engage a specific individual to oversee the schedule, to make sure everyone and everything is in place and on time, and to double- and triple-check all the details all the time. The person to handle this job—the event manager—might be someone who works for you. It should be a person who is good with details, can push the troops when they need pushing, and can solve problems under pressure without getting flustered or angry.
- Are there people in place who will take care of the attendees' problems? Most of the businesses we work with invite lots of their employees to attend their annual events and talk to the attendees, answer their questions, and take care of any problems that might arise. Often, these problems have nothing to do with the event itself. They might be hotel or travel problems. They might be health issues or family concerns that arise. It doesn't matter what the issues are: If your employees come to the event with the idea that they are there to make sure everyone has a great, fun time, they will be willing to do whatever they can, and that will leave a very good impression about your company in the minds of all those who attend.
- How well-planned is the check-in process? The first impression your customers will have when they attend your event will likely be the one they receive while checking in on the first day. If you haven't properly planned the check-in process, or are understaffed

to handle the initial rush of that first-day check-in, you'll create a negative impression that will be hard to erase, even if the rest of the event runs smoothly.

- Do you have a fail-safe audiovisual system? Don't rely on the hotel's AV staff to deliver 100 percent of what they promise. There are always surprises when it comes to electrical, mechanical, or computerized components. Make sure that you have back-up systems in place and insist that technical support is always available at a moment's notice throughout the event, in case of an emergency.

- Do you have a truly welcoming welcome package? You will reduce the number of problems you run into by preparing for each attendee a welcome package that tells them everything they need to know about the program, the activities, the hotel facilities and amenities, and just about anything else you can think of. Include a local map and information about local shopping, spa services, and restaurants. Include emergency contact information and the names and phone numbers of staff members who are available to answer questions and assist attendees during specific hours.

TAKE ADVANTAGE OF EVERY MARKETING ACTIVITY

As you've seen from the examples we've already given, your business can benefit in several ways from marketing special events.

Customer Knowledge: First and foremost is the knowledge you will acquire about your best customers. It's not only the demographic information you can get from the registration forms, but the psychographic data you can gain by analyzing their actions during the event. Which workshops were most heavily attended? Which speeches got the highest ratings? Which presentations provoked the most controversy? And last but not least, which products (and which price points and which pitches) sold most strongly during the event?

Attendance Fees: When we first began promoting conferences in the early 1980s, attendance fees were the only stream of revenue we had for them. Back then, we were selling offshore banking advice to American investors. Because of the lack of good information on that subject, we were able to charge attendees about $800. Since then, we've learned a lot about setting attendance fees. In general, the more esoteric the conference topic, the more expensive the price of admission. ETR runs at least three conferences a year. The prices have ranged from $240 to $10,000. As a rule, we like to generate between $500,000 and $1 million in attendance fees per conference.

Exhibitor Fees: If you have a good-sized attendance, you can set up an exhibit hall adjacent to your main conference room. There, attendees can look at and purchase products from exhibitors that are related to the subject of the conference. Exhibitor fees can be a significant source of extra income. To ensure that the exhibition adds to—rather than detracts from—the quality of the conference, you should be picky about which exhibitors you allow in. Also ensure that a large part of their sales process is educational, so your customers will benefit from the exhibit experience, even if they don't buy any products. To make sure that the exhibitors have a good experience (i.e., enjoy reasonably good sales activity, at least enough to pay for their costs), it's a good idea to maintain a healthy attendee/exhibitor ratio. In our industry, that is about ten to one.

Sponsorship Fees: You can make some extra income by having exhibitors or outside vendors sponsor such things as meals, cocktail parties, and entertainment as part of your event. Sometimes, you may be willing to allow the sponsor to speak to the audience during their sponsored soiree. And sometimes, they will be happy merely to be prominently listed as its sponsor.

Podium Sales: In the information industry, it's now customary to allow some of your speakers to sell information products as part of their presentation. When this is done crudely, it has a negative impact on attendee satisfaction and will likely result in refunds. When it is done well, by a practiced professional, it goes over without a hitch and can result in significant extra bottom-line income. There are no fixed rules to guide you in determining how much platform selling you should allow at an event. Our policy has been to keep it to a minimum (fewer than one out of four presentations), and to only allow it when it is both an integral part of the presentation, and when the product being pitched will be beneficial to our customers.

Vertical Back-end Sales: Generally speaking, the largest single source of income at our conferences these days comes from the marketing of a single, high-priced back-end offer that allows those in attendance to purchase our latest, best, and most desirable products, bundled together, for a one-time, highly discounted price.

Developing this sort of "bundled" product requires a good deal of thought and planning. It should include some new and very exciting product that attendees are likely to want to purchase anyway, along with lots of other good quality products that they may not have, and then some special, limited-availability services that bind the offer together and give it a VIP feeling. Generally speaking, the bundled, VIP offer that you make at an annual conference will be the most expensive package you offer that year.

Ancillary Sales: In addition to all of the above, there are numerous extra sources of revenue that you can derive from a yearly conference. You can (and should), for example, sell an audio- or video-taping of the event to all those who attended (to keep as a reference) and to every one of your customers who was not able to attend. You can establish a little bookstore outside the main conference room where you sell your entire product line. You can even break down the presentations into individual products and sell them separately to existing customers, and even test them to create new customers.

INFORMATION CONFERENCES VERSUS SPONSORED SALES PRESENTATIONS

At this point, we should distinguish between an information conference and a sales event.

- If you are BMW and want to unveil a new sports car, you will probably want to send out invitations to your best customers and charge nothing for the event. This is because the purpose of the event is clearly to sell cars. It is a sponsored sales presentation.

You know it and your customers know it, too. Because they are being invited to spend another $60,000 to $160,000 with you, it would seem excessively greedy to charge them a fee to attend.

- An information conference is a very different sort of event. Its primary purpose is to teach customers more about your products, how to use them, and how to benefit from them, and also to offer them great deals that they won't find at any other time. Sales can be made at information conferences. In fact, you can make lots of money with information conferences. But to make them valid for the customer, they must always be primarily about *information*.

CONFERENCE FEES: YES? NO? HOW MUCH?

Generally speaking, the lower the price you charge, the more attendees you will get. But that consideration must be weighed against the considerable cost of producing a conference and the likelihood that free admission will bring in lots of nonresponsive browsers. It has been our experience that fee-based conferences produce much greater benefits all around—for the sponsor, for any vendors that are involved, and for the attendee, as well. Yes, charging a fee reduces the quantity of attendees, but usually by eliminating people who otherwise would be wasting your time and consuming your resources, without any reciprocity in terms of current or future sales.

How much you charge for attendance depends on the disposable income of your customers and the quality of the program you are offering. Attendance fees for the conferences we have run have ranged from $100 to $10,000. Interestingly, this corresponds roughly to the price range of products in our industry (information marketing). So that may be a guide. If you set your fee at the lower end of the range, you will likely attract a bigger audience, which might allow you to make money from selling exhibitor space. If you set your fee at the upper end, you will not be able to bring in outside vendors, but the in-conference sales of back-end products will likely be much greater. Ultimately, choosing a price is an art, not a science. A prudent course of action for first-time conference promoters would be to pick a mid-range price—such as $500—and then make adjustments in subsequent years.

OTHER TYPES OF MARKETING EVENTS

So far, we have discussed only two types of events: sponsored sales presentations and information conferences. In addition, there are many other types of events you can market:

- **Free local seminars:** Many financial and legal professionals market their services by putting on free local seminars on subjects such as investing, estate planning, business tax avoidance, and so on. The challenge with free local seminars is attracting qualified attendees. If you make the event free and give away coffee and donuts, you will have a lot of moochers showing up. If all you are giving away is good information and you are marketing the event strongly, you'll get the attendees you are looking for and they will convert to customers at a satisfying rate.

- **Teleseminars and virtual seminars:** Using modern audio and Internet technology, you can run telephone or Internet seminars to a large number of people—prospects or customers—at a relatively low cost. What you need is an exciting topic, an experienced speaker, some special product to offer to those who "attend," and a cost-effective way to generate attendance.

- **Trade shows:** Whether you set up a booth at a large event or host your own and sell booths to partners and even competitors, trade shows are a great way to raise your company's profile and the profile of your industry as a whole. Of course, you can't expect attendees to simply roam around checking out products and hearing sales pitches. You need to give them networking parties, well-known speakers (even if they are just well-known in your industry), and other "entertainment."

- **Exclusive retreats:** These are held in either high-end resorts and hotels or secluded locations. They're less an "event" and more a meeting of the minds. They are more expensive than standard events because they feature one-on-one contact between expert speakers and attendees. They are usually more informal and give attendees a great opportunity to find like-minded business partners. The Michael Masterson Business-Building Conference held at the Ritz-Carlton in Palm Beach is a good example. It was $10,000 per person, and all the attendees were accomplished entrepreneurs or businesspeople. Michael Masterson pinpointed problems in each of their businesses and suggested improvements. There was a lot of "after hours" networking as well.

- **Charity and fundraising events:** In the old days, when a nonprofit wanted to raise money, they simply asked potential donors for it, using either the phone or direct mail. Today, raising money is a multi-channel marketing event.

  Let's use the Susan G. Komen "Race for the Cure" as an example. In South Florida, this event is held every January. However, the advertising starts about nine months prior to the race. It is advertised on the Web, on the radio, on TV, and in print—including local newspapers, national magazines, and even mall displays. A huge number of people participate. And no one is excluded. There are categories for individuals, families, and children, to either walk or run. The sponsorships alone are a substantial part of the bottom line.

- **Niche specific/Club events:** Many clubs put on events for their members to get together and trade stories. For example, a colleague's grandmother recently returned from her Green Thumb conference, where the featured presentation was a session that taught attendees how to raise orchids. In this case, the event was not held to make money. Members paid their own way, plus a fee for the instructor.

- **Associations:** Many associations, such as the American Management Association (AMA) and the Specialized Information and Publishers Association (SIPA), put on events to help members advance in their careers. Often they will ask experts to donate their time and charge the attendees so that they can keep the association afloat.

ONE OR ONE MILLION, THE STEPS MUST BE TAKEN

Marketing an event is like any good marketing campaign: If you are planning one, the steps you take are the same, regardless of whether you are hosting 20 people or 500 people. Yes, onsite preparation is more challenging for a larger number of attendees. However, your preparations are the same.

The following section is a reference guide that you can work with when planning any marketing event. This one may go into far more detail than you will ever find necessary. However, you can easily tailor it to suit your specific needs.

Event Timeline

Assemble a team for each event. The team should include:

- **Event planner:** This must be someone who is organized and who can push to get everyone to do what needs to be done. Experience helps here, but the right kind of personality—calm, detail-oriented, and thoughtful—is essential.
- **Marketer:** Any good direct-response marketer can do the job. Event planning, from a marketing point of view, is pretty simple.
- **Copywriter:** As with any direct-response promotion, good copy can double or triple response rates. Don't skimp when it comes to paying for copy.
- **Profit center manager or business director:** The event itself should be profitable. So put its profits in the hands of someone who has experience creating profits.
- **Emcee:** The choice of emcee is very important for seminars and conferences. Although emcees don't usually provide any content, they are in front of the audience a great deal of the time. A great emcee is much better than a good one. Invest the time and money to get a great emcee.
- **Speakers and presenters:** Every speaker and presenter will either enhance or detract from your reputation, so be very careful in deciding who you are going to put in front of your best customers.

Determining the Four Ws and One H

Next, determine the Who, What, Where, Why, and How for the event. Ask yourself:

Who is our demographic?
- What lists are appropriate to promote to?
- Are there any joint-venture opportunities?

- Who is eligible to attend? Do they have to fit within certain guidelines? What level are they—beginner, intermediate, or advanced?
- How many attendees will we have? What number will allow us to maximize revenue, but also provide the best information and services to attendees?

What type of event is this going to be?
- Will it be high end (all-inclusive) or low gate fee (less amenities provided)?
- Will the general goal be to help our readers obtain extra income? Educate them on marketing techniques? Become more Internet savvy?

Where will the event be held?
- How do the possible locations/venues compare? Do these locations/venues meet our pre-determined goals? Can the hotel provide our event-specific needs on specific dates?
- Have we considered all the information we need to negotiate a contract? Room rates. Meeting space requirements. Attendee logistics (time zone, airport locations, etc.). Attrition issues, group blocks. A/V requirements. BEO (banquet event order) requirements.
- Are we prepared to maintain constant contact with the hotel rep regarding group block, cut-off dates, food and beverage requirements, spacing needs, etc.?

Why are we doing this—in other words, what is the purpose of the event?
- What is the general purpose of the event?
- What is the desired outcome?
- Does this make sense revenue-wise?

How will we execute this event?
- How will this event be executed in the most cost-effective manner for our company as well as for our attendees?
- Does it make sense to partner with others or to use in-house resources?

Marketing Considerations

The promotion
- Work with copywriters to ensure that promises made in the sales copy can be delivered during the event.

Order form/conference module set up
- Set price points.
- Set "status grouping" (i.e., VIPs and special guests).
- Set cancellation/refund dates.
- Set processing fees.

Schedule of marketing efforts
- Make sure promotions are out on time.
- Ensure that promotional teleconferences and any additional marketing efforts are coordinated.

Campaign ideas and brainstorming sessions
- Make sure necessary external meetings are coordinated.
- Make sure event staff provides constant updates and encourage them to generate new ideas.

Marketing/attendee reports
- Make sure reports are shared and analyzed.
- Make sure historical data/timelines are considered.

Evaluation of marketing methods. You want to know:
- Which promotion worked?
- Which list gave us the most return?

Attendee Considerations

Attendee count
- Make sure the count is constantly updated with cancellations, credit card declines, refunds, etc.

Conference communication
- Make sure reminders are sent out to attendees and speakers.
- Make sure preparation needs (for speakers, coaches, and attendees) are constantly updated.

Special requests/needs
- Keep track of all special requests/needs from attendees, speakers, and staff.

Communicate all details to customer service
- Make sure all credit card rejections are addressed.
- Make sure payment plans are implemented and fulfilled.
- Make sure all customer service questions are answered in a prompt and professional manner.

Event Schedule

Skeleton agenda
- Have a working agenda provided to all involved.
- Make sure the agenda is constantly updated and improved.
- Make sure appropriate topics are covered for the best "flow" of information.
- Make sure cocktail parties, networking events, and off-site events are represented properly and cost-efficiently.

Agenda finalization
- Send the final agenda to attendees, staff, hotel, and speakers.

Theme

Work with a designer on the event concept and ensure that it is implemented appropriately throughout the event.

Collateral materials
- Make sure all collateral materials are created in the best manner possible (with quality and content being key).

Ensure that deadlines are met for:
- Copy
- Promotional and marketing efforts
- Design
- Hotel
- Printer
- Speakers

Provide the following materials:
- Name tags
- Attendee binders
- Signage/banners
- Order forms
- Any additional collateral materials needed
- Evaluation forms/surveys

Vendors

Create and maintain trustworthy and lasting relationships with the following:

- Printers
- Audiovisual providers
- Entertainment/awards vendors
- Decorations providers
- Technology rental providers
- Hotel representatives

Speakers

Work with your event staff and marketing team to decide which speakers are appropriate. Then take care of the following details:

Speaker contracts
- Have them drafted.
- Make sure they have been signed and returned.
- Make sure appropriate issues and legalities have been covered.

Speaker logistics
- Schedule presentations according to each speaker's availability.
- Make sure their travel and hotel accommodations (and other necessary arrangements) are made.
- Make sure their presentation preparation deadlines are met.
- Make sure necessary materials will be provided during each speaker's presentation.

The Actual Event

Plan ahead to try to foresee any issues that may arise—and coordinate the following at the event itself:

- Registration.
- Execution of the final agenda—ensuring that speakers are on time with their presentations and end on time.
- Hotel logistics. (Troubleshoot any issues that come up to ensure that the event flows seamlessly.)
- The handling of offsite "happenings."
- Cocktail parties/networking events. (Make sure they are handled appropriately.)
- Concierge services. (Make sure they are provided when needed.)
- Deliverables.
- Communication with hotel staff on any changes or problems that come up.

Staffing
- Ensure that each aspect of the event is staffed appropriately.

Conference materials
- Make sure that all conference materials arrive on time and are handed out at the appropriate time.

Transportation
- Make sure all staff and speakers are on time and provided with transportation to and from event.

Audiovisual
- Make sure that all sessions are taped, that microphones and A/V equipment is set and ready, that PCs (if needed) are set up and ready, and that tech equipment is supplied.

Contact sheets
- Make sure registration sheets, sign-in, and attendee networking sheets are all provided.

Back-End Sales

Products sold
- Make sure product codes and order forms have been created.
- Make sure sales are processed via credit card machine and kept track of.
- Make sure petty cash is on hand for cash transactions.
- Make sure inventory has arrived at the hotel.

Profit splits
- Follow up on profit splits according to your contracts.

Staffing
- Make sure staff and sales teams are briefed on products, order processing, and logistics.

Marketing materials
- Make sure appropriate marketing materials are given out to purchasing customers.
- Follow up on deliverability and promises made.

Financial Considerations

Preliminary budget
- Work with your profit center manager on the overall event revenue goals.
- Follow through with meeting and exceeding budgetary needs.
- Have a preliminary profit and loss statement prepared.

Final profit/loss statement
- Determine the final profit or loss from the event.
- Include all attendee revenue, joint-venture revenue, profit splits (in-house versus outstanding dollars).
- Include an expense report breakdown.
- Show final net versus gross revenue.

Invoice settlement and payments
- Make sure all vendor invoices are paid.
- Make sure speaker compensation is delivered on time.

Divisional revenue
- Make sure all expenses/revenues are coded properly, with accounting to reflect the correct profit center's gains/losses.

Follow-Up

Final cancellations/refunds
- Make sure all cancellations, refunds, and credits are accounted for.

Postconference materials
- Make sure final evaluations are sent out and analyzed.
- Make sure thank-yous are sent to speakers and other participants.
- Make sure follow-up communication is sent to attendees, including e-mail updates.
- Build a members-only web site and other exclusive content.
- Work with A/V to make sure DVD recordings of the event are edited to specifications, artwork is created, and materials are sent to customers in a timely manner.

Final financial report
- Detail the final count of money brought in by the event, with all profit splits, joint ventures, and expenditures accounted for.

Postmortem with event team. Address these questions:
- What went wrong?
- What went right?
- How can the next event be better?

With the above reference guide and everything else that you have learned thus far, you're now in a good position to either put on your first event or make an annual event that you've been running more profitable.

But before you do that, study the following three excerpts from promotions for events put on by *Early to Rise*. (We strongly encourage you to review these three ads in their entirety in the Appendix to this book, as well as the additional ETR promotions you'll find there. They will serve as a valuable resource for you as you implement or improve your multi-channeling marketing campaign.) We consider each of our events to be very valuable for our customers. We believe you will see why after you see how we promote them.

The first excerpt is for our annual web site building and Internet business coaching event, "5 Days in July."

Coming This Summer, The Event You've Been Waiting For...

Give Us Five Days in July... and We'll Give You Income for Life

**Walk in Tuesday Morning with NOTHING...
(No Product, Website, or Technical Experience)...**

**Walk Out Saturday Afternoon With
Your Own REAL Internet Business.**

The next excerpt is for a wealth-building retreat in Orlando, featuring expert speakers from a variety of industries, including real estate, investments and online businesses.

**Come to Early to Rise's 2008 "Spring Fling"
and Get Over $17.3 Million in
Unique & POWERFUL Money-Making Secrets...**

Profits In Paradise!

**Introducing Dozens of Great _New_ Income-
Generating and Entrepreneurial
Adventures...**

The final excerpt is for our longest-running (and best-attended) event—a bootcamp we hold every year. It's a one-stop shop for entrepreneurs looking for the easiest way to start a very profitable Internet business. (Remember, you can see all three of these sample ads in their entirety in the Appendix to this book.)

Last Year, 145 Million People Spent Over
$108 <u>BILLION</u> Online!

Where Did All That Money Go?

The "Other Side"
of The Internet!

Now, Here's Your Chance to Switch
Over to the <u>WINNING SIDE OF THE WEB</u>...

- "Other Side Entrepreneur" J.W. Earned $306,043 in <u>3 Days.</u>

- "Other Side Entrepreneur" P.H. Earned $2,292,001 in <u>2 Weeks.</u>

- "Other Side Entrepreneur" G.G. Earned <u>Over $8,500,000 in 1</u>
  <u>Month!</u>

OUR EVENTS ARE BACKED UP BY THE
PROMISES WE KEEP

As you can see, very big promises have been made in each of the above
sales letters . . . and ETR has exceeded every one.

This should be your main takeaway: If you promise 10 things at
your event, deliver 11 or 12. Never underdeliver on your promises.
Your refunds will destroy your margins.

If you are new to event marketing, start on a small scale and make
sure your first event is word-of-mouth-worthy!

CHAPTER FOURTEEN

PUBLIC RELATIONS

Man Bites Dog; Man Gets Famous

Two men walked into a small restaurant in Nebraska. They sat down at the counter and ordered hamburgers. When their check came, one of the men paid it and put money on the counter to pay for everyone else who was eating there that day. The bill came to about $2,000.

When the waitress asked him why he was being so generous, he sheepishly replied that he had just won the lottery. "What lottery?" she wanted to know.

"The Powerball Jackpot," he said.

"You mean *the* Powerball Jackpot?" she said. "The one for $365 million?"

He nodded.

People gathered around him. They wanted to know how he had been so lucky. He held up the book he had been carrying. It was called *The Attractor Factor*. "I owe my success to this," he said. "I found the winning numbers in the book."

Local media immediately picked up the story, and then passed it on up the chain until it went nationwide. In each interview and news report, the man talked about *The Attractor Factor*.

But when lottery officials were finally contacted by fact-checking reporters over the next couple of days, they refuted the man's claims. He hadn't won the lottery after all. The entire thing was a hoax. A hoax designed to make *The Attractor Factor* a nationally recognized title.

The ruse worked, and subsequent news stories continued to talk about the book and its author, a Texan by the name of Joe Vitale. Vitale himself was interviewed several times, and pictures of the book's cover were included in many of the newspaper articles.

Vitale admitted that he had hired a pair of professional pranksters to pull the hoax. He admitted it was a very unusual way to promote a book. But, he pointed out, it was also very effective. *The Attractor Factor* was talked about coast-to-coast, and featured by major news outlets such as *Good Morning America* and the Associated Press. And it became a best-seller.

Vitale's stunt was outrageous, but it was far from unprecedented. The history of modern public relations (PR) is full of such theatrics. Think of John and Yoko's sleep-in. Or Janet Jackson's "wardrobe malfunction" during the Super Bowl. Or just about anything that Howard Stern does in public.

Being outrageous (even a little duplicitous at times) is a good, quick way to get on the airwaves. But more traditional PR marketing tactics can work as well.

Of the many channels of marketing, public relations is one that no business should ignore. That's because it is nearly free (the only costs are the events themselves), and when it works, it can work like wildfire, going from local to regional to national—and even to international audiences—faster than it takes to write up a marketing plan for a conventional advertising campaign.

And because PR is nearly free, it is an ideal channel for small and start-up businesses. Its huge potential, however, makes it a viable option for larger businesses, too—especially those that have big ambitions.

PUBLIC RELATIONS IN ACTION

In our own businesses, we have used public relations campaigns to promote a variety of information products, including books, special events, and seminars.

To boost the sales of *Automatic Wealth* and *Ready, Fire, Aim*, for example, our publishing partner, John Wiley & Sons, employed a public relations expert to generate dozens of reviews in magazines and newspapers, in-flight publications, and online business reviews. Both of these books became best-sellers on all the major listing services, including Amazon, Barnes & Noble, *The Wall Street Journal, Business Week,* and *The New York Times.*

We routinely use public relations campaigns to boost attendance at regional seminars and sales events by sending out press releases to local publications.

Daily Reckoning, an Internet-based investment advisory publication, used PR to promote its brand and one of its products, a book titled *Empire of Debt.* Addison Wiggin, *Daily Reckoning's* publisher, accomplished this by producing a documentary film (*IOUSA*) that premiered to critical acclaim at the prestigious Sundance Film Festival.

On a smaller scale, to promote his ballroom dance instruction business, Paul Lawrence, an entrepreneur in South Florida, got to know local entertainment reporters and began inviting them to dance events that he hosted. Most declined his invitations at first, but when one reporter did a story on him, the others followed suit. In a few short months, he was featured in the *South Florida Sun-Sentinel,* the *Miami Herald,* and several local newspapers. He went from teaching eight lessons a week to over 50.

There are all sorts of clever strategies for getting free publicity for your company and your products. But they are all guided by a few commonsense principles:

UNDERSTAND WHAT THE MEDIA IS LOOKING FOR

You start a new company, launch a new product, hire a new marketing director—but that's not news. News is "Britney Spears Shaves Her Head" or "Hillary Clinton Throws a Gutter Ball." It's pathetic, but that's news.

It's unlikely that the media will be interested in any sort of news about your business. Yes, you may be able to get news about your company published in an industry trade journal, but what good is that? Your customers aren't reading trade journals. They are watching TV and reading *USA Today.*

So how do you get on television and in the newspapers?

You start by understanding what they are looking for. Generally speaking, they are looking for two things:

- News about subjects their readers are already interested in (i.e., Paris Hilton—not you).
- Captivating and/or curious tidbits to fill in the gaps.

It is only into this second category of "news" coverage that you can hope to find a welcome place for your public relations campaigns. Just keep in mind that by taking advantage of America's obsession with lottery winners, Joe Vitale's trickery propelled his book into national prominence in a matter of weeks.

So begin with this: What you won't do. You won't waste your time and resources sending out press releases to the national media about company news. And if you do announce corporate news in industry periodicals, it will not be with any hope that it will boost your sales.

What you will do is figure out, first and foremost, which news media you want to be in, and then figure out how to create curious and captivating stories that relate to your business.

A GUY IN A WEDDING DRESS

One way to get free publicity is to be totally outrageous. A big, burly guy wearing a wedding dress might fit the bill.

In 1997, Dennis Rodman, the 6-foot-8-inch bad-boy basketball player, wore a wedding dress (and blond wig) to a book signing at a New York bookstore to promote his autobiography, *Bad as I Wanna Be*. Did we mention he arrived at the signing in a horse-drawn carriage? Pictures of Rodman flooded national and international news outlets and helped fuel book sales.

WHICH NEWS MEDIA DO YOU WANT TO BE IN?

Ask 10 entrepreneurs which news media they want to be in, and nine will give you the same answer: "That's easy. I want the major media— the biggest newspapers and television news programs."

Trouble is, the national news media are not going to run "news" about your company. And they have reams of curious and captivating filler stories already. They don't need the story you will send them. The chances of having them pick it up are slim to none.

You have a much better chance with local or specialized media (both television and printed publications). They favor local and specialized coverage, and if your story is good enough, they might run it.

When you get some local coverage, you can hope to see it extend itself naturally. The regional media look to local media for human-interest stories. And the national media look to regional coverage for the same. A good illustration of how a good local story can organically expand is the story of Alex Tew, a once-struggling college student from the United Kingdom.

Tew was having trouble paying his college tuition bill when he thought of a novel solution. Sell ad space on a web site for $1 per pixel, in bundles of 10. His goal was to sell $1 million worth of space. MillionDollarHomepage.com took 48 hours to build, and Tew started selling ads on it immediately.

Family and friends were his first customers, attracted by a sales letter he sent to everyone on his personal e-mail contact list. Then he sent a press release to local media. Those stories generated more visits to his site and more orders for ad space. He sent out more press releases and media coverage increased.

Soon the story was national and then international. Within a month, Tew sold $40,000 worth of ads. Five months in, he had sold enough ads to individuals and businesses around the world to reach his million-dollar goal.

Tew had not only made more than enough money to pay for college, he had learned a valuable lesson about unconventional PR.

FIGURE OUT HOW YOUR COMPANY OR PRODUCT CAN MEET THAT DEMAND

To figure out how to create successful stories, you have to know the media you want to reach and understand what kind of stories their audience delights in. That's actually pretty simple to do. Just see what they have used in the past.

If you want your story to be picked up by *USA Today*, for example, you might consider coming up with one that ties into a current trend. If you study *USA Today*, you will see that most of the smaller, human-interest stories are angled that way. The editors at *USA Today* know what they are doing. They can't compete with *The New York Times* or *The Wall Street Journal* in terms of serious news, but they tend to overtake them when it comes to social fads of almost every type. In the health area, for example, *USA Today* keeps tabs on all the trendy diet and exercise programs. They don't care so much about the scientific import of diet and exercise, but they do care about the kind of diet and exercise that's growing in popularity.

If your media target is specialized periodicals—maybe about golf or electronics or office furniture—you will have to study the best-read publications that go to the consumer you are trying to reach. If one of those publications likes to run stories about industry statistics, for example, you could do your own industry study and tie that into your product in some creative way. The study needn't be exhaustive in terms of research. Such publications are seldom as concerned with the quality of the research as they are with the interest it will create with their readers.

So it's very important to target your press releases to the specific publications and media outlets whose audiences you want to reach. Rather than sending out 1,000 general press releases about a story that has general appeal, it's much more effective to send out a dozen or so targeted press releases containing stories that are exactly right for the intended consumers.

And while we're on the subject of targeting your press releases, let's observe a parallel truth about successful publicity today: Sending your releases to an individualized list of 100 people with whom you have talked or corresponded is infinitely more effective than buying a list of 10,000 people who don't know you from a hole in the ground.

Public relations today, like marketing and advertising, is much more effective when it's done with intelligence, personalization, and individualization.

TAKING ADVANTAGE OF THE INTERNET

The rise of Internet communications has changed much of the world of marketing, advertising, and public relations. The fundamental rules of selling still apply, but many of the rules of marketing and PR are different now, because of all the ways there are to reach consumers online.

When President Clinton entered the White House in 1993, there were only 50 sites on the World Wide Web.[1] Today, there are hundreds of millions. What that means, in terms of public relations, is that there are literally millions of ways to promote your company and product for free!

As David Meerman Scott points out in *The New Rules of Marketing and PR*, old-fashioned press releases issued impersonally to large lists of PR agencies—in print and online—are much less effective today than they were in the past. The omnipresence of blogs and web sites and e-zines has made it much, much easier for information providers to locate and distribute interesting stories to their audiences. People in charge of deciding which stories get published and which don't are deluged with impersonal press releases. They just don't have the time to review them—or the need to.

Scott says that, as a contributing editor at *EContent* magazine, he receives hundreds of broadcast e-mail press releases each week from "well-meaning PR people who want me to write about their widgets." But in five years of working there, he has never published a single one. "I'm not the only one who doesn't use unsolicited press releases," Scott says. "I think about a subject that I want to cover in a column or an article and I check out what I can find on blogs and through search engines. If I find a press release on the subject through Google News or a company's online media room, great. But I don't wait for press releases to come to me. Rather, I go looking for interesting topics, products, people, and companies. And when I do feel ready to write a story, I might try out a concept on my blog first, to see how it flies. Does anyone comment on it? Do any PR people e-mail me?"[2]

Essentially, the new rules of Internet publicity are the same as the new rules of print and media publicity:

- Target a very specific audience.
- Find out exactly what kinds of stories they enjoy.
- Create a story that they might be interested in.
- Tie that story to your product in a clever way.
- Develop a list of personal PR contacts.

- Focus 80 percent of your energy and resources on the 20 percent of the media market that you know well, especially the people in the business who know you and are likely to help you.

And finally, if you have it in you, put on a wedding dress and get yourself photographed.

CHAPTER FIFTEEN

THE INCREDIBLE POWER OF A MULTI-CHANNEL CAMPAIGN

Four employees, two computers, and one telephone—that's how *Early to Rise* started in 1999. For several years, the company grew slowly, generating revenues but barely breaking even. Eventually, it hit $8 million a year in revenues, but stalled.

Then, in 2006, there was a paradigm shift. Multi-channel marketing was introduced to the company and implemented throughout. Revenues soared from $8 million to $26 million in a matter of 18 months. And today, this multi-channel philosophy is adopted by every employee who joins the company, regardless of their job title.

That's our story, and why we're so excited about direct-response multi-channel marketing.

So now that you've read this book to this point and understand the individual marketing tactics and strategies, it is time to put it all together. You should not feel as though you have to use every marketing channel in every campaign—you don't.

If you have never done a multi-channel campaign, start with two or three channels. Make sure you include your greatest strength—the channel that you already excel at—as well as the low-hanging fruit available to you: channels such as PR or dedicated e-mail blasts, which are relatively inexpensive and have massive reach.

Here are the 10 steps to launching your multi-channel campaign.

COUNT TO 10 AND GO!

If you understand the fundamental principles of direct-response marketing and the importance of multi channel marketing, all you need to do is count to 10. These 10 steps are the core of your multi-channel campaign and should be followed, although you can rearrange the steps into the order that works best for you.

1. **Determine the purpose of the product you intend to sell.** There are two kinds of products: "need to have" products and "want to have" products. Understanding which you are selling is critical to your success. "Need to have" products include houses, furniture, and food. Selling these products is usually a matter of providing good value at a fair price. "Want to have" products include jewelry, cosmetics, and art. To sell these products, you have to create a perceived value for them.

   Before you begin to market, you need to make sure that your product meets a certain need or want or solves a particular problem that resonates with your prospects.

2. **Establish marketing priorities via a timeline.** You are about to put your new product on the market and you want to make the biggest splash possible. The best way to do it is with a product launch timeline. Regardless of whether you are working alone or with a team, you may feel a little overwhelmed by your mental to-do list. This is why a timeline is a vital part of ensuring your campaign's success.

   A timeline is a visual representation of a number of events and their chronological occurrence. It tells you what happened, or is going to happen, and when.

   The timeline will help keep your planning efforts on track.

   You can tailor the timeline we discussed in Chapter 7 for direct-mail copy to every channel and task of your multi channel campaign. If you are a first-timer, see if you can get advice from

THE SEVEN STEPS OF A FAILED PRODUCT LAUNCH

These are the seven steps of a failed product launch:

1. Get an idea for a product.
2. Write or design the product.
3. Print or manufacture the product.
4. Advertise the product.
5. Watch the marketing campaign flop and generate no sales.
6. Sell or give away the product to family members and colleagues.
7. Store the unsold inventory until it is thrown away.

Never try to launch a product by using the "I know best" approach that is illustrated above. Remember that what you *think* means nothing. It is what you *know* that counts.

So, how do you know your prospective customers will want your product? You test and test and test and test some more.

In this Internet age, testing is easier than ever before. If you are torn between two products, don't go with your gut, and don't go with what your friends tell you. Test a couple of pay-per-click ads and see which one gets more clicks.

That is exactly what we did to determine the title of this book. We had five potentially good titles, so we put all five in Google PPC ads to determine which one would really resonate with people who needed the kind of information we're providing here.

Well, based on the results of those ads, the title on the cover of this book won hands down. And it is a title that neither of the authors came up with; it came from someone on the *Early to Rise* staff. The ones we created bombed.

Don't worry about not having your product ready while you're testing your PPC ads. Develop the ads and let them run for five to seven days. When potential customers click, let them know that you are building a "hot list" and will contact them as soon as the product is ready. Or give them something else in the meantime. That's what we did with our book-title PPC ads. We opted our responders in to a subscription to ETR.

(continues)

THE SEVEN STEPS OF A FAILED PRODUCT LAUNCH (*Continued*)

You can use the same plan with banner ads, text ads, and even dedicated e-mails to ensure you are on the right track—before you spend the time and money to develop your product.

Last year, *Early to Rise* developed a comprehensive Internet business start-up program for $4,000. We had two possible names for the program. We put up banner ads not only on our web site, but on competitive sites, as well. After a week, we had a clear winner and The Internet Money Club was born. And because the product was not quite ready to go out the door, we built a hot list and communicated with those people for two months before we actually launched our campaign. When we were ready to send out our sales letter, we didn't have to go any further than that hot list.

This is a cheap and easy way to test product ideas without expensive R&D costs. Plus, you have the added benefit of simultaneously building a list of interested prospects.

Remember: When you test anything, make sure the results of your test scream, not whisper.

THE HOT LIST

In direct marketing, a hot list is made up of customers and/or subscribers on your e-mail list who opt in to receive information about an upcoming event or product launch. By creating and targeting this refined list of people interested in receiving your promotions, you will boost your response rate. The people on this list are essentially "pre-qualified" and more likely to buy.

an experienced marketer to get an idea of how long each step may take. But to be realistic about your own launch, take their estimate and double it.

Once you have set deadlines for each component of your launch, respect those deadlines. Even when you think something could be done better, there comes a point of diminishing returns. Those little tweaks you make that will postpone or push back your launch will cost you more than they're worth.

3. **Determine your goals.** Before you go any further, make sure you know exactly (or close to it) what your efforts will yield. This is called making assumptions or forecasting.

Keep in mind that your goal does not have to be the same for each channel. You may intend to make money on many

---

DO YOU REALLY WANT TO MAKE MONEY?

It may seem as though the purpose of every marketing campaign is to make a profit. However, many marketers and business owners actually lose money on acquiring new customers.

There are three basic scenarios when launching a marketing campaign. You need to determine which scenario fits your business best.

1. Do you want to bring in customers at breakeven? This means that for every dollar spent, you get that dollar back, but no more. For example, if you spend $1,000 and you make $1,000 with your marketing efforts while acquiring new customers, you have done so at breakeven.

2. Are you willing to take a loss up front in order to obtain more customers who can make you more money on the back end? For example, if you spend $1,000 and you make $800 while acquiring new customers, you are taking an initial loss. But you can continue to sell more—and more expensive—products to those new customers, making additional money on the back end.

3. Is your goal to make money on the initial sale? For example, if you spend $1,000 and you make $1,250 with your marketing efforts while acquiring new customers, you have done so at a profit.

(continues)

DO YOU REALLY WANT TO MAKE MONEY? (*Continued*)

The following chart illustrates a basic breakeven forecast:

	Assumptions
Mail quantity	95,000
Projected response rate	1%
Projected orders	950
Average unit of sale	$100
Cost of goods	10%
Projected revenue	$95,000
Expenses:	
Cost of goods	$9,500
Projected promo costs	$85,500
Net profit per channel	$0.00

It's very important to do a forecast like this when determining your marketing channels, as well as your media plan.

---

of your online channels, while you're willing to take a loss on your direct-mail campaigns because of the lifetime value of the customers you expect to bring in.

4. **Get your sales copy written.** You may think it is counterintuitive to get your sales message written before you determine your channels, but it is not.

In Chapter 7, we discussed the copywriting process. You know that dealing with copywriters and getting final copy can take a while—in some cases, several weeks. So you need to start this process as soon as possible.

Use the timeline for copy that we discussed in Chapter 7.

Remember that the copy has to grab the attention of your prospects from the very beginning. It has to make them understand their need for the product. And it has to help them visualize the product in their minds and imagine how it will enhance their lives.

Also, the copy must anticipate and answer any questions or concerns your prospects may have. Don't leave this to chance.

Make sure all the critical information about the product is supplied early in the sales letter, while minimizing any risk and instilling confidence in the product and the company behind it.

Lastly, make sure it's easy for the customer to purchase the product. How many times have you read a sales letter in which the mailer wants you to call and order, but you cannot find the phone number? That's a rookie mistake. On your web sites, make the order button prominent. In direct mail, a postage-paid envelope will always out-pull one that requires the prospect to use their own stamp.

5. **Determine your channels.** If you will be marketing your product to your house list, the campaign probably will do well. (As discussed in Chapter 3, your house list is made up of names you have permission to market to.) Your house list already knows you and your company, so you can predict a higher response rate, resulting in a better ROI.

   You can also market your product to outside lists. These are names that you do not have permission to market to directly, but who have agreed to receive third-party advertisements. In this case, you will assume a lower response rate, resulting in a lower ROI . . . depending on the cost of the product and the cost of marketing.

   The first thing you must do to determine which marketing channels to use is to ask basic questions regarding your prospects. Ask yourself how you originally acquired their names and how you have been communicating with them recently.

   Chances are good that your prospects will see your advertisement in more than one channel. Therefore, remain consistent with your marketing. Keep the offer and message the same. Even things like color and images should be consistent on all channels. The idea is to ensure that the prospect knows it is *you* each time they see your advertisement, regardless of the channel.

   Did you know that a direct-response consumer sees an ad an average of three times before making a purchase? Repetition is very important. If your prospect doesn't respond to your dedicated e-mail right away, communicate with her through another channel. By approaching her from multiple directions, chances are she's likely to see your ad often enough to buy your product.

Whenever possible, use e-mail first to communicate with customers and prospects. This is going after low-hanging fruit. If you have a permission-based list, e-mail will be the easiest, fastest, cheapest, and most effective method of marketing your product. So start by getting as many responses as possible from this channel. Then, when you go to your next channel, you can purge your responders from the list and market only to the people who have *not* responded to your e-mail efforts. This makes marketing via your next channels more cost effective.

Don't forget to do an assumption forecast (as shown earlier in the chapter) for each channel.

6. **Develop your media plan.** Now that you know which channels you will use for your campaign, you will need to select the media for each. Start by checking out your competitors'

MULTI-CHANNEL MARKETING FOR A HIGH-END CONFERENCE

Early to Rise held a high-end business-building retreat last year, with a ticket price of $10,000. We started by selecting a group of customers to market to—customers who met certain criteria that made it likely they would be interested in the conference.

We first sent them announcements via e-mail. We had 25 slots filled in 30 minutes. The next day, we called some of the people on the list and filled another five slots. A week later, we sent a direct-mail package to the rest of the prospects on our list and filled seven more slots.

Because we started with the fastest, easiest, and cheapest channel, it cost us very little to bring in the first $250,000.

The cost of calling was higher, yet nowhere close to the $50,000 our calls produced.

Finally, our mailing was the most expensive channel. It cost us $1.50 per prospect. However, we sent out only 250 invitations, for a total cost of $375. Yet the mailing ended up filling seven slots at $10,000, or $70,000.

Had we stopped marketing after our dedicated e-mail blast, we would have left $120,000 on the table. And had we started with direct mail, our profit margin would have been significantly lower.

web sites. Do they accept outside banner ads? Do they send third-party advertising to their lists? Perhaps they have a print publication associated with their business. If they have repeat advertisers who are selling something similar to your product, your ad will probably do well with them, too. This is the "birds of a feather flock together" approach that we spoke of in Chapter 8.

7. **Secure JV partners.** To find potential joint-venture partners, get on the phone, send e-mails, make lunch appointments, and attend industry conferences and events. Remember: Your potential partners will always want to know "What can you do for me?" If you project an "I'm willing to give more than I get" attitude, you will have a much easier time. Consider the following points in every JV deal:
   - The costs and the risks
   - How the costs and the risks will be shared
   - Specific goals and objectives
   - Product and company synergies
   - How goals and objectives will be achieved, and which parties will be responsible for each
   - An approximate timeframe and a clear exit strategy
   - How to continue to cultivate and develop the relationship with your partner

8. **Slice and dice your copy.** The hard work is done; your marketing copy is finished. The copy may be 12 to 24 pages long, and—with some minor changes—you should be able to use it for a direct-mail sales letter, a dedicated e-mail blast, and a landing page on your web site.

   You can send the same copy to in-house and outside lists with little more than a salutation change. You should be able to use the headline for your PPC ads, and the headline and lead for your text ads. If you are planning an outbound telemarketing campaign, you should have the makings of a script, too, in that long copy.

9. **Tech talk.** Understanding operational issues from a technical perspective will give you a better sense of the constraints and possibilities for implementing marketing ideas. However, never let technology dictate your marketing. Instead, it should support

the needs of your campaign. But make sure your tech people understand your goals and have all the information they need to serve you better.

10. **Measure, track, and analyze.** None of the above steps will do much good if you're not keeping metrics on your progress. If you are not tracking and analyzing, you are simply wasting time and money. Your online marketing efforts can offer you almost immediate feedback. And if you've done your testing properly, you can roll out instantly with your winner, while continuing to test different elements that can bring in more bottom-line dollars.

Here are some definitions and formulas for critical online and offline marketing metrics:

- **CPA (cost per acquisition).** Your cost divided by the number of orders (sales). This calculation will help determine how much money it costs to acquire a customer.
- **CPL (cost per lead).** The cost divided by the number of leads (e-mail addresses). This calculation will help you determine how much money it costs you to acquire a lead.
- **CPM (cost per thousand).** The charge per thousand for direct-mail names or banner impressions.
- **ROI (return on investment).** Total revenues divided by cost. This calculation will help you determine how much money you are making or losing (or if you're breaking even) on your advertising campaigns.
- **CTR (click-thru rate).** Total clicks divided by impressions. This tells you the rate at which people who viewed your ad clicked on it to follow the link, expressed as a percentage.
- **Open rate.** How many people opened your e-mail divided by the number of e-mails sent. This calculation will let you see if your e-mails are getting opened.
- **Bounce rate.** How many e-mails were returned divided by the number of e-mails sent. The bounce rate is important to measure the credibility of a list.

SHOW ME THE MONEY

Throughout this book, we have discussed many different channels of marketing. We don't expect you to use all of them all the time. The idea is for you to know what your options are. Test different channels and different channel combinations, and roll out with what is most effective for you and your business.

Do not, however, make the mistake of thinking that if a specific channel does not meet your campaign ROI, you should disregard it.

Take a look at Table 15.1. In this example, you are selling your product for $100. You had $85,000 to spend on marketing, and your goal was to make $1.25 for every dollar you spent (an ROI of 125 percent).

You had tremendous success with your online efforts—your endorsed e-mails, banner ads, and PPC campaigns.

Your teleconference yielded a 90 percent ROI and lost $500.

And your direct-mail campaign produced only an 80 percent ROI, losing a whopping $10,000.

Because two of your five channels lost $10,500, are you going to cut them from your multi-channel campaign? Of course not. Those two channels brought in nearly 42 percent of your customers . . . customers you now have the opportunity to bond with and sell more products to. It has been our experience that customers who come in through the mail have a higher lifetime value. This means that the 400 customers from your direct-mail campaign will most likely be your best long-term customers. On top of this, you met your goal of 125 percent ROI on your campaign. So there's no reason to cut these two channels.

TABLE 15.1 Channel and ROI Amount

Channel	Cost	Revenue	# of Orders	ROI
Endorsed e-mail	$10,000	$30,000	300	300 percent
Banner ads	$10,000	$16,000	160	160 percent
PPC	$10,000	$15,700	157	157 percent
Teleconference	$5,000	$4,500	45	90 percent
Direct mail	$50,000	40,000	400	80 percent
Total	$85,000	$106,200	1,062	124.9 percent

AN OLD-SCHOOL RETAILER GETS A MULTI-CHANNEL MAKEOVER

When you think of cutting-edge multi-channel marketers, retail giant and mall stalwart JC Penney probably doesn't come to mind.

But in recent years, the company has used a multi-channel approach. They encourage in-store customers in their baby department to shop online (where they have a larger selection) by highlighting their web site in display signs. When they launch new store brands or private-label products, they publicize them on micro-sites (small web sites dedicated to one particular product) through print media and e-mail, as well as in-store ads.

They are also going after younger customers through integrated multi-channel campaigns using web videos, web sites featuring fashion tips, contests in which kids compete to create the best back-to-school look, in-store promotions, print ads in teen magazines encouraging readers to enter the contest, as well as viral and "guerilla" marketing efforts.

And the results have been promising. Referral sales on baby items from stores to the JC Penney web site (www.JCP.com) went up 107 percent at the locations where the concept was tested. There was a 30 percent increase in Internet and phone sales across the board at those test stores, as well.

This is good news for JC Penney. Their Internet sales represent $1.3 billion in sales per year, and is their fastest growing channel. And the company considers their web site key to capturing customers who didn't find what they were looking for in the brick-and-mortar store. To this end, the company also makes it easy for store employees to look up the availability of items online.

At the same time, JC Penney maintains its traditional direct-mail effort: the hefty catalog. Although circulation has dropped, catalog sales still bring in more than $1 billion a year.

As you can see, JC Penney has embraced the multi-channel approach. It can work in almost any industry, with the elements used dictated by the type of product, the type of company, and where the company's customers shop.

Source: Chantal Todé, "JCP.com is linchpin in JCPenney's multi-channel strategy," DMNews, July 26, 2007.

The channels you use in your advertising campaigns will produce varying results. The idea is to subsidize some channels with the channels that have greater ROIs, in order to bring in additional customers who will make future purchases from you.

GET STARTED—NOW

Yes, you may already be making money by using only one marketing channel. But think of the potential revenue and prospective customers you could be missing—all because you are stuck exploring only one small piece of your market. If you're using only one channel, you are most likely leaving millions in potential revenue behind.

To grow your company, your customer base, and your profits, start expanding your marketing efforts to different channels. And don't wait until next quarter or next year. Get started today. As we've discussed, it can take little more than a few minutes to get started in some of these channels. Throw up a couple of PPC ads . . . call up a competitor and suggest that you do a mailing to his list . . . have lunch with an industry expert, and ask if she'd be interested in doing a joint venture. . . .

As soon as you close this book, talk to your publisher, your marketing director, or your marketing team about which channels you should be using. Then, start testing your new, expanded, multi-channel marketing campaign right away.

Your company—and your bank account—are sure to thank you.

CONCLUSION

SMOKING AT JOE'S

By Michael Masterson

About two blocks from our office in Delray Beach, Florida, is a cigar shop called Cigar Connoisseur. Actually, it's much more than a cigar shop. It's a little bit of heaven for stressed-out executives, overworked tradesmen, and underappreciated high school teachers. It has a marble-topped bar with eight stools, a seating area with seven comfortable leather chairs, two café tables, and an outside patio that people use when it gets too crowded inside.

Which it does ... often. It's getting busier every week.

The owner, Joe Fiori, is a big man who wears jeans, Italian shoes, and very expensive watches. He started his first cigar shop in Wellington, Florida, about an hour northwest of here. That store became successful quickly, so he let his partner run it and opened up this one.

Everybody likes Joe. And it's not just because he makes you feel at home. Cigar Connoisseur is the ultimate cigar haven. It's stocked with every product and amenity a cigar smoker could hope for: a cozy environment, a great selection of wine and beer, world-class espresso, and a walk-in humidor that is as good as any in South Florida.

Cigar Connoisseur is also a place where you can listen to jazz on Friday evenings or attend a cigar or wine sampling on Saturday night. There is always some interesting event taking place at this little shop, and as a valued customer you are always invited. Cigar Connoisseur provides its customers with a pleasing combination of homey comfort and casino-styled entertainment on a small scale. And, yes, you can smoke inside.

That's what I'm doing right now. Smoking a Padron Anniversario at the bar and typing out this final section of the book, looking for a way to sum up everything we've been talking about. Although many of the examples we used were from the information publishing industry, the principles and practices we showed you apply to almost any business. Even to a little retail business like Joe's.

Cigar Connoisseur's impressive growth is directly attributable to Joe's belief in multi-channel marketing. A short conversation with him about how he started and grew his stores makes that very clear.

Joe executes a five-channel marketing program that combines joint-venture deals, radio and television advertising, and direct print and event marketing.

He buys space ads in upscale local magazines that offer him the chance to publish advertorials alongside the ads. When he launched each one of his stores, those ads promoted the grand opening as a special event featuring professional models, hand-rolled cigars, special discounts, and bonuses to those who came early. Then he backed up those print ads with local television and radio coverage that referred prospects to a web site that gave more details about the event and provided plenty of promises and benefits for coming on down to the opening.

Joe is well aware that he can get good (i.e., much better than advertised) rates on media buys. To track the results of his advertising, he directs people who respond to his various marketing efforts to separate online homepages, and uses that feedback to determine which time slots and media (stations and channels) work best.

When new customers arrive at his shop, Joe and his staff collect names and addresses and transfer them to a database that he subsequently uses to mail out promotions about upcoming special events and offers. (What he hasn't been doing so far is collecting their e-mail addresses. But I'll get to that in a minute.)

As for joint ventures, he partners with cigar manufacturers to give his customers great deals on cigars. And he teams up with luxury goods producers, as well as local businesses, to cross-promote products and services.

In the South Florida area, there are hundreds of cigar shops servicing local communities. Most of them are eking out a living. Many open

---

CUSTOMER SERVICE JOE-STYLE

One evening last year, as Joe was closing the store, a car drove up and a man jumped out.

"Is it too late to buy a cigar?" he asked.

"It's never too late," Joe said. He unlocked the door and let the guy in.

"What's that you're smoking?" the man asked.

"It's a Perdomo Silvio maduro," Joe said.

"Good?"

"Yes it is."

The man bought one. It was a $25 sale. He lit it up on the spot.

"Take your time," Joe said. "Enjoy it."

Joe lit up another cigar and sat down with the man and talked. Turns out he was a newcomer to town. Joe gave him the lay of the land, recommended restaurants, and asked him about his interests—golf, wine, work, and cigars.

"This is a damn good cigar, Joe," the stranger said. "Got any boxes?"

As it happened, a shipment had just been delivered. Joe had six boxes in the humidor. Joe's new customer took all six. Total sale: more than six thousand dollars.

"He's been a great customer ever since," Joe says. "Imagine if I had turned him away. How dumb a move would that have been?"

---

and close within two years—the usual longevity for start-up retail enterprises. But a few do very well. And Joe's two shops are at the top of the list.

Ask Joe what the secret to his success is and he'll tell you: "Success in business is really very simple. Get new customers in by smart marketing. And keep existing customers coming back by great customer service."

PLAN FOR THE FUTURE

Joe is semiretired. He is living the entrepreneurial dream—making a great living doing what he would be happy to do for free. He doesn't need to open up any more cigar shops, but he probably will if he can find capable people to run them. To continue his impressive success, he needs to keep on doing exactly what he's been doing so far—developing new customers and then optimizing them with a coordinated multi-channel marketing approach.

The first rule of successful multi-channel marketing is to continue with what is already working—and in Joe's case, the list of what's working is impressive:

- Joint-venture marketing
- Event marketing
- Local radio advertising
- Local television advertising
- Direct-print advertising
- Direct mail to existing customers

Joe is already doing a great job. His business offers a unique and attractive product. His customer service is top notch. And his growth and marketing strategies have been very successful.

If I were advising Joe (not that he needs my advice), I'd recommend that he expand on his existing channels, and then add a few new channels to his already well-developed multi-channel marketing platform. He could probably rule out two channels that don't make sense for a local, retail business: teleconferencing and social media marketing. But he should certainly explore telemarketing, direct e-mail marketing, and search engine marketing.

JOE'S EXISTING CHANNELS

Joint-venture marketing: Joe is an expert at using joint ventures to add value to both sides of his business: marketing and customer service. He should continue to make deals with cigar companies that are offering specials that would appeal to his customers. He should also continue to cross-market luxury goods that might interest his customers. These would include fine watches, wines, and other upscale products typically featured in cigar magazines.

Joe has had success promoting local businesses that are outside the normal scope of cigar magazine advertising. These include the Delray Beach film festival, a new upscale men's barber, and a car detailing service. One very successful event he hosted this year involved a local spa. He arranged to have massage therapists from the spa give free shoulder rubs to his customers—and the house was packed. Joe's customers enjoyed it. Joe sold lots of products. And the spa handed out free passes to qualified potential customers.

Event marketing: Again, this is a marketing channel Joe has nearly perfected. Right now, as I sit here in Cigar Connoisseur, Joe is advertising no fewer than three upcoming cigar promotions featuring live music, food, raffles (with prizes that include free trips to the Dominican Republic—another joint-venture relationship), professional models, and "great memories." Also on the calendar is "Hookah Night," featuring Middle Eastern music and a belly dancer.

Local television and radio advertising: Joe should continue placing short-form ads on local television and radio. These would promote his special events and special offers. Because the commercials would be event-specific, he would know which media worked (i.e., brought in enough new customers to pay for the advertising), and which didn't.

Joe could compare the cost of each ad to the number of customers it brought in, multiplied by the estimated lifetime value of each. If, for example, a particular commercial cost him $1,600 and brought in eight people, he would be in the money so long as the average lifetime value of a customer is worth more than $200 to him. If Joe wanted to be conservative in rolling out with television and radio, he would cut the lifetime value in half for the purposes of his calculations. So, in this case, he'd need to bring in 16 customers from a particular ad before it would make sense to place another one with the same station.

Direct-print advertising: Joe would use that same arithmetic to roll out his direct-print advertising. To polish his existing programs, I'd advise him to read Chapter 8 of this book, and then allocate a reasonable budget (a week's worth of sales would be reasonable) toward testing a variety of offers and copy approaches.

Direct-mail marketing: Currently, Joe uses the post office to notify customers of special events. For each event, he prints postcards that he sends to the mailing list he's been compiling when customers make their first purchase in one of his stores. He should train his assistants to be vigilant about getting those addresses. These are potentially very valuable names (as Joe well knows). He should be sure he is getting every name possible.

He should also consider expanding his direct-mail efforts to generate new customers. It would be relatively easy for him to rent zip code-specific mailing lists and target promotions to affluent neighborhoods where his ideal prospects live. I'd also advise Joe to test other formats in addition to postcards. The efficiency of a postcard may be hard to beat, but he won't know that until he tries other options. One format that begs to be tested is a personalized invitation that offers new prospects a can't-say-no opportunity to enjoy his store.

NEW CHANNELS FOR JOE TO EXPLORE

Although Joe has implemented multiple channels, there are other marketing avenues that he can explore to make more money with his business.

Telemarketing: Although I would not usually recommend telemarketing for a retail business, Joe's success in creating a friendly, at-home atmosphere means that his customers would be very responsive to a phone call now and then. With the right easy-going, low-key pitch, Joe and his assistants could bring his best customers to special events in greater numbers than he has likely achieved by any other means.

Direct e-mail marketing: This is a big opportunity for Joe. With his base of loyal customers, and given all the events and special promotions he runs, it would be easy for him to collect hundreds, if not thousands, of e-mail addresses. He could then publish a weekly "Newsletter from Joe," in which he might talk about cigar industry news, recount stories he's heard from customers, and talk about specials that are coming up at Cigar Connoisseur. Joe wouldn't need to hire anyone to write his newsletter. He's a natural. I'd advise him to write about whatever interests him, in his own words. And I'd recommend that he write regularly about the two business subjects he believes in most: marketing and customer service.

His marketing pieces would include editorial pieces that "sell" his core franchise—the pleasure of smoking good cigars and the fun of using all the accessories that cigar smokers buy. That would mean stories about new cigars that Joe likes, old cigars he still favors, cutters, lighters, ashtrays, humidors, and more. When a new product comes in, Joe should try it out. And if it meets his high standards, he should let his customers know about it, with enthusiasm and in detail.

Joe's customer service pieces would include announcements about new products and services (which are, after all, products and services that his customers desire), as well as announcements about upcoming events (e.g., a special cigar or wine sampling where gifts are being given away), new policies (e.g., a free sampler pack of cigars for each box of cigars bought), and special services for new or existing customers.

I might even suggest that Joe create a VIP club of some sort, and tie it into the program he now has that includes a special lockbox for customers to store their cigars, a free magazine subscription, special discounts, and advance purchase opportunities.

What could Joe expect from adding such a comprehensive direct e-mail channel to his existing marketing and customer service efforts? Plenty. Think of it this way: Currently, Joe's customers find out about most of these great benefits (opportunities to spend) when they walk into his store and talk to him or one of his assistants. But with an e-mail marketing program, Joe would be in charge. He wouldn't have to wait for them to walk into his store. He could talk to them as often as he liked.

Joe estimates that his average customer comes into one of his stores eight times a month. That is 96 times a year that he has the chance to stimulate additional sales from them. By adding a direct e-mail channel to his efforts, Joe could contact them every day if he wanted to. What would happen to his sales if he increased his sales presentations by 280 percent? They'd skyrocket!

My bet: Joe's sales will increase by 50 percent to 100 percent in his first year of direct e-mail marketing—and his cost would be a few hundred dollars plus the half-hour a day he would spend writing to his customers.

Search engine marketing. Joe's new direct e-mail channel would have a huge impact on increasing the lifetime value of every customer that came into his store. Implementing an effective search engine marketing program would dramatically increase the number of new customers that would come through that door.

Search engine marketing is a great way to get prospective customers to "land" on your web site. As MaryEllen and I pointed out in Chapter 5, it is a way of drumming up business that might otherwise never take place. Search engine marketing includes four key techniques or operations:

1. Link building
2. Tagging
3. Pay-per-click (PPC) marketing
4. RSS/Syndication

But . . . before Joe can take advantage of search engine marketing, he has to clear up a red flag on his web site (www .cigarconnoisseur.net). That red flag is Flash. It's a multimedia program that makes great-looking web sites, but the search engines can't read any text that is in Flash. Which means that any keywords on the Cigar Connoisseur web site will be wasted in terms of its ranking in search results.

So Joe's site managers should go back and do a redesign with a lot less Flash. Some Flash elements can be used, but any pertinent articles, links, and so on, should be in text and html. If a redesign is not possible, a quick fix could be for Joe to add a blog to his online presence that would be regularly updated with keyword-rich content.

To get the most response from his web site, Joe must make it engaging, informative, and sales-oriented. He will do this naturally by having the e-mails that he's writing and sending to his customers posted on the web site. In addition to that, he should hire a local search engine optimization (SEO) specialist to work with his copy through tagging and link building—something Joe's business can benefit from without a huge expenditure of time or money. Link building could be focused by trying to acquire links from local Chambers of Commerce, local clubs, Yellow Pages sites, and Google local listings, as well as local review sites such as Yelp.com.

He should also consider RSS and pay-per-click (PPC) marketing as his business expands. He will want to restrict these efforts to his local area since he is primarily a retail operation. But if the SEO expert he hires to do the link building and tagging is on his game, Joe can expect success in those areas as well.

THE ARITHMETIC OF JOE'S LONG-TERM MULTI-CHANNEL MARKETING PLAN

Legendary marketing expert Jay Abraham is famous for pointing out that there are only three ways to increase sales:

1. Increase the number of customers.
2. Increase the frequency of purchases.
3. Increase the amount of the average sale.

Creating a direct e-mail channel will increase both the frequency of purchases made in Joe's shops and his average sale. Improving the performance of his web site through search engine marketing and optimization will increase the number of new customers he gets every month.

Here's some math for Joe to consider. Assume that he currently services, on average, 100 customers per day. (These assumptions are invented. Joe's actual numbers are higher.) And assume, further, that each customer spends $30 per day. Joe could easily double both the number of customers he services every day and double (more likely quadruple) the amount they will spend per year.

Increasing his daily traffic by 100 customers a day means 600 more per week or 30,000 more per year. At $60 per purchase, that equals $1.8 million a year in extra sales, plus another $900,000 in added lifetime value for existing customers. That's a total of $2.7 million in sales per store. And because so much of that is the result of back-end marketing (which has a very high margin), Joe's yearly profits would go through the roof.

WRAPPING THINGS UP

MaryEllen began this book with a story about buying a home. I ended with a look at a retail business that sells cigars. In between, we gave you lots of examples from the information publishing industry (because that's what we know best), but we also provided dozens of examples from other types of businesses in many different industries.

The point is that the world of marketing in the twenty-first century is significantly and profoundly different than it was in the twentieth century. The big change happened in the late 1990s, and it has accelerated at warp speed ever since.

Today's advertising world is bigger, freer, and more fluid than it ever was. The Internet has made the entire world every marketer's oyster. It has made it possible to communicate with prospects and customers frequently and cheaply. Very cheaply. Because of that, nothing in marketing will ever be the same.

To be competitive today, we must embrace the sea change that technology has brought. We must accept the fact that we can't control what we once controlled, though we can reach farther and further than we ever could have in the past.

More specifically, we must implement a multi-channel approach to all of our marketing efforts, giving priority to our core selling competence but, at the same time, taking advantage of other marketing channels to expand our customer base and deepen the relationships we develop with our customers.

Computer-, satellite-, media-, and Internet-related technologies have changed the way people shop in the twenty-first century. It stands to reason that marketers have to adjust to those changes by changing the way they market. To be successful, you now have to be a smarter, stronger, and more agile marketer than your twentieth-century counterpart. Adopting a multi-channel approach to marketing today will guarantee you a successful tomorrow.

APPENDIX

———

EXAMPLES OF ADS

This appendix is intended to provide you with the full text of several ads and promotional sales letters listed in Chapters 3 and 13. Please refer to them as indicated when you come to those sections. Reading the full version of each ad is key to understanding the concepts discussed in each chapter.

THE ENDORSED AD

Below are the complete versions of two of the types of ads mentioned in Chapter 3: the squeeze page and the dedicated e-mail ad. As the chapter indicates, endorsed ads are the heart of direct e-mail marketing. The content and copy of endorsed ads can be leveraged and used in *all* of your other tactics and channels, including squeeze pages and dedicated e-mail ads.

The Squeeze Page

The ad in Figure A.1 is for *The Healing Prescription*, a product offered by Total Health Breakthroughs, a division of Early to Rise. This illustrates the "squeeze page" and can serve as a valuable model for you as you implement or improve your multi-channel marketing campaign. See Figure A.1 starting on page 237.

The Dedicated E-Mail Ad

Now that you have seen the squeezed version of the endorsed ad, Figure A.2 shows its longer and more detailed version—the dedicated e-mail ad. Although you saw an excerpt of this ad in Chapter 3, review the full version of this endorsed ad for *The Healing Prescription*, a product offered by Total Health Breakthroughs, a division of Early to Rise. See Figure A.2 starting on page 241.

THE EVENT AD

Before you begin the event checklist, which Chapter 13 describes, review these excerpts from promotions for three events put on by Early to Rise. We have reprinted approximately the first two pages of each sales letter in the Figures A.3 and A.4. We consider each of our events to be very valuable for our customers. We believe you will see why after you read the promotional copy below.

Figure A.3 is from our annual web site-building and Internet business coaching event, known as 5 Days in July. See Figure A.3 starting on page 259.

Figure A.4 shows a sales letter from a wealth-building retreat in Orlando, titled Profits in Paradise and featuring expert speakers from a variety of industries—including real estate, investments, and online business. See Figure A.4 starting on page 261.

The sales letter for our longest-running event, our annual Information Marketing Bootcamp, is shown in Figure A.5. It's one of our best-attended events: a one-stop shop for entrepreneurs looking for the easiest way to start a very profitable Internet business. See Figure A.5 starting on page 264.

FIGURE A.1

"6 months ago, I was constantly fatigued, overweight, and heading toward diabetes. Today, I'm healthy, energetic, and can fit into jeans I wore before I gave birth to three kids...."

Ex-Supermarket Employee Reveals the Secrets of How to Reprogram
Your Body's "Metabolic Code"
for Optimal Health

Record Numbers of Patients Avoid Cancer, Arthritis, Diabetes, Alzheimer's, and Other Devastating Illness ... for Decades ...

Dear Health Resources Reader,

Are you sick and tired of feeling sick and tired?

That's exactly the way I felt last year ... all the time.

I'm a 46-year-old mother of three young kids ages 3 to 9.

As the CEO of a $25 million publishing company, I juggle motherhood with a rewarding but stressful executive career.

So severe was my fatigue, every afternoon I had to close my office door and put my head on the desk in sheer exhaustion.

Being tired all the time made me irritable. I constantly fought with my husband ... blew my stack with my staff ... and snapped at my children all the time.

I was going to the gym for an hour every morning. But it didn't boost my energy. Worse, I had gained lots of weight ... and could not lose a pound.

Then one evening, I ate a dinner that resolved all my health problems -- and utterly changed my life forever.

It wasn't the food on the plate.

FIGURE A.1 *(Continued)*

It was one of my dinner companions, one of the country's foremost medical experts-- let's call him "JL" for now -- who listened attentively to my tales of woe as I complained how stressed, tired, and miserable I felt.

JL handed me a business card and told me: "Make an appointment to see me at my clinic. We can help you get better."

This clinic boasts an incredible track record of helping patients overcome insomnia -- chronic fatigue -- arthritis -- asthma -- obesity - cancer -- allergies -- diabetes -- high blood pressure -- osteoporosis -- and other debilitating and life-threatening conditions.

To my surprise, the clinic he sent me to wasn't the Mayo Clinic ... Mount Sinai ... Johns Hopkins ... or any other "famous" hospital.

Instead, it was my good fortune to be sent to his private clinic in Cincinnati, Ohio.

Saving Ryan's Life: Cracking the Healing Code

When I arrived there, I discovered that over 7,000 patients have already been treated at this clinic by JL and his team of medical experts.

My name is Mary Ellen Tribby, and I am the Executive Publisher of Early to Rise an online health, wealth and success newsletter reaching over 400,000 readers.

I'm writing to you today to tell you that JL's innovative approach to healing has changed my life for the better.

In fact, he has achieved results that patients and medical professionals alike are calling nothing short of miraculous:

David, a 56-year-old executive, had an enlarged prostate that was causing him to get up to urinate 3 or 4 times a night. He desperately wanted to avoid prostate surgery, which could potentially leave him impotent. The clinic treated him with bioactive compounds that blocked production of DHT, a hormone that causes the body to over-produce its normal amount of prostate cells. David shrank his prostate, avoided surgery, and can now get a peaceful night's sleep without waking to use the bathroom.

———————

Ryan came to the clinic as an 11-year old boy with recurring bone cancer metastasized in his lungs. His doctor had given up on him and told his parents he had less than a year to live. Today, at 18, he has not had a lung metastasis in 3 years, and is leading the normal life of a healthy teenage boy; recently, Ryan stopped by the clinic for a visit, bringing with him his first girlfriend.

———————

FIGURE A.1 *(Continued)*

AL, a middle-aged woman 100 pounds overweight was insulin resistant, pre-diabetic, and unable to control her food cravings. "After visiting the clinic, I feel in control of my body for the first time in a decade," says AL. Her cravings are gone. She has already lost 40 pounds and continues to shed weight each week.

SF, an 11-year old with Tourette Syndrome, had uncontrolled outbursts and tics over 50 times a day. After three neurologists failed to quell his symptoms, SF's parents were at a dead end. But after treatment at the clinic, SF leads a far happier life, his symptoms almost completely under control.

These and dozens of other stories like them are so compelling ... and the unique treatments at this clinic so thoroughly grounded in the revolutionary new science of *achieving optimal health by balancing human metabolism* ...

... that when faced with a potentially fatal illness myself (I was pre-diabetic, and my father had died from diabetes when I was in my early 30's), I got on a plane, flew to Ohio, and put myself in this medical team's hands.

I was so impressed by the treatment I received -- and the dramatic improvement in my health and well-being -- that I pledged I would use my "pull" as a publisher to bring these life-transforming medical breakthroughs to health-conscious readers like you.

You can review this special report absolutely risk-free and also receive a complimentary subscription to *Total Health Breakthroughs* --a twice a week health and wellness email newsletter offering alternative solutions for the mind, body and soul.

Please enter your first name and email address below to view the rest of this special report and to begin your free subscription to Total Health Breakthroughs.

Your First Name: [   ]

Your E-Mail: [   ]

FREE REPORT!

FIGURE A.1 *(Continued)*

We Respect Your <u>Privacy!</u>

We will never sell, rent, or otherwise abuse your e-mail address. It will be used solely for the purpose of sending you the Total Health Breakthroughs e-letter and occasional advertising letters. (We send these letters ourselves; we do not share your address or any information about you with the advertiser.) Should you wish to unsubscribe at any time, instructions on how to do so are included with every e-mail.

FIGURE A.2

FIGURE A.2 *(Continued)*

It was one of my dinner companions, one of the country's foremost medical experts--let's call him "JL" for now -- who listened attentively to my tales of woe as I complained how stressed, tired, and miserable I felt.

JL handed me a business card and told me: "Make an appointment to see me at my clinic. We can help you get better."

This clinic boasts an incredible track record of helping patients overcome insomnia -- chronic fatigue -- arthritis -- asthma -- obesity - cancer -- allergies -- diabetes -- high blood pressure -- osteoporosis -- and other debilitating and life-threatening conditions.

To my surprise, the clinic he sent me to wasn't the Mayo Clinic … Mount Sinai … Johns Hopkins … or any other "famous" hospital.

Instead, it was my good fortune to be sent to his private clinic in Cincinnati, Ohio.

Saving Ryan's Life: Cracking the Healing Code

When I arrived there, I discovered that over 7,000 patients have already been treated at this clinic by JL and his team of medical experts.

My name is MaryEllen Tribby, and I am the Executive Publisher of ETR's Total Health Breakthroughs.

I'm writing to you today to tell you that JL's innovative approach to healing has changed my life for the better.

In fact, he has achieved results that patients and medical professionals alike are calling nothing short of miraculous:

David, a 56-year-old executive, had an enlarged prostate that was causing him to get up to urinate 3 or 4 times a night. He desperately wanted to avoid prostate surgery, which could potentially leave him impotent. The clinic treated him with bioactive compounds that blocked production of DHT, a hormone that causes the body to over-produce its normal amount of prostate cells. David shrank his prostate, avoided surgery, and can now get a peaceful night's sleep without waking to use the bathroom.

Ryan came to the clinic as an 11-year old boy with recurring bone cancer metastasized in his lungs. His doctor had given up on him and told his parents he had less than a year to live. Today, at 18, he has not had a lung metastasis in 3 years, and is leading the normal life of a healthy teenage boy; recently, Ryan stopped by the clinic for a visit, bringing with him his first girlfriend.

FIGURE A.2 *(Continued)*

AL, a middle-aged woman 100 pounds overweight was insulin resistant, pre-diabetic, and unable to control her food cravings. "After visiting the clinic, I feel in control of my body for the first time in a decade," says AL. Her cravings are gone. She has already lost 40 pounds and continues to shed weight each week.

SF, an 11-year old with Tourette Syndrome, had uncontrolled outbursts and tics over 50 times a day. After three neurologists failed to quell his symptoms, SF's parents were at a dead end. But after treatment at the clinic, SF leads a far happier life, his symptoms almost completely under control.

These and dozens of other stories like them are so compelling ... and the unique treatments at this clinic so thoroughly grounded in the revolutionary new science of *achieving optimal health by balancing human metabolism* ...

... that when faced with a potentially fatal illness myself (I was pre-diabetic, and my father had died from diabetes when I was in my early 30's), I got on a plane, flew to Ohio, and put myself in this medical team's hands.

I was so impressed by the treatment I received -- and the dramatic improvement in my health and well-being -- that I pledged I would use my "pull" as a publisher to bring these life-transforming medical breakthroughs to our loyal THB readers.

I wined and dined JL ... twisted his arm considerably ... and now, I want to send you the first issue of his new monthly advisory, *The Healing Prescription* -- the most important health publication you will read this year.

"Gee, Mom, you're not so cranky anymore..."

As a result of JL's innovative *metabolism-based approach* to medicine, I not only avoided the disease that took my father's life while I was young, but I am healthier -- and feel better -- than I have in years.

My insomnia, from which I suffered every night of my life for the past few years, is gone. I'm out like a light within minutes of my head hitting the pillow ... and sleep like a baby throughout the night.

My weight loss is in the double-digits, and I am wearing jeans I wore before I had my kids.

Best of all, I have my old drive and vitality back! I am at my desk at 6:30 am full of energy and ready to face the day. After I put in my usual 10 to 11-hour day running my business, I can enjoy going to my kids' sports games. Recently my oldest daughter said, "Gee, Mom, you're not so cranky anymore!"

FIGURE A.2 *(Continued)*

As I watch the games, I look around me, proud in the knowledge that I accomplish more each day than most of the other moms there who are 15 years younger than me.

My trip to the clinic in Cincinnati put me back on the road to health and wellness, absolutely changing my life and my future, so I'll be able to live my dream: being alive and well to babysit for my grandchildren when they come -- something my dad never lived to see.

Now, I want to show you how to benefit from JL's latest health breakthroughs and natural therapies -- and you won't even have to fly to Ohio like I did to learn about them!

But first, let me introduce you to the passionate and brilliant doctor who brought me back from illness and fatigue to health and vitality....

"America's best-kept health secret"

"JL" is Dr. James LaValle, a remarkable healer who started his career working as a pharmacist at an Ohio supermarket.

It was there -- in a pharmacy surrounded by food -- that James first began to master his revolutionary nutritional approach to correcting deficiencies in human metabolism.

Today, he is a Doctor of Naturopathic Medicine, board-certified clinical nutritionist, and the Founder of the LaValle Metabolic Institute (LMI) -- perhaps the nation's premiere integrative health institution for treatment of diabetes … insulin resistance … cancer … allergies … insomnia … and a host of other conditions triggered by metabolic imbalances.

At LMI, James LaValle and his staff of medical doctors, licensed dieticians, nurses, and therapists specialize in treating, curing, and preventing illness by *rebalancing the patient's metabolism.*

During my initial examination, Dr. LaValle amazed me by repeating everything I had told him about my health history at our dinner meeting. (I wish my other doctors had listened half as well when I was in their exam rooms!)

He then began the process of making me well with a rigorous assessment of my metabolism, physical condition, and blood chemistry.

My test results showed that 40 out of 41 of my readings, including blood sugar and key hormones, were "off the chart" and outside of normal range. The results frankly shocked me. For example, as a Floridian, I spent quite of time in the sun with my kids in the pool and on the playground. Yet my tests showed that my vitamin D levels--the vitamins you get from sunlight--were shockingly *low*!

Getting better was a gradual process that combined changes in eating habits, an exercise

FIGURE A.2 *(Continued)*

routine, and the replenishments of certain bioactive compounds in my blood stream through diet and supplementation.

But feeling positive, tangible results from my treatment by Dr. LaValle and his team *wasn't* gradual: within 24 hours of beginning the prescribed regimen, I felt noticeably better, less tired, and more energetic.

And that's just the beginning. Within six weeks my life had completely turned around. I was hopping out of bed before dawn, ready and raring to go. At the office I was bursting with energy … and breezing through tasks in half the time they'd taken me earlier.

Then came the real payoff: Early dinners at home with my family, and still plenty of time for reading with my children or simply relaxing with my husband.

When I realized the power of this change in my life, that's when I pledged to tell everyone I knew about Dr. LaValle and his revolutionary metabolic approach to health improvement.

So in this letter, I want to show how Dr. LaValle -- and his team at the LaValle Metabolic Institute -- can guide YOU on the "metabolic path" to optimal health … without ever leaving the comfort of your home!

Cracks the "metabolic code" for optimal health

"The chemical reactions of metabolism take the food we eat and transform it into the fuels and building blocks for our bodies," explains Dr. LaValle.

These chemical reactions are necessary for providing energy for activities such as movement and thinking … and for organ functions (e.g., digestion) and building new tissue.

"Your metabolic code is your personal body chemistry," says Dr. LaValle. "**Virtually all health problems are caused by a metabolic imbalance resulting in undesired changes in body chemistry**."

But it's reassuring to know that if your metabolism is off-kilter, there are many measures that can be taken to restore balance among the metabolic pathways within the body.

You *don't* have to settle for a medical fate preset by genetics. By modifying your diet, medications, lifestyle, exercise habits, and with nutritional supplementation, your health is largely within *your* control.

Dr. LaValle's approach to health is sensible, straightforward, and has worked for me and thousands of his patients and readers:

FIGURE A.2 *(Continued)*

- Through an extensive assessment, Dr. LaValle **helps you pinpoint the metabolic imbalances that are affecting your health today** and setting you up for future problems. (The metabolic changes leading to cancer, diabetes, arthritis, and other serious disease often begin to make themselves known *8 full years or more* before they actually cause you to be ill. By catching and correcting them now, you can bypass serious illness and live a long, disease-free life.)

- Dr. LaValle and his team then **recommend lifestyle and dietary changes, along with supplementation to correct metabolic deficiencies and optimize body chemistry**. These recommendations often include nutritional supplements many doctors in the U.S. don't even know about (but are widely used in other countries) -- many of them clinically tested at the LaValle Metabolic Institute years before you hear about them.

- By making the prescribed changes, you **get your body chemistry back on track** … make pain and other symptoms vanish … restore energy … lose weight … overcome insomnia and depression … lower cholesterol … improve blood sugar levels … and ensure that you don't become sick years down the road.

And now, reading Dr. LaValle's monthly health letter *The Healing Prescription* can help you benefit from his cutting edge metabolic research -- *without ever* making the trip to Ohio for an examination at Dr. LaValle's private clinic.

Order Now!

Why doctors go to classes taught by this ex-supermarket employee

James LaValle, R.Ph., CCN, MS, ND, the founder of the LaValle Metabolic Institute, has more than 20 years of clinical practice experience in natural and integrative therapeutics and functional metabolism.

He is a licensed pharmacist, board-certified clinical nutritionist, diplomate in homeopathic medicine and pharmacy, and doctor of naturopathic medicine.

Dr. LaValle began his lifelong study of human metabolism -- and his career of helping people achieve optimal health by correcting metabolic deficiencies -- largely by accident.

Trained as a traditional pharmacist, his first job in pharmacy was working the midnight shift at the drug counter for Kroger's supermarket.

The store was located in a poor neighborhood. Many of Jim's customers were not highly educated, and as a consequence, did not know how to prepare nutritionally balanced meals.

FIGURE A.2   *(Continued)*

When I was visiting with him, Jim told me an interesting story that I want to share with you now....

One day "Loretta," a middle-aged woman, came to his pharmacy counter to pick up her diabetic medication.

"I took one look in her shopping cart and saw instantly that almost every food she was buying was exactly the kind of stuff a diabetic *shouldn't eat* -- corn syrup, foods loaded with trans-fat, white flour, white sugar, soda, fruit juice, cookies, potato chips, the fattiest cuts of meat -- you name it," says Dr. LaValle.

Out of concern for her health, James took Loretta around the store, made her put back the bad foods she had chosen, and replaced them with foods that would help control her insulin and blood sugar levels. Now her cart was filled with healthy, wholesome foods.

As word of this "healing pharmacist" got around, Loretta's friends began visiting the supermarket, asking James for nutritional and dietary advice.

To his delight, James discovered that teaching people how to live a healthy lifestyle was more satisfying than simply dispensing prescription medication. From this initial interaction he developed a food tagging system that empowered thousands of people with diabetes and cardiovascular disease to choose healthier foods. Before long he was being asked to spend more time advising shoppers.

How a classically-trained pharmacist discovered a much better way to combat illness and stay healthy

"My family had a horrible history of diabetes," says James LaValle. His grandmother died of diabetes, blind and with her toes gone. His father had also become diabetic along with all of his brothers. "I didn't want to follow in their footsteps."

Jim had been sickly in childhood with severe allergies. As a young man in college, Jim started experiencing his own problems with blood sugar regulation: he had severe hypoglycemia, a condition that increases your risk of becoming diabetic.

So Jim took a different approach. A family member had told him about a doctor in his area who used nutrition to address health issues.

With this doctor's help, changes in lifestyle and diet, plus the use of nutritional supplements, Jim stopped his blood sugar levels from fluctuating, and has never become diabetic, and never suffered from hypoglycemia again.

This experience prompted James to take the knowledge gained from pharmacy and apply it to learning more about adjusting human metabolism through diet, nutritional supplements, and

FIGURE A.2   *(Continued)*

exercise.

He slowly figured out why, even though he was not overweight, his body chemistry had become off-kilter, and how the natural products had worked to rebalance that chemistry.

It was the beginning of his lifelong study of how traditional medicine and nutritional therapy could be combined to achieve a greater effect on the human metabolism than either individually.

Pharmacists are taught about the biochemistry of the body and how drugs and natural products work to change that chemistry. So as a trained pharmacist, James already knew that many drugs on the market are actually derived from natural products, and that pharmacy actually had roots in natural substances.

His pharmaceutical studies, combined with his experiences of personal illness during childhood and young adulthood, had set the stage to change his destiny and become a pioneer in natural metabolism-based healing....

Companies like CVS, Cardinal Health, the Rite Aid Vitamin Institute, and Long's Drug Chain started asking James to write guides on natural health for their pharmacists and customers. Health magazines and book publishers contracted with him to write articles and books for them on natural therapies and wellness. Roche and Bayer asked James to consult with them on the formulation of new lines of natural health products.

Known to his colleagues as "the pharmacist's pharmacist," James LaValle is the one health care practitioner even medical doctors turn to when they get sick or need advice. He has taught metabolic medicine at the University of Cincinnati's Colleges of Pharmacy and Medicine. More than a thousand health care professionals have attended his classes and lectures to learn the secrets of improving health through better body chemistry.

In the 1980s, Dr. LaValle became a full-time practitioner specializing in natural therapies, and has never looked back. Today, the LaValle Metabolic Institute is one of the largest integrative medicine practices in the country, with a strong track record of success.

Dr. LaValle is a member of the American College of Clinical Pharmacy and was named one of the 50 most influential pharmacists in the U.S. by *American Druggist* magazine. He is the author of over a dozen books including *Cracking the Metabolic Code: 9 Keys to Optimal Health* and *The Nutritional Cost of Drugs.*

Dr. LaValle is only one of nine people in the world chosen as a Founding Board Member of the Dietary Supplement Education Alliance. In addition, he was the nutrition expert on "Bodyshaping," the #1 fitness program on ESPN. He has also appeared as a guest on hundreds of radio and TV shows.

Benefit from tomorrow's medical breakthroughs TODAY

The LaValle Metabolic Institute is not just a clinic. It is also a cutting-edge research facility in metabolic pharmacology and nutrition.

FIGURE A.2 *(Continued)*

"We are often chosen as a clinical test site for new dietary supplements," says Dr. LaValle. "That way, we know about new nutritional therapies for correcting metabolic deficiencies that cause disease--sometimes years ahead of other health care practitioners."

One of the most exciting of these nutritional therapies is a branded supplement that Dr. LaValle has prescribed for hundreds of his patients, including me. And here's why....

If you have trouble sleeping at night, one of the reasons could be excessive stress in your life -- from stress at work, to problems at home, to worries about money and health. All of these can contribute to your insomnia.

Chronic stress over-stimulates your brain, making it difficult for your mental functions to "quiet down" at night when it's time for sleep.

You know the feeling: you either can't fall asleep at night because you're thinking about work or other problems. Or, you fall asleep but wake up in the middle of the night with your mind racing.

But stress is not just mental and emotional. It can affect your very physiology... depleting key neurotransmitters, leading to disturbed sleep patterns and uncontrollable cravings -- which can cause changes in growth hormone production, blood sugar imbalances, and can compromise your immune system.

The under-publicized supplement that Dr. LaValle uses to help reduce stress and restore deep, restful sleep contains a unique blend of patented plant extracts, some of which have been used as sedatives in traditional Chinese medicine for more than 2,000 years.

In a clinical study with 773 patients, 90% said this unique bioactive compound helped them reduce fatigue caused by lack of sleep -- and 93% said it helped them relax. I've been taking this phytonutrient since Dr. LaValle recommended it; I don't wake at night any more, and I fall asleep promptly after going to bed.

"Felt and looked better in 2 to 3 weeks"

Another natural health breakthrough Dr. LaValle was recommending to patients two years before it was on the market in the U.S. is a little-known dietary supplement made in Hungary from fermented wheat germ -- and approved as a medical food in Europe.

A huge body of clinical data -- including more than 100 published papers -- overwhelmingly demonstrates the benefits of taking fermented wheat germ for cancer patients and for those with autoimmune disorders.

The active ingredient in the fermented wheat germ slows the uptake of sugar in cancer cells, effectively starving the tumor. It also helps to prevent cancer cells from reproducing out of control.

FIGURE A.2 *(Continued)*

In addition, this nutrient can even improve the efficacy and reduce the side-effects of chemotherapy. Dr. LaValle recommended it for Ryan, his 11-year-old cancer patient I told you about earlier.

"Two to three weeks after beginning the program, Ryan felt and looked better than he had in the previous year," says Ryan's dad. "He continues his tremendous physical recovery with the help and support of James LaValle and his staff at the LaValle Metabolic Institute."

Like the many patients quoted above -- and thousands more -- I made the journey from illness to health at the LaValle Metabolic Institute.

Now, I want to extend to you the same opportunity to benefit from the pioneering therapies innovated at the LaValle Metabolic Institute … even if you can't make the trip to the clinic yourself … by accepting my offer to join us as a Charter Member to ….

..The Healing Prescription :
The Official Health Alert of the LaValle Metabolic Institute

Today we are proud to announce we're going to bring Dr. LaValle's natural therapies for achieving optimal health to YOU -- **in the privacy of your own home** -- with *The Healing Prescription*: *the Official Health Advisory of the LaValle Metabolic Institute.*

Each month, *The Healing Prescription* brings you the latest research findings … breakthroughs in metabolic therapy … new supplements … weight-loss programs … healthful recipes … case studies … and other ideas for achieving optimal health -- direct from the LaValle Metabolic Institute.

Here's just a sampling of what you get as a Charter Member:

- **Can eating a big meal boost your libido -- or even make you horny? The surprising connection between food and sex.**

- Four natural stress busters. Take these 4 dietary supplements tonight -- and feel more relaxed and mentally sharp starting tomorrow. Also helps eliminate food cravings, promote weight loss, prevent insomnia, and get rid of headaches.

- **Achieve optimal cardiovascular fitness by exercising *less*, not longer. Quick and easy 5-step exercise routine takes just 12 minutes a day.**

- Two foods you should remove from your diet today to avoid joint pain, fatigue, and a host of other health concerns.

- **The 3 biggest lies about ab exercises … and what you really need to do to get a six-pack stomach.**

FIGURE A.2 *(Continued)*

- This little-known herb can help asthma sufferers breathe easier … *without* an inhaler.

- **Why drinking too much cola can cause severe joint pain -- and even bone loss.**

- These 5 amazingly effective natural remedies can clear up your children's ear infections faster than they can say, "Mommy and daddy, my ear hurts!"

- **Diagnosed with fibromyalgia? 12 natural remedies that can relieve tenderness, stiffness, aches, pains, and other symptoms.**

- Throw away your Band-Aids! A common vitamin you find in grapefruit can speed your recovery after injury -- and help wounds heal up to 50% faster.

- **Get rid of hot flashes, depression, vaginal dryness, and loss of libido with 5 safe, all-natural alternatives to hormone replacement therapy (HRT).**

- Consumer rip-off alert: the awful truth about canola oil … energy bars … farm-raised salmon … soy … frozen yogurt … and other popular "health foods" that are anything but.

- **Why diet soda makes you fat -- even though most diet sodas contain no sugar and no calories.**

- This best-selling blood pressure medication can deplete your magnesium, zinc, sodium, and potassium to dangerously low levels. If you must take it, here's what you should do to counter-balance drug-induced nutrient depletion.

- **Can drinking a glass of ordinary store-bought cranberry juice really clear up a serious urinary tract infection? The answer will surprise you!**

- The best foods to eat for reducing breast cancer risk … despite the AMA's advice to the contrary.

- **A simple change in diet dramatically reduces your risk of losing vision due to age-related macular degeneration.**

- 4 ways to relieve urinary problems and shrink an enlarged prostate -- without prescription drugs, radiation, or risky surgery.

- **The dangers of taking antacids to relieve heartburn -- and why you should not.**

- St. John's Wort can be an adequate alternative to Prozac for mild depression. But if your serotonin levels are low, try this natural remedy instead. Plus: beat the

FIGURE A.2 *(Continued)*

winter blues with this special light bulb (ordinary incandescent bulbs don't work).

- **The 4 early warning signs of serious magnesium deficiency … and what to do about each.**

- One out of five women who fractures her hip dies from complications within 90 days. Here are 3 bioactive compounds that can increase bone density -- and lower your risk of fracture from a fall.

- **This delicious beverage is proven to increase longevity in scientific studies. Hint: it's NOT green tea.**

- Strengthen your immune system with this natural, painless colon cleanser. You take it orally at home -- no unpleasant or invasive procedures required.

- **5 steps to reducing the food cravings and hunger pangs that make you put on weight.**

- The little-known yet extremely common vitamin deficiency that's more of a risk factor in deaths from ischemic heart disease than smoking, high blood pressure, or even high cholesterol levels. Available at the supermarket, a pill a day can stop atherosclerosis in its tracks.

- **The 10 common causes of insomnia and other sleep problems … and 9 proven ways to overcome them … and get a good night's rest.**

- Taking antibiotics can actually make you sicker. Here's how to get the full benefits of the antibiotics your doctor prescribes -- with none of the side effects.

- **Are anger and rage making you fat? 5 ways to gain control of your emotions -- and take off the pounds.**

- Your cells are absolutely dependent on coenzyme Q10 to produce energy. But taking any of these 35 common prescription drugs can cause angina, high blood pressure, stroke, and other illness brought on by CoQ10 depletion.

- **Is the diabetes medication your doctor prescribed slowly destroying your heart? Here's a safe, effective, and all-natural bioactive alternative.**

- 9 ways to adjust your metabolism to normalize body chemistry, stave off illness, increase energy, and achieve optimal health. If even one of these metabolic factors is out of whack, it can make you deathly ill.

- And much, much more…

Whether you are 18 or 80, male or female, in good health or poor, Dr. Lavalle's advice in

FIGURE A.2 *(Continued)*

The Healing Prescription: *Restoring and Maintaining Vitality, Wellness, and Longevity* can make a dramatic and almost immediate change in your life.

Best of all, you don't have to wait weeks for an appointment at his clinic, like I did. Because as a *Healing Prescription* Charter Member, you can benefit from Dr. LaValle's metabolic health breakthroughs right now....

Order Now!

Your best health starts today

Here are the privileges and health benefits that are yours when you accept my offer to become a Charter Member to *The Healing Prescription* on a no-risk trial basis:

- *The Healing Prescription* ... a 1-year membership brings you 12 monthly issues of the official 8-page research bulletin and health alert of the LaValle Metabolic Institute delivered via U.S. Postal Service to your mailbox. Topics covered include: aging ... stress ... diabetes ... insulin resistance ... glucose tolerance ... energy ... sleep ... men's health ... women's health issues ... joint pain ... hormones ... metabolism ... herbal remedies ... diet ... nutrition ... lifestyle ... fitness ... and more.

- *Members-Only Discounts* ... savings of 10% and more on dietary supplements sold and recommended by Dr. LaValle at the LaValle Metabolic Institute online store. This alone can save you hundreds of dollars a year -- and pay back the cost of your membership to *The Healing Prescription* many times over!

- *Insight from LMI's Team of Medical Experts* ... our members get regular communiqués on medical research, health, and wellness from LMI's 80-member staff including: strength trainer Carlo Alvarez, former conditioning coach for the Cleveland Indians ... Maureen Pelletier, M.D., author of the *Complete Idiot's Guide to Menopause* ... Dr. Gary Huber, a board-certified emergency medicine physician ... Laura LaValle, a registered and licensed dietician ... dietician Katherine Wight ... and nurse Pam Cordes.

6 life-saving special reports -- yours FREE

In addition to all of the above -- the monthly newsletter, members-only discounts, and information from clinic's staff on the most current health breakthroughs-- you also get this valuable health library of 6 Special Reports written by Dr. LaValle absolutely free:

- *Special Report #1: The 5 Foods You Should Never Eat* ... compelling reasons why you should avoid high-fructose corn syrup ... trans-fat ... refined sugar ... and other foods that may be making you sick. Plus: 3 artificial sweeteners you

FIGURE A.2   *(Continued)*

should never use -- and the only one that's safe.

- ***Special Report #2: Natural Remedies for Lowering Cholesterol and Risk of Cardiovascular Disease*** ... more than 2,600 Americans die from cardiovascular disease daily. The two most common dietary factors putting you at risk? Fat and cholesterol. This report is your guide to foods that lower your cholesterol and risk of heart disease as well as foods to avoid. Get the straight talk on olive oil ... omega-3 ... salt ... alcohol ... folic acid ... potassium ... garlic ... green tea ... L-carnitine ... and more.

- ***Special Report #3: Cold War: Your Defense Against Cold and Flu Season*** ... does taking vitamin C really reduce the duration and severity of colds? You'll find the answer -- and the science behind it -- in this report. It also gives you the truth about zinc lozenges, echinacea, garlic, golden seal, and common homeopathic cold and flu remedies. Do they work ... or are they simply a waste of your time and money?

- ***Special Report #4: Four Steps to Diet-Free Weight Loss*** ... approximately 70% of the U.S. population is overweight, and Americans spend billions of dollars annually on diets and weight loss programs. The 4 bioactive compounds revealed in this report can help you lose weight safely and naturally, without fad diets or dangerous prescription weight loss pills.

- ***Special Report #5: Nature's Valium*** ... instead of popping Valium or Xanax to relieve anxiety, try this safe, gentle, natural botanical agent instead. It helps to balance the stress on your adrenals -- to keep your cortisol levels in check.

- ***Special Report #6: Drugs That Make You Starve*** ... dozens of common prescription medications actively deplete magnesium, chromium, and other vital nutrients in your body to dangerously low levels. In this special report, you'll get a checklist of these drugs ... the bioactive compounds they rob you of ... and how to overcome their nutrition-depletion effects.

All 6 of these special reports are yours FREE when you accept my offer to become a Charter Member to *The Healing Prescription* on a 60-day no-risk trial basis.

To download your 6 FREE Bonus Reports immediately, just click below now:

Get Your 6 FREE Reports Now!

What does it cost to benefit from Dr. LaValle's cutting-edge nutritional health research and therapies?

FIGURE A.2 *(Continued)*

Normally Dr. LaValle is booked solid with patients a month or more in advance, and it takes 3-4 weeks to get an appointment for a personal consultation.

The initial exam is $300 and does not include the cost of supplements, round-trip airfare to Cincinnati, and food and lodging -- not to mention losing a day or two at work. You can easily spend hundreds or even thousands of dollars to receive the doctor's expert advice and follow the treatment plan he creates for you.

But there's no waiting -- and you won't have to drain your bank account -- to get your hands on the premiere issue of Dr. James LaValle's newsletter, *The Healing Prescription* and benefit from his metabolic health breakthroughs right away.

As a Charter Member, your cost for a full year of *The Healing Prescription* is just $49. Or, subscribe for a full 2 years for only $79 -- our lowest rate available. You save nearly 20%.

A membership to *The Healing Prescription* brings you ongoing advice and support from Dr. James LaValle -- and his entire staff at the LaValle Metabolic Institute -- all year long for as little as 11 cents a day.

Surely, improving your health and wellness throughout the year is worth a dime and a penny a day, right?

Order Now!

Satisfaction guaranteed or your money back

Your Charter Membership to *The Healing Prescription* comes without commitment or obligation of any kind.

If you are not 100% satisfied with *The Healing Prescription*, just let us know within 60 days for a full and prompt refund of your entire membership fee.

After 60 days, *The Healing Prescription* must continue to please you. If not, you may cancel at any time for a full refund on the unused portion of your membership.

That way, you risk nothing.

Whatever you decide, all issues and bonus materials received are yours to keep FREE ... it's my way of saying "thanks" for giving *The Healing Prescription* a try.

James LaValle gave me back my life.
Now I want him to help *you*

FIGURE A.2 *(Continued)*

enjoy optimal health every day of the year.

There are lots of people out there posing as health experts and pretending they have all the answers for what ails you.

I know, because when I became pre-diabetic, gained weight, and was suffering from fatigue, I searched far and wide ... and tried more things that didn't work than I care to count.

With this launch of Total Health Breakthrough's new health newsletter, *The Healing Prescription*, I wanted to be certain that we were offering health advice that actually worked -- not just health advice I thought we could market.

So after telling Dr. James LaValle my entire medical history at a dinner last year, I decided to make myself the guinea pig -- and become his patient before committing to publishing him.

In short order, James' treatments got my blood sugar, triglycerides, cholesterol, hormone, and other levels all within normal range ... helped restore my energy, mood, and vigor ... eliminated my insomnia ... and even helped me lose pounds I'd been unable to shed on my own despite vigorous daily exercise.

Now, although I am still the oldest mom at my kids' soccer games, I am no longer the most tired -- even though I'm one of the few with both young kids and a high-pressure executive career.

Instead, I have the energy to enjoy both my work and my personal life with enthusiasm ... and I haven't even mentioned how things have changed in my marriage! (I'll leave it at that, but let me just say both me and my husband are smiling more these days.)

And with the metabolic adjustments Dr. LaValle's treatments achieved for me, I am no longer insulin resistant. The early death my father suffered from diabetes while I was still in my 30s isn't in my future any more. I fully intend to babysit some day for my future grandkids -- something my dad never lived to do.

As a happy patient, I am supremely confident that Dr. James LaValle, his team, and his writing can make a positive impact on *your* health and your life ... quickly, easily, and without straining your wallet.

Over 7,000 patients and health care professionals have already benefited from Dr. LaValle's unique metabolic approach to achieving optimal health. Now, I am delighted to bring the breakthrough healing therapies of this world-class expert right to your home.

So what are you waiting for?

FIGURE A.2 *(Continued)*

To activate your risk-free Charter Membership to Dr. James LaValle's *The Healing Prescription,* call toll-free **1-800-681-6476**. Or click below now:

Order Now!

You'll be glad you did.

Sincerely,

MaryEllen Tribby
Patient of Dr. James LaValle
Publisher, ETR's Total Health Breakthroughs

P.S. Remember, order your risk-free 60-day trial membership to *The Healing Prescription* today and get 6 FREE Bonus Reports:

1. *Five Foods You Should Never Eat.*
2. *Natural Remedies for Lowering Cholesterol.*
3. *Cold Wars.*
4. *Four Steps to Weight Loss.*
5. *Nature's Valium.*
6. *Drugs That Make You Starve*

These valuable health reports are yours to keep, regardless of whether you become a member of *The Healing Prescription.*

To activate your no-risk charter membership ... and get your FREE bonus reports ... just click here now:

Order Now!

P.P.S. Quick-Response Bonus. Order within 72 hours and get an additional special report, *No More Arthritis Aches and Pains.*

Glucosamine and chondroiton are the "800 pound gorillas" of natural remedies for relieving arthritis pain. But would you be better off taking SAMe, MSM, Boswellia, or CMO? You'll find the answers here. Some patients report improvement in arthritic symptoms of over 63%!

To get your free quick-response bonus report, click here within 72 hours. After that, it's too late:

FIGURE A.2 *(Continued)*

FIGURE A.3

Coming This Summer, The Event You've Been Waiting For...

Give Us Five Days in July... and We'll Give You Income for Life

Walk in Tuesday Morning with NOTHING... (No Product, Website, or Technical Experience)...

Walk Out Saturday Afternoon With Your Own REAL Internet Business.

Dear Skeptical Reader,

We're looking for a few good people.

A few good people who aren't afraid of some hard work - maybe even *very* hard work - for a couple of days this summer.

A few good people **ready for success**.

It's this simple: Decide right now you want to be one of these people, and less than 75 days from today you **WILL** be the proud owner of your own, REAL Internet business.

When you join us at our Early to Rise Internet Business-Building Conference this July, we'll take you by the hand and together we'll build the foundation for your own **life-long Internet income stream**. And we intend to accomplish it all in just five days.

We won't give you knowledge you can't use.

We won't give you "feel good" stuff that leaves you pumped... and nowhere to go afterward.

FIGURE A.3 (*Continued*)

Instead, we're going to run you through a very intense, results-oriented training program where together we'll build your own Internet business in just five days.

Don't worry if you're not a "techie" or a marketing expert, because we'll be giving you all of our **proven** Internet success techniques in this super easy-to-understand step-by-step program.

I say "proven success techniques" with confidence, because the blueprint we're handing over to you has brought in over $250 million a year to a handful of our closest affiliates in each of the past 5 years.

But here's the interesting part... ANYONE can re-use this formula provided 1) you understand the secrets we'll give you, and 2) you're willing to put forth the effort and commitment to actually make it happen.

This Is a REAL "Rocky Mountain High"
That Will Last Your Whole Lifetime...

FIGURE A.4

Come to Early to Rise's 2008 "Spring Fling"
and Get Over $17.3 Million in Unique & POWERFUL Money-Making Secrets...

Profits In Paradise!

Introducing Dozens of Great <u>New</u> Income-Generating and Entrepreneurial Adventures...

Dear Fed-Up Friend,

A so-called expert once said, "You can't mix business with pleasure".

Brother, are we going to prove HIM wrong!

You are cordially invited to join Early to Rise and a few hundred of our closest friends for a tropical 3-day weekend adventure in breakthrough profit-taking!

Spirits will be high... and the chance for **extraordinary gains** in your income... your savings... and your portfolio will be even higher.

Our mission is to give you the inside scoop on some very hush-hush secrets for turning a nifty buck in the slightly scary economic times we're all going through right now.

In what promises to be an incredibly exciting and energetic 72-hour wealth-building summit, we're going to hand you the SAFEST and most PROFITABLE income-generating and entrepreneurial opportunities you've **never heard of**.

And because we know you're watching your budget these days, we are making this our most affordable event ever!

FIGURE A.4 *(Continued)*

It's Like ETR's "Spring Break on Steroids"

We'll all be gathering in sunny and warm Orlando, Florida this spring - home to world-class golf, tennis, and theme park attractions - to give a small army of eager Early to Risers dozens of recession-busting, retirement-saving, and breakthrough income-boosting strategies.

We've cornered an elite team of Entrepreneurial Wizards, Real Estate Experts and Wealth-Building Gurus for our **"Profits in Paradise"** spring summit.

Come join us in Florida this April and it will be their privilege to show you their very unusual but very practical and powerful off-the-radar wealth-building techniques - including how you could...

- **Dramatically build or grow your retirement nest egg by making up to 92% returns - SAFELY - on an investment which goes up just 2%!**...

- **Start an Internet business (even with no prior experience) that taps into an "underground" multi-billion dollar niche just ripe for the picking**...

- **Find all the money you'll ever need to do your deals and never have to fool around with a bank**...

- **Learn how one man turned his MONTHLY income into his HOURLY income of $1000's - and how you could do the same**...

Make a fortune in the exploding fields of personal growth, health and healing, enlightened spirituality, self-help and self discovery...

- **Discover the keys to making $1.3 million+ a year from the housing foreclosure boom**...

- **Sit back and watch as your computer does the heavy lifting - all you have to do is make offers and cash checks in this dynamite "personal profit center"**...

- **How you could retire from the proceeds from a single deal**...

FIGURE A.4 *(Continued)*

> **And much, much more!**
>
> And that's just a small taste of what's in store for you...
>
> When you join us in Orlando this spring, you'll be positioned to take advantage of dozens of **hidden profit opportunities** from some of the nation's leading experts in their respective fields.
>
> Nothing like this has ever been offered - anywhere, by anyone - including Early to Rise. So come on down, because right now is YOUR time to discover how you could amass alarmingly large profits in record time!
>
> ## Prosperity Amidst the Palm Trees

FIGURE A.5

Last Year, 145 Million People Spent Over $108 <u>BILLION</u> Online!

Where Did All That Money Go?

The "Other Side" of The Internet!

Now, Here's Your Chance to Switch Over to the <u>WINNING SIDE OF THE WEB</u>...

- "Other Side Entrepreneur" J.W. Earned $306,043 in 3 <u>Days.</u>

- "Other Side Entrepreneur" P.H. Earned $2,292,001 in <u>2 Weeks.</u>

- "Other Side Entrepreneur" G.G. Earned <u>Over $8,500,000 in 1 Month!</u>

Dear Ambitious Reader,

Today, I'd like to show you how you can create a business (or transform the one you already have) that will make between $1 million and $100 million a year.

It takes advantage of a *trillion-dollar* industry. It is related to the secret that a small group of people I know have used to build *extremely* successful businesses.

Once you understand this powerful secret, you will be able to build your own income-generating business, propelled by a huge explosion that is currently taking place in this trillion-dollar industry. You will be able to. Whether you do or not will depend on you.

But if you do, then I'll be able to welcome you to this remarkably easy place for succeeding in business I've dubbed, "The Other Side of the Internet".

FIGURE A.5 *(Continued)*

You see, for far too many people this wonderful invention called the Internet is slowly transforming into a disturbing distraction. Hours spent surfing the web endlessly, rising Internet fees… in short, nothing but your time and your money flowing out your door.

But when you switch to the "Other Side" of the Internet, you move from the *giving* side to the *getting* side. You move from the *spending* side to the *earning* side. In short, you'll be on the *winning* side of the Internet!

And when you get there, you can enjoy its many benefits, which include power, prestige, freedom and an income that is only limited by your ambition.

Of the many paths to wealth, this one has all the advantages you want if you are starting from scratch: simplicity, an extremely low entry cost, and a huge and growing potential for extremely high profit margins.

Today, I'm going to divulge the one, great underlying secret my colleagues have used to create their fortunes, large and small… and invite you to learn more about it (if you like) at an event I'm planning this October.

An Exploding Opportunity in a Huge and Growing Market

Right now, you have a rare and exciting opportunity to take advantage of one of the largest industries on earth. And it is – most experts agree – the one that has the greatest growth potential.

It capitalizes on the Internet, which is perhaps the fastest-growing mega-trend in the history of commerce. And it has – as far as I know – the lowest production costs of any industry in today's world.

Because of that low cost-of-entry and growth potential, it is the ideal vehicle for getting wealthy in the 21st century. Whether you intend to make your fortune on your own (as an entrepreneur) or within the context of a corporate environment (as an intrapreneur), taking advantage of these forces is the best and easiest way to achieve fast success and acquire great wealth.

I am referring to, of course, the Information Publishing industry.

Now don't be intimidated by that term. You won't need a printing press, typesetting gear or even employees! Information Publishing is simply about marketing products based not on hard goods (flowers, baskets, computers, etc.) but instead on ideas (e-letters, teleconferences, special reports, etc.).

FIGURE A.5 *(Continued)*

For companies based in the U.S. alone, the market is well over $200 billion. Around the world, it is at least another $800 billion. Italy, Scandinavia, Eastern Europe, all of Latin America, South America, India, Africa and the Middle East, plus Australia, New Zealand and the Far East bring the total to over a trillion dollars.

But it's not the whole industry I'm talking about here. It's the fastest-growing part of it, the part that has (far and away!) the greatest wealth-building potential.

I am talking about the explosion of online information-related businesses that has been taking place for about ten years now in the areas of publishing, marketing, media, news, entertainment and many personal services like directories, advisories, research facilities, personal and professional networks, etc.

And, more specifically, the Internet-based applications of these businesses, including, for example:

* The Knot, a site that offers wedding-related blogs, advice, and budget planning, which has a market value of over $746 million and 3.2 million monthly visitors.

* IMDB (the Internet Movie Database), which has 47 million visitors each month.

* BankRate.com, a financial news and information site, which has a market capitalization of $674 million and had over 467 million page views last year.

* WebMD, a health information site, which has a market capitalization of over $2.8 billion and nearly 35 million unique monthly visitors.

The numbers are astonishing. And what is the potential of this part of the information industry? A single anecdote will give you a quick idea...

YouTube.Com, founded only two years ago, was said to be worth somewhere in the neighborhood of $600 million last summer. Now, following its continued explosion in popularity, they've been bought out by Google for $1.6 BILLION in Google stock. All this from one single idea, in about 24 months!

When a business has that kind of success, you can be sure there will be many, many imitators. Already, in fact, Guba.Com has signed deals with Sony and Warner Brothers... and start-up Eefoof.Com is offering to pay contributors depending on how many viewers a video attracts.

But when you join my colleagues and I on "The Other Side of the Internet", you won't have to worry about competition.

Why?

FIGURE A.5 *(Continued)*

Because 98 percent of the people who get into this industry don't understand the secret I'm about to reveal to you.

The Secret Is Knowing What People *Really* Want!

NOTES

CHAPTER 1: MARKETING IN THE TWENTY-FIRST CENTURY: HOW QUICKLY THINGS HAVE CHANGED

1. Direct Marketing Association, www.DMAChoice.org. (Accessed: June 9, 2008)

CHAPTER 5: SEARCH ENGINE MARKETING: BUSTING MYTHS AND DRIVING SALES

1. "Pay Per Click Tools," www.payperclicktools.com. (Accessed: May 23, 2008)

CHAPTER 6: TELECONFERENCES: ALL YOU NEED IS A PHONE AND GOOD IDEAS

1. Robert Cialdini, *Influence: The Psychology of Persuasion* (New York: William Morrow and Company, 1984), 17–18.
2. Ibid, 57.

CHAPTER 7: DIRECT MAIL: AN OLD DOG THAT STILL KNOWS A FEW TRICKS

1. American List Counsel Inc., "Cyclical Analysis of the Direct Mail Market," July 2001. www.alc.com/pdf/final_study_consecutive_pgs.pdf. (Accessed: June 12, 2008)
2. Graphic Arts Online, "Direct Mail Spending Up," Feb. 29, 2008. www.graphicartsonline.com/article/CA6536898.html. (Accessed: June 12, 2008)
3. Ibid. (Accessed: June 12, 2008)

CHAPTER 8: DIRECT PRINT: GETTING MORE THAN EVER FOR YOUR AD DOLLAR

1. Audit Bureau of Circulation, "About ABC," www.acessabc.com/aboutabc/index.htm. (Accessed: June 10, 2008)
2. Canadian Heritage, "Advertising Sales Tools—A Guide for Small Publishers," www.pcdh.gc.ca/progs/ac-ca/pubs/guides/ad_tools/02_e.cfm. (Accessed: June 10, 2008)

CHAPTER 9: DIRECT-RESPONSE TELEVISION: WHY SUPER BOWL ADS DON'T WORK

1. Diego Vasquez, "A Downside to Funny Super Bowl Ads," *Media Life Magazine*. Jan. 30, 2008, www.medialifemagazine.com/artman2/publish/Research_25/A_downside_to_funny_Super_Bowl_ads.asp. (Accessed: April 4, 2008).
2. Denny Hatch, "General Advertising vs. Direct Marketing and Vin Gupta's Victory," *Business Common Sense*, Oct. 29, 2007: Vol. 3, Issue No. 75.
3. Ibid.
4. Ibid.
5. Ibid.
6. Kim Gordon, "As Seen on TV," *Entrepreneur Magazine*, February 2002, www.entrepreneur.com/magazine/entrepreneur/2002/february/48312.html. (Accessed: May 27, 2008).
7. Ibid.

CHAPTER 10: DIRECT-RESPONSE RADIO: MUSIC, NEWS, SPORTS, AND TALK = MONEY

1. The Project for Excellence in Journalism, "The State of the News Media 2007," www.stateofthenewsmedia.org/2007/narrative_radio_audience.asp?cat=2&media=9. (Accessed: June 5, 2008).

2. Radio Advertising Bureau, "Radio Sectors Yield Diverse Revenue Results," www.rab.com/public/pr/revenue_detail.cfm?id=97. (Accessed: June 6, 2008)
3. David Wallechinsky and Irving Wallace, *The People's Almanac* (New York: Doubleday, 1975–1981). Reprinted by www.trivia-library.com.
4. Ibid.
5. "Report Says Online Advertising Dollars Will Be Twice Radio Advertising Dollars," Aug. 28, 2007, Webmetro.com, www.webmetro.com/PPC-Management/news1detail1819.asp. (Accessed: June 10, 2008).

CHAPTER 14: PUBLIC RELATIONS: MAN BITES DOG; MAN GETS FAMOUS

1. Anne B. Keating and Joseph Hargitai, *The Wired Professor* (New York: NYU Press, 1999), 68.
2. David Meerman Scott, *The New Rules of Marketing and PR* (New Jersey: John Wiley & Sons, 2004).

ABOUT THE AUTHORS

Michael Masterson is not your typical businessman. An ex–Peace Corps volunteer, he never took a class in business, doesn't read the business press, and doesn't like to talk business. He spends his spare time writing poetry, collecting fine art, and practicing Brazilian Jujitsu. His neighbors call him a bohemian capitalist. And with good reason. He wrote his first poem when he was 10 years old and started his first business a year later. Since then, he has written more than a thousand poems and short stories and played an integral part in dozens of successful businesses in a variety of industries.

In 1999 Michael helped launch is EarlytoRise.com, an Internet-based company that provides advice and training in "health, wealth, and wisdom." Started initially as an informal weekly e-mail to a handful of his protégés, it quickly morphed into a $28 million enterprise.

In addition to consulting with ETR, the primary focus of his business life these days is as consultant to Agora Inc., a $300 million, Baltimore-based publisher of information products with offices in England, France, Spain, Germany, South Africa, and Australia.

Notwithstanding clandestine luncheons that erupt into new multimillion-dollar ventures, Michael insists that he has been spending most of his time teaching and writing since he retired, for the second time, when he turned 53.

He writes poetry and fiction ("somewhat badly," he says), as well as books on business and wealth building (all of which have been *Wall Street Journal*, Amazon.com, or *New York Times* best-sellers). "I have a readership that appreciates the way I look at things," Michael says. "And that is gratifying."

His nonfiction books include *Ready, Fire, Aim: Zero to $100 Million in No Time Flat; Seven Years to Seven Figures: The Fast-Track Plan to Becoming a Millionaire; Automatic Wealth for Grads . . . and Anyone Else Just Starting Out; Automatic Wealth: The Six Steps to Financial Independence; Power and Persuasion: How to Command Success in Business and Your Personal Life;* and *Confessions of a Self-Made Multi-Millionaire.*

Changing the Channel is his eleventh book and his sixth with John Wiley & Sons. He continues to write about starting and developing small businesses on a weekly basis in the EarlytoRise.com e-zine.

MaryEllen Tribby has led the Early to Rise team since May of 2006 as Publisher and CEO. She has over 20 years of publishing and business experience, most notably in direct marketing. Since coming on board, she has more than tripled ETR's revenue in her first 15 months.

Her extensive experiences in the publishing industry began at 10 years old, when she delivered her local daily newspaper in her hometown of Parsippany, New Jersey. Of course, at the time she did not realize that one day she would be working for some of the largest publishing companies in the world.

Before joining ETR, Ms. Tribby served as President of Weiss Research in Palm Beach Gardens, Florida, and Vice President of Globe Communications in Boca Raton, Florida.

Prior to moving to Florida, New York City was where Ms. Tribby truly gained her publishing expertise. While working at Times Mirror magazines, she learned many channels of marketing and implemented hundreds of successful marketing campaigns through direct mail, radio, television, and print.

At the age of 26, she managed a division of *Forbes*. From there she was recruited to head of marketing and circulation for *Crain's New York Business*.

MaryEllen often speaks on expert panels at industry specific events, including those hosted by the Specialized Information Publishers Association (SIPA), Financial Information Publishers Association (FIPA), and Direct Marketing Association (DMA).

Changing the Channel: 12 Easy Ways to Make Millions for Your Business, coauthored by Michael Masterson, is her first book.

She currently resides in Boca Raton, Florida, with her husband of 12 years, Patrick, and their three beautiful children, Mikaela, Connor, and Delanie.

When she is not working, you will find MaryEllen at one of her children's sporting events or relaxing on the beach with her family.

INDEX

SPECIAL Free Bonus for Readers of *Changing the Channel*

Learn Even More of Michael Masterson and MaryEllen Tribby's Multi-Channel Marketing Secrets

Congratulations! You've just learned hundreds of multi-channel marketing secrets for skyrocketing your business in *Changing the Channel: 12 Easy Ways to Make Millions for Your Business.* You are now equipped to find new customers through all the marketing channels, media, and methods discussed in this book.

And it gets even better. Experts agree that learning is a continuous process. So why not continue your education with a subscription to the Internet's most popular daily success e-zine, *Early to Rise*?

Michael Masterson was involved in the founding of this information-packed publication, remains its chief advisor, and contributes daily articles about business, entrepreneurship, and, of course, marketing. MaryEllen Tribby is the publisher and CEO of the company, as well as a frequent contributor. They are joined by an extraordinary team of world-class entrepreneurs, marketing experts, copywriters, and industry leaders who will provide you with constant encouragement and smart new ideas that will augment the wisdom you've already gained from reading *Changing the Channel.*

Delivered to your inbox bright and early each morning, *Early to Rise* is your daily dose of actionable information on wealth-building, entrepreneurship, marketing, advertising, copywriting, and key success topics that are essential to taking your business to the next level. *Early to Rise* offers cutting-edge and contrarian business ideas that are actually working in the marketplace right now.

As a reader of *Changing the Channel*, you are eligible to immediately sign up for a complimentary subscription to Early to Rise. You can unsubscribe at any time with no obligation. So why not try it out? Please visit www.earlytorise.com/changingthechannel right now, and you'll receive your first issue tomorrow.